Related Books of Interest

Rapid Portlet Development with WebSphere Portlet Factory
Step-by-Step Guide for Building Your Own Portlets

by David Bowley
ISBN: 0-13-713446-0

The Step-by-Step Guide to Building World-Class Portlet Solutions—Fast!

Expert developer David Bowley walks you through several of today's most common portlet development scenarios, demonstrating how to create powerful, robust portlets quickly and cost-effectively. Each walkthrough contains all the step-by-step instructions, detailed guidance, fast answers, and working sample code you need to get tangible results immediately.

The best resource available on WebSphere Portlet Factory, this book reflects Bowley's unsurpassed experience constructing large enterprise portals. Bowley covers everything from back-end integration to user interface and AJAX techniques, helping you choose the right builder tool for each task, and define high-level instructions that generate superior code artifacts. His example projects are simple enough to understand easily, but sophisticated enough to be valuable in real-world development.

WebSphere Business Integration Primer
Process Server, BPEL, SCA, and SOA

by Ashok Iyengar, Vinod Jessani, and Michele Chilanti
ISBN: 0-13-224831-X

Using WebSphere® Business Integration (WBI) technology, you can build an enterprise-wide Business Integration (BI) infrastructure that makes it easier to connect any business resources and functions, so you can adapt more quickly to the demands of customers and partners. Now there's an introductory guide to creating standards-based process and data integration solutions with WBI.

WebSphere Business Integration Primer thoroughly explains Service Component Architecture (SCA), basic business processes, and complex long-running business flows, and guides you to choose the right process integration architecture for your requirements. Next, it introduces the key components of a WBI solution and shows how to make them work together rapidly and efficiently. This book will help developers, technical professionals, or managers understand today's key BI issues and technologies, and streamline business processes by combining BI with Service Oriented Architecture (SOA).

Related Books of Interest

The New Language of Business
SOA & Web 2.0

by Sandy Carter
ISBN: 0-13-195654-X

In *The New Language of Business*, senior IBM executive Sandy Carter demonstrates how to leverage SOA, Web 2.0, and related technologies to drive new levels of operational excellence and business innovation.

Writing for executives and business leaders inside and outside IT, Carter explains why flexibility and responsiveness are now even more crucial to success — and why services-based strategies offer the greatest promise for achieving them.

You'll learn how to organize your business into reusable process components — and support them with cost-effective IT services that adapt quickly and easily to change. Then, using extensive examples — including a detailed case study describing IBM's own experience — Carter identifies best practices, pitfalls, and practical starting points for success.

 Listen to the author's podcast at:
ibmpressbooks.com/podcasts

Executing SOA
A Practical Guide for the Service-Oriented Architect

by Norbert Bieberstein, Robert G. Laird, Dr. Keith Jones, and Tilak Mitra
ISBN: 0-13-235374-1

In *Executing SOA*, four experienced SOA implementers share realistic, proven, "from-the-trenches" guidance for successfully delivering on even the largest and most complex SOA initiative.

This book follows up where the authors' best-selling *Service-Oriented Architecture Compass* left off, showing how to overcome key obstacles to successful SOA implementation and identifying best practices for all facets of execution—technical, organizational, and human. Among the issues it addresses: introducing a services discipline that supports collaboration and information process sharing; integrating services with preexisting technology assets and strategies; choosing the right roles for new tools; shifting culture, governance, and architecture; and bringing greater agility to the entire organizational lifecycle, not just isolated projects.

 Listen to the author's podcast at:
ibmpressbooks.com/podcasts

IBM
Press™

Visit ibmpressbooks.com
for all product information

Related Books of Interest

Service-Oriented Architecture (SOA) Compass
Business Value, Planning, and Enterprise Roadmap

by Norbert Bieberstein, Sanjay Bose,
Marc Fiammante, Keith Jones, and Rawn Shah
ISBN: 0-13-187002-5

In this book, IBM® Enterprise Integration Team experts present a start-to-finish guide to planning, implementing, and managing Service-Oriented Architecture. Drawing on their extensive experience helping enterprise customers migrate to SOA, the authors share hard-earned lessons and best practices for architects, project managers, and software development leaders alike.

Well-written and practical, *Service-Oriented Architecture Compass* offers the perfect blend of principles and "how-to" guidance for transitioning your infrastructure to SOA. The authors clearly explain what SOA is, the opportunities it offers, and how it differs from earlier approaches. Using detailed examples from IBM consulting engagements, they show how to deploy SOA solutions that tightly integrate with your processes and operations, delivering maximum flexibility and value. With detailed coverage of topics ranging from policy-based management to workflow implementation, no other SOA book offers comparable value to workingIT professionals.

IBM WebSphere and Lotus
Lamb, Laskey, Indurkhya
ISBN: 0-13-144330-5

Enterprise Messaging Using JMS and IBM WebSphere
Yusuf
ISBN: 0-13-146863-4

IBM WebSphere System Administration
Williamson, Chan, Cundiff, Lauzon, Mitchell
ISBN: 0-13-144604-5

Outside-in Software Development
Kessler, Sweitzer
ISBN: 0-13-157551-1

Enterprise Master Data Management
Dreibelbis, Hechler, Milman, Oberhofer, van Run, Wolfson
ISBN: 0-13-236625-8

Enterprise Java Programming with IBM WebSphere
Brown, Craig, Hester, Pitt, Stinehour, Weitzel, Amsden, Jakab, Berg
ISBN: 0-321-18579-X

Application Architecture for WebSphere®

The developerWorks® Series

The IBM Press developerWorks Series represents a unique undertaking in which print books and the Web are mutually supportive. The publications in this series are complemented by their association with resources available at the developerWorks Web site on ibm.com. These resources include articles, tutorials, forums, software, and much more.

Through the use of icons, readers will be able to immediately identify a resource on developerWorks which relates to that point of the text. A summary of links appears at the end of each chapter. Additionally, you will be able to access an electronic guide of the developerWorks links and resources through ibm.com/developerworks/dwbooks that reference developerWorks Series publications, deepening the reader's experiences.

A developerWorks book offers readers the ability to quickly extend their information base beyond the book by using the deep resources of developerWorks and at the same time enables developerWorks readers to deepen their technical knowledge and skills.

For a full listing of developerWorks Series publications, please visit: **ibmpressbooks.com/dwseries**.

Application Architecture for WebSphere®

A Practical Approach to Building WebSphere Applications

developerWorks® Series

Joey Bernal

IBM Press
Pearson plc
Upper Saddle River, NJ • Boston • Indianapolis • San Francisco
New York • Toronto • Montreal • London • Munich • Paris • Madrid
Capetown • Sydney • Tokyo • Singapore • Mexico City
ibmpressbooks.com

IBM Press Program Managers: Tara Woodman, Ellice Uffer

Cover design: IBM Corporation

Associate Publisher: Greg Wiegand
Marketing Manager: Kourtnaye Sturgeon
Publicist: Heather Fox
Acquisitions Editor: Katherine Bull
Development Editor: Kevin Howard
Managing Editor: Kristy Hart
Designer: Alan Clements
Project Editor: Chelsey Marti
Copy Editor: Paula Lowell
Indexer: WordWise Publishing Services
Compositor: Gloria Schurick
Proofreader: Leslie Joseph
Manufacturing Buyer: Dan Uhrig

Published by Pearson plc

Publishing as IBM Press

IBM Press offers excellent discounts on this book when ordered in quantity for bulk purchases or special sales, which may include electronic versions and/or custom covers and content particular to your business, training goals, marketing focus, and branding interests. For more information, please contact:

U.S. Corporate and Government Sales
1-800-382-3419
corpsales@pearsontechgroup.com.

For sales outside the U.S., please contact:

International Sales
international@pearsoned.com.

Library of Congress Cataloging-in-Publication Data

Bernal, Joey.

  Application architecture for WebSphere : a practical approach to building WebSphere applications /
Joey Bernal.

    p. cm.

  ISBN 978-0-13-712926-3

  1. WebSphere. 2. Software architecture. 3. Application software—Development. I. Title.

  TK5105.8885.W43B48 2008

  005.1—dc22

                                    2008035862

        Pearson Education, Inc.
        Rights and Contracts Department
        501 Boylston Street, Suite 900
        Boston, MA 02116
        Fax (617) 671 3447

        ISBN-13: 978-0-13-712926-3
        ISBN-10: 0-13-712926-2

Text printed in the United States on recycled paper at R.R. Donnelley in Crawfordsville, Indiana.
First printing September 2008

To Christiane, my better-half of 22 years who has found her cheese and fully demon-strated the philosophy of embracing change. I'm so proud of your recent graduation from nursing school and continuation toward a graduate degree—Hook 'em horns! To Daniel and Christopher, I want you to enjoy your time away at college, and know that I'm turning your rooms into a billiards room and a media room. For Julia who continues to blossom into a beautiful young woman while still appreciative of my jr. high sense of humor. And to Oliver, who is becoming an independent young gentleman and my last chance to have a fellow geek in the family. Finally, of course, to my faithful Lulu, who brings me my paper (slightly wet) every Sunday without fail, whether I want it or not.

Contents

Foreword

The late comic Rodney Dangerfield made an entire career out of stating that he never got any respect. Sometimes I think that the lot of an application architect is just as bad. They are the ones who get blamed when applications are late, when the applications don't meet all the sometimes unrealistic expectations of the users, when the application crashes (even if it was the infrastructure, and not the application that was at fault), or generally when anything else bad happens in software development. The job title "application architect" might not have all the flash of the title "enterprise architect," but nonetheless they are the backbone of most large software development organizations. The weight of the world is on their shoulders, and it sometimes seems like a thankless job.

Let's face it—given how much an application architect is expected to master these days, his job is cut out for him. He has to understand not only the details of the application requirements, but is expected to be an expert on the facilities provided by the application server environment, a myriad of open source projects that are available to him, the development environment, and a host of other smaller details. In this book, Joey has made a concerted effort to teach people not just what application architecture entails, but more importantly, how to be a *good* application architect. He provides a concise roadmap to the areas that application architecture covers, and then gives real, practical advice on how to make the right choices when designing an application.

Joey begins by convincing potential architects of the benefits of a layered architecture, and then goes on to provide concrete examples of how all the layers work, with copious sample code and explanation of the pros and cons of the major decisions that have to be made in each layer. He also discusses the all-important nonfunctional requirements that go into building an application, and discusses how you can take advantage of sometimes little-known WebSphere features to meet those requirements for performance and security.

If you are currently an application architect and need to implement on WebSphere Application Server or WebSphere Portal Server, you need not only to read this book but to keep it close to your desk for when those tricky questions arise. Likewise, if you're an application developer who needs to implement a WebSphere solution, you need this book also. And finally, if you are an enterprise architect who needs to comprehend the problems faced by your application architect colleagues so that you can understand how an enterprise architecture for your entire organization should be built, you need this book too. I'm glad that Joey has written this, and trust that you'll get as much out of this as I have.

Kyle Brown
Distinguished Engineer
IBM Software Services for WebSphere

Acknowledgments

You've heard it before: A book like this doesn't get published by one person. Dozens of people work really hard to ensure that what is finally delivered to you, the reader, is of the highest quality possible. From IBM Press, Tara Woodman for navigating the IBM maze of people and permissions, and to Ellice Uffer, for her awesome marketing and blogging insights. Thanks to Katherine Bull, Kevin Howard, and Cindy Teeters from Pearson. Katherine held my virtual hand every step of the way.

Thanks to the technical reviewers Sam Pearson, Ashok Iyengar, Ron Lynn, Scott Davis, Richard Gorzela, Peter Blinstrubas, Brad Bouldin, Jim Sides, and Julia Weatherby for keeping me honest. I know how much real work you have to do, so taking the time to help on special projects means a lot. Extra special thanks to Julia, Scott, and Richard for doing double duty on some of the chapters at the last minute.

My executive sponsor within IBM for this effort was John Allessio, VP Software Services for Lotus—thank you, John, for sponsoring this work. Also thanks to my management chain, Bennie Gibson and Ken Polleck for supporting this effort and providing time here and there (albeit unofficially) to make continued progress. Many thanks to Kyle Brown for reviewing the final draft and writing the Foreword. After 7+ years at IBM I continue to be amazed by the vastness of opportunities available, and the support of management to pursue them. Too many to name are the many friends, coworkers, mentors, mentorees, managers, executives, customers, and others who I work with in my day job who provided insight and examples of how to do things right. You are why I continue to enjoy this profession after many years.

About the Author

Anthony (Joey) Bernal is an executive IT specialist with Software Services for Lotus, and a member of the WebSphere Portal Practice. Senior certified with IBM as an IT specialist, he has an extensive background in the design and development of portal and web applications. He is the coauthor of several books, including *Programming Portlets 2E; Programming Portlets, the IBM Portal Solutions Guide for Practitioners;* and from a previous life, *Professional Site Server 3.0.* He also contributes to his popular blog, WebSphere Portal in Action.

Mr. Bernal helps to lead the Software Services team in many areas, including application architecture and design, performance, and assisting clients with their cross-brand challenges that leverage WebSphere Portal. By its inherent nature of being a platform to integrate applications at the desktop, WebSphere Portal projects require significant cross-brand expertise. All WebSphere Portal projects have products from multiple brands, and many have products from all five brands in the solution. Specifically, he works to reduce the challenges presented by the cross-brand nature of WebSphere Portal projects, especially in the use of newer technologies such as the integration of WebSphere Portal with services-oriented architectures.

Prior to joining IBM, Mr. Bernal was the director of IT for an incentive and performance improvement company. Mr. Bernal was also the lead technical advisor and architect of multiple high-profile Internet and intranet applications for several Fortune 500 companies.

Preface

As we grow our skills as professional developers and architects, we tend to forget that our profession is constantly churning with new people, ideas, and technology. This churn, and the fact that software engineering is not like any other type of engineering is why we continue to build poor applications time and time again. What is a poor application? A poor application is any application that does not live up to its design in terms of performance, security, usability, or function. It should not be that hard for any of us to think back on a project we have worked on, or led, that meets this criterion.

The science of software engineering should be composed of the same rigorous set of rules and standards that other sciences have to live by. No other engineered product is released to the general public without inspection, yet software inspections take place a small fraction of the time, and at that are often cursory and incomplete.

I wrote this book because I continued to see problems in the way that customers designed and built WebSphere and WebSphere Portal applications. I was convinced that by writing some of my concerns down many of these problems would magically disappear. Well perhaps it is not that easy, but hopefully reading this text and considering some of its suggestions will help you on your way to obtaining software excellence. I have purposely written this book to be something you can sit down and read, rather than as a reference of sample patterns to be looked at when needed. The concept of application architecture embodies not only how projects are approached but also all the preparation that goes on before any coding begins. Read through this book and as you begin to understand some of the issues involved with building good applications, take that understanding and apply it to your current or next project with vigor. Just building an application is not enough; we have to strive to build *good* applications.

One approach with a book like this is to build up an application throughout the different chapters until you end up with a complete albeit complex example. While I think there is value in this approach, it does not often appeal to me as a reader. If I get lost in the middle of a section, then sometimes later chapters don't make as much sense. With this in mind I chose a central theme, "Classic Models," but chose not to build a single monolithic application. Rather I just offer up bits and pieces of sample code as appropriate. I hope you find this approach useful as you drop some of the examples into your own project code.

Enjoy!

Chapter 1

Application Architecture

This book is about building good application architectures. Before diving too far into the details of how to accomplish the goals of this book, it is important to answer the question of why. Application or software architecture in the J2EE space is a challenging business. It seems the more software engineers or Application Architects learn, the more there is to learn, and we welcome newcomers into our fold everyday who are trying to catch up and keep up with changes in direction and technology. Some constants, however, such as overall approaches and good decision-making practices, can help you along the way. That is what this book, and this chapter, are about—helping to guide you in making solid decisions that if nothing else, won't hurt you as the technology swirls around us all.

People often have different viewpoints on application architecture depending upon their role within the organization. Architects with responsibility for multiple projects within the organization often try to set up global standards and constraints in the hopes of getting everyone to follow the same set of basic patterns and processes. This approach is often the right one; however, the architects on the ground who are focusing on their project and dealing with day to day issues, also understand that you can never account for all the issues faced by a specific project team, and some degree of flexibility is required. The key is to merge those views and allow for feedback across the entire organization in order for it to grow as a unit. This chapter outlines the roles and responsibilities of the application architect and tips on accomplishing those goals.

What Is Application Architecture?

Application Architecture is the act of defining the structure and framework within which an application can be developed and delivered. It seems that the idea of application architecture (also called software architecture) is confusing to some people. This must be the case; if it is not, then application architecture is so overlooked within the bigger picture of building and deploying enterprise applications as to be essentially nonexistent. The latter often seems to be the case, because much of the time application architecture seems to be considered as an afterthought in many of the projects that I have helped with over the last few years. Maybe it is a disease that marketing has spread in its constant effort to make everything seem easy—and for simple applications, demos, and proof of concepts, it is easy. But the truth is for an application of substance, regardless of the technology, approach, or methodology, architecture and design are important. I am continually surprised at people's attitudes when I discuss this topic; many smart people just assume that nothing will go wrong, when without the right planning, they would be better off assuming that things *will* go wrong.

Don't get me wrong—having a positive attitude on your projects is important. In general you should love what you do; the project won't succeed without your dedication to success. Working with negative people can be very challenging; however, some degree of wariness is also necessary for success. This wariness could be considered the wisdom that comes with experience; every profession has a requirement for the ability to recognize potential problems and understand the risk that they may occur. I am not referring to the kind of risk assessment that becomes another unread work product delivered by your architecture team or an external consultant, but about the kind of risk that you understand inherently when a set of requirements is dropped on your desk that makes you and your team responsible for building a new enterprise application.

Helping organizations and architects understand the importance of application architecture as well as how to accomplish the desired goals within the context of the organization or project are the reasons I wanted to write this book. If you are using WebSphere in your project, then this book can help you focus on the key areas for consideration as well as provide examples of where and how to code many of the approaches discussed. This book is based on the concept of something called sleeves-up architecture, which means it is written for architects who find it necessary to roll up their sleeves and work directly with the code by building, tweaking, explaining, or reviewing code artifacts within the project. I'm not sure who to credit for that phrase, but he or she deserves a medal, as it perfectly typifies the right approach for building a successful application.

Architects and Architecture

Many people agree that the title *architect* is overloaded. I worked with an organization recently where everyone had the title architect, simply because that was the only way to meet the salary requirements of many of their IT staff. I'm okay with over use of the term, as I have never been big on titles. More important than a title is fully describing the role that an architect and other technical team members fills. Does the word *enterprise* really fit into your job title? For example, are you directly responsible for the success of a specific project? Or is it just your concern to deal with the bigger picture of the organization or Enterprise, leaving other architects with the responsibility of a specific project?

It is easy for practitioners in this field to become distanced from the technology, yet still be looked at as some type of guru. This position is very difficult, and in many cases trying to get re-engaged with the details of the technology can be intimidating. Technology moves so fast that not keeping up can easily result in your obsolescence. I know that many of you would agree that many high-level or enterprise architects don't know things like Java very well. And perhaps they shouldn't, depending upon their role within the organization, but if that is the case, then there are gaps the organization needs to fill (Application Architects) to allow for all the skills that are needed. Jokingly, high-level architects are sometimes referred to as "hand wavers" who with the wave of their hands or by drawing some boxes on the white board can determine an application's fate from day one. But they should also know when to abdicate that responsibility to someone better prepared to help make the right decisions on the ground.

Most of the time I think there is a huge disconnect between the folks who rightly carry the title *enterprise architect* and the lowly folks on the development team. I say "lowly" jokingly because my own career path is of that of an IT specialist, but to many up and coming techies, *architect* is the way to go if for no other reason than the title. Application architecture sits much lower in the software engineering hierarchy and is the type of architecture that is better performed by a specialist or a lead developer than a high-level architect. The point is that in most cases, application architecture should be performed by someone who is a working developer in that specific technical area.

Types of Architects

Figure 1.1 illustrates one view of the roles within an organization. Obviously, different roles than these exist and they are often given different names, but the concepts are valid in most cases.

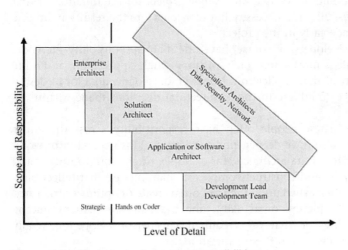

Figure 1.1   Technical roles and responsibilities

Each role in Figure 1.1 has a unique responsibility. Cases may exist where some people provide expertise for multiple roles, but it is important that the someone with skills in all the roles participate in the entire project. The following list describes the roles:

- **Enterprise architects:** These people have responsibility across the entire organization. They work closely with business decision makers and executives to understand the vision of the organization and drive IT to help achieve this vision. They also work with other teams and architects to understand points of interaction, available services, and help make decisions that affect the entire organization. The scope of their work is necessarily broad; however, they should have some deeper skills in some of the technologies they are evaluating or recommending.
- **Solution architects:** This title is a bit overloaded. In this context it defines someone who outlines the product set and major functions of an application. For example, an enterprise architect may just put a box in the design document that says "portal." It is the solution architect who may then start to decompose or flesh out that box and apply an application server, an HTTP server, security context, applications, and other components that help define the scope of the overall solution or environment. The scope of this person's work is generally focused across multiple projects; however, he or she may be focused on a single project or environment at any given time.
- Application or software architects: This role is really the focus of this book. The application or software architect is the person(s) who outlines the details of the application under development. Often this responsibility falls upon the development lead, but sometimes an application architect is assigned to the project. In either case, the application architect and the development team work hand in hand to ensure that what is developed is actually what was outlined in the architecture. This person's scope should be focused on a single project for the duration of that project. End-to-end visibility is a necessity in order to ensure the results are in line with the decisions made early in the project.
- Development lead: Developers, of course, have one main responsibility—to code. The scope of their role is most often solely within a single application, and quite often just a small part of that application. However, developers do a lot of design and all the while need to adhere to the architectural decisions made within the project.
- Specialized architects: These people often have responsibility across the entire organization, but they also have deeper implementation skills necessary for working within their specialty. Data architects, for example, often work to understand the needs of the business and construct complex domain models that reflect business needs; however, when called upon they can often create or optimize Structured Query Language (SQL) queries, or actually tune the database (DB) by adding indexes, changing settings, or whatever is required. This person's scope is generally across many or all projects within the organization.

This list should give you an idea of the type of roles that are necessary within the organization. Again, none of these roles are set in stone, but they are probably close to what you see within your organization. It seems sometimes that everyone is striving to be an architect, and better yet, an enterprise architect. Organizations proliferate this notion because often the only way to grow within the organization and on projects is to take on those roles. But the reality is that the higher you go, the harder your job should be as you struggle to keep up with enough technological details to make sound architecture decisions. Too often organizations end up with architects doing lots of hand waving and not making detail-based, sound decisions.

Some General Advice for Application Architects

So now that you have a set of defined roles, let me make a few suggestions to the technical leads within a project:

- Not knowing Java (I use the word Java here generically to mean any technology that may be used in your application; it could also be WebSphere, Spring, or whatever) does not relieve you of the responsibility to ensure that the application being designed and built follows best practices and good coding standards and conventions, and in general to warranty the application fit for the intended use. On the contrary, it increases your responsibility to ensure that the right people, skills, and rules are put in place to provide these assurances. Fortunately, this book provides some focus topics and guidelines to help you achieve these goals regardless of your experience level.
- Don't believe all the marketing hype: Vendor architects can sell you on a solution only for you to find out that it doesn't work quite as well for your application. In the last seven-plus years I have been working with WebSphere, I have never found a problem that could not be solved, but a small proof of concept early in the effort can go a long way toward minimizing your risk and ensuring you have estimated the effort correctly. This problem can be especially true when relying on tooling and wizards. A wizard can build a simple application in a few seconds that can connect to a database or web service and allow the user to interact with the data. This result does not mean that this generated example should then be moved into a production environment. There is a big difference between a generated example and production-ready code.
- If you are responsible, then act responsibly. Sometimes even if you are not responsible you should assume responsibility for the quality of your project. Many years ago during the dot-com boom, I wanted in on the action and switched from working in operations to becoming a consultant with a well-known boutique consulting firm. For my first project I was brought in on a team as one of the technical specialists to help during the requirements phase. In a team of about 20 people I was literally the low man on the totem pole. Six months later I was running the entire project with a team of about 40 developers. How did this happen? It wasn't through the ladder-climbing or attention-grabbing activities that many of my co-workers were involved in. While entertaining, these approaches generally ended up being nonproductive. My responsibilities grew by my assuming those responsibilities that

my coworkers ignored. Executive management recognized this and knew that I was mostly running the project anyway, and over time they made my role official. By the way, although I was largely successful on this project, it was my last official attempt at technical project management. I think it is way more fun to be digging in the trenches than peering over the side trying to plan the depth and length of the trench, even if the digging does sometimes appear to be harder.

• Don't ignore the little things, and sometimes the big things. Too often important details are left until later in the project, which can often be a source of trouble. What can be considered is often subjective to the architect or the project. Often it is one thing or another that we think we can figure out later in the project, such as standards. I love it when I hear, "we'll work out our standards as we go" when getting started on a big project. In some cases the big things can get ignored as well. For example, I'm surprised how often the discussion of performance and caching is pushed off until later in the project. Understandably, everyone has a lot to do at the beginning of a project, but too often "later" never comes, and if it does the effort to address the delayed issue is understandably more than if it had been designed for properly in the beginning.

Communicate Every Day

Daily communication is an important tool that too often gets lost in the day-to-day shuffle. When I am assigned as a lead in a project I make it a point to talk to the team every day. Usually I do so individually during the course of the day as I walk around and discuss different points or items in progress. This effort probably stems from my time as a squad leader in the army, where you can imagine that constant communication is extremely vital.

A while back I was helping with a project that had eight different project managers (PM) to manage different parts of the project as well as a senior project manager responsible for the entire project. My role as a consultant was to provide guidance into the application architecture, design, and development of the project. During the course of the day I would meet the members of the different teams to discuss their status, any problems, and solutions or next steps. Sometimes a team would report to its project manager that some component was finished, only to realize later on in the discussion that something either was not working as required or needed to be changed. These issues were not major; actually they were very routine items during the course of the development cycle.

Often the senior project manager would stop by my desk to get an update on what was going on during the day. I would tell him who I was working with and about any problems we had found with a particular component. As you can imagine this infuriated the subteam project managers who would go to the daily status meeting and report the status of a component as complete, only to be questioned by the senior project manager because I had mentioned the component was perhaps not quite totally complete. This was not done in a negative way, or to challenge anyone's competence, or to get anyone in trouble; it was merely the result of the incessant need for constant and informal communication.

I tried to explain to one PM who questioned me on this communication technique that he simply needed to do what I did—talk to his team's members instead of relying on status emails. Asking me why I was giving the senior PM conflicting information from what was in the emails, I replied simply, "Because he asked."

Often I see a virtual light bulb go on when I discuss application architecture topics with customers or project teams, and it is nice to see when someone is really starting to understand the concepts around Application Architecture. But often this fleeting moment soon gets lost in the hustle and bustle of the daily grind. For architects, project managers, and lead developers (really anyone associated with building enterprise applications) this should be the main focus of your daily grind, rather than a subtext to be "gotten to" when there is more time available.

As you grow your skills as a professional developer or architect, you may tend to forget that the profession is constantly churning with new people, ideas, and technology. This churn, and the fact that software engineering is not really like physical engineering concepts, is why poor applications continue to be built. In physical engineering the quality of a product can be measured directly, however in software engineering this can be very difficult. What is a poor application? It is any application that does not live up to its functional and nonfunctional requirements in terms of performance, security, usability, or function. It should not be that hard for any software engineer to think back on a project he or she worked on or led that did not meet that minimum set of criteria.

Application Architecture and Engineering

The science of software engineering should abide by the same type of rigorous rules and standards that other sciences and engineering disciplines abide by. No other engineered product is released to the general public without deep inspection and testing, yet in the software world, inspections take place only a small fraction of the time, and those are often cursory and incomplete.

I have purposely written this book to be something you should sit down and read, rather than as a reference of patterns to be looked at when you think they are needed. By this I mean that I hope you can learn from actually reading the chapters and not just trying to look up the answers when you think you need them. My goal is to change your way of thinking slightly when it comes to software architecture and building web applications. The concept of application architecture involves thinking about how projects are approached and the preparation that goes on before any actual coding begins. As you read through this book and begin to understand some of the issues with building good applications, I hope you can take that understanding and apply it to your current or next project with vigor. As the title suggests, knowing just how to build an application is not enough—knowing how to build good applications is the ultimate goal.

WebSphere and IBM

A1.1

Sometimes the word WebSphere can be a little confusing to people new to the IBM products suites; however, allow me to try to clarify the concept. WebSphere is both a brand and a set of products. As a brand, it is the trademark for IBM's integration and middleware line of products, but it is also a trademark that is applied to individual products within the WebSphere product line. This includes many of the products discussed in this book, as well as services and tools that might be available, such as development tools.

Figure 1.2 illustrates many of the areas where WebSphere Application Server or other WebSphere products can be used.

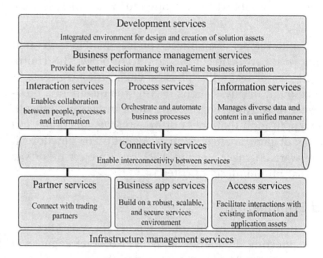

Figure 1.2   IBM integration reference architecture

Here are brief descriptions of some of these areas:

- Business application services: Business application services are the components and services that deliver the functionality to drive your business. In the Java world these are now standard web applications, which normally deliver a user interface enabling your employees, customers, or business partners to interact with and perform your core business functions. Essentially, you can think of this as an application server and it is at the core of the discussion within this book.
- Interaction services: In clear terms interaction services refers to the interface or front end that is used to directly interact with applications and back-end systems. It can be a web page, a portal, or some type of mobile device such as a PDA or cell phone.
- Process integration: Business process choreography is the new wave of IT. Understanding, modeling, and choreographing, and most importantly, improving business processes, is the key to a service-oriented approach and enabling the needs of the business through information technology.
- Information and application integration: System interoperability is key to getting an environment full of disparate systems to work together cohesively. Most organizations are full of systems running on different platforms, written in different languages. Integrating these systems with new systems allows IT to be more flexible when business requirements demand systems integration in new and sometimes unusual ways.

To get an idea of how comprehensive the products in the WebSphere brand are you can take a look at where they fit into this reference architecture (see Figure 1.3). In theory each of these areas can map to one or more products, services, or accelerators that can speed the delivery of functionality within the WebSphere brand.

The focus of this book is on WebSphere Application Server. It is the base product in the WebSphere brand and provides a strong application server solution based upon the Java Standard Edition. This subject is more than enough for a single book; however, I do touch on related functionality in other products and try word to help you make some decisions around the use of these products.

IBM WebSphere Application Server

IBM's WebSphere Application Server (WAS) is one word of the leading application servers on the market today. Like most application servers, WebSphere has many features in common with current competitors, but it also has many additional features that offer advantages to using it. Figure 1.3 shows many of the features, application programming interfaces (APIs), extensions, and capabilities of WebSphere Application Server. As of this writing WebSphere Application Server V6.1 is the latest version with version 7 not far away. This book tries to provide helpful information outside of any version-specific information; however, as much as possible the discussion focuses any examples and suggestions on version 6.1 with a look toward the extensions and new capabilities available in version 7.

A1.2

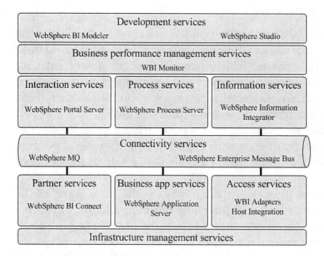

Figure 1.3   Reference architecture with product mapping

Generally you can think of WAS in simple terms as a product that has a web container and an Enterprise Java Bean (EJB) container. This simple definition helps us sleep better at night. But as you can see in Figure 1.4, WebSphere Application Server is a complex product with not only multiple containers, but many core services and infrastructure facilities. If you are working with a layered product such as WebSphere Portal, WebSphere Commerce, or WebSphere Process Server, then often you are focused on the specific functionality and requirements for that product. However, let me reinforce that base WebSphere Application Server knowledge can still help you build better WAS applications.

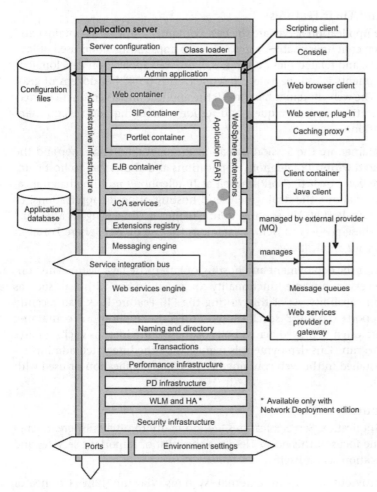

Figure 1.4   WAS V6.1 product architecture

The Base Containers and Their Features

At the core of WebSphere Application Server are the base containers—the web container and the EJB container. The web container enables you to run web apps mostly composed of Java Server Pages (JSPs), servlets, and related files or libraries. Basic web application development and building these components is well beyond the scope of this book, but dozens of great books on the topic exist. The web container handles all the application server functions necessary to host your application, such as request and response handling and session management for your application.

Included in the web container are the Session Initiation Protocol (SIP) container and the portlet container. SIP is used within IP telephony applications and allows you to host components that can manage voice over IP (VoIP) as well as IP telephony multimedia applications. The portlet container allows the deployment and hosting of portal applications, or portlets, that follow the Java Portlet API specification. Chapter 6, "Investing in a Portal," offers more detail about these portlets as well as examines the use of WebSphere Portal in the presentation layer of your applications.

The EJB container allows for the deployment and hosting of Enterprise Java Beans. This container provides all the necessary runtime functionality for an EJB to live within it, such as threading and transaction capability. As of this writing the EJB Feature Pack had recently been released, which supports the EJB 3 specification. Enterprise applications containing servlets, JSPs, and EJBs are often deployed across both of these containers as each requires its unique environment to run. This deployment is managed by the integrated administration console, which is installed in the web container as a separate application or used with the deployment manager.

Other WebSphere Features

The rest of WebSphere Application Server's features are too many to discuss in great detail here, even if they were the focus of this book. Here is a short list of important services and features within the application server itself:

- JCA Services provides access to external systems via the J2EE Connector Architecture (JCA) specification. Database connections are created through the JCA services interface, through other external enterprise applications, and through specialized connectors such as message bean connectors for the Java Messaging Service (JMS) communication. The JCA service provides a connection manager that pools and manages resources to external data systems. JCA resource providers may be provided by external vendors to allow access to these systems.
- Messaging resources allow you to support asynchronous messaging within your applications. Providers are included for both WebSphere MQ and for generic JMS providers that adhere to messaging specifications. The Service Integration Bus (SIB or SI Bus), as part of the messaging engine, provides a reliable way to integrate messaging services with the rest of your architecture. For example, the SI Bus allows web services to introduce or receive messages within your application.

- Security plays a large part in applications today and as such is not treated lightly by WAS. In many applications, security is turned on by default and should be turned on by any applications you deploy, no matter how small. Chapter 9, "Keeping Things Secure," offers some basics and guidelines to make sure you start off on the right foot toward security, although admittedly it is probably another topic that needs its own book to be handled correctly.

Due to space constraints they aren't discussed here, but several APIs and services are available within WAS such as Java Naming and Directory (JNDI) service, JavaMail API, the WebServices engine, and transaction services.

A Word about Specifications

Open standard specifications provide guidelines to creating portable applications. I have to admit that even though sometimes they may seem horribly boring to read, I am a big proponent of reviewing technology specifications, especially those for features expected to be part of a new product release. When a spec is released for a new feature that IBM is implementing, reading it is one approach for quickly getting up to speed on the new feature's functionality. By reviewing the specification and perhaps even presenting a little information about it to some coworkers, you can obtain a better understanding of it. Some of the specifications covered in this book are currently being released as tech previews and will be fully released in WebSphere products as of this book's release:

- Enterprise JavaBeans Specification 3: Currently released as a WAS V6.1 Feature Pack and should be part of WAS V7
- JSR 286 (Java Portlet API V2): Recently approved and will be part of WebSphere Portal V6.1
- Service Data Objects (SDO) V2.1: Currently released as a WAS V6.1 Feature Pack and should be part of WAS V7
- Service Component Architecture (SCA) V1.0: Currently released as a WAS V6.1 Feature Pack and should be part of WAS V7
- Java API for XML Web Services (JAX-WS) V2.0: Currently released as a WAS V6.1 Feature Pack and should be part of WAS V7
- Java Architecture for XML Binding (JAXB) V2.0: Currently released as a WAS V6.1 Feature Pack and should be part of WAS V7

How Close to the Specification Should I Stay with My Architecture?

WebSphere provides many features and functions that are beyond any current specifications. Probably one of the reasons your project or organization is using WebSphere is because IBM has a lot of smart people developing the application server and related products within the WebSphere brand of products. If you run into trouble, or one of the features does not work as designed, then you have the full power of IBM (which can be impressive when put into action) working to fix your problem.

For example, suppose you decide to implement an object caching strategy using a custom approach rather than taking advantage of the built-in dynamic caching ability of WebSphere, such as the distributed Map (dMap). Any problems you encounter would likely be considered custom code and although IBM would help you diagnose and understand the problem, it would most likely not be on the hook for application design changes. If, however, you were using the distributed Map technology and it was not working correctly, a lot of people would be lining up to help resolve your issue as well as make sure that other customers did not encounter the same problem.

WebSphere Extensions to Consider

Understanding what is available to you is half the battle. If you know of a specific service or extension to consider then you can evaluate the use of that service within your application. Does it fit your needs, or how close is it considering you won't have to reinvent the wheel? The following are extensions that I find compelling:

- Eclipse Extension Framework allows you, IBM, and other vendors to provide extensions to its applications that can be adapted to your requirements. For example, the WebSphere Portal V6 URI resolution service uses the Eclipse Extension Framework to allow you to build custom extensions for portal URI mapping. Although seemingly trivial, this feature provides the ability to access specific resources within the portal via externally created URLs.
- The Dynamic Caching Service is one of the most compelling capabilities available within WAS. The ability to cache at all levels within your application (internal and external) using minimal code is something that should be built into every application. Chapter 8, "Caching and Performance," covers caching in detail, but for now consider it something that is non-negotiable in your application design.
- The WAS Scheduler is a cron-like scheduling service for J2EE applications. Scheduling has traditionally been a problem for Java applications, which provide batch operations or need to run at a specific time. Application servers are uniquely designed to be real time, request and response type of applications so fitting the two competing requirements has been problematic. The scheduler allows you to extend specific interfaces with your application and then manage specific intervals via the WAS administration interface.

Certainly other extensions exist that you may consider, such as Business Process Model, ActivitySessions, Startup Beans, and Object Pools; however, these components are used in some very specific cases and are not addressed in this book.

Sometimes organizations want to adhere very closely to the specification because of the very respectful goal of ensuring portability across vendors or platforms. Many times I see this with customers who are developing with IBM's JWL (JavaServer Faces Widget Library), but who want to use something like Apache MyFaces instead. Optionally in other projects there might be some indecision about portlet messaging standard within a portal framework.

Should we build a custom portlet communication method, instead of IBM's portlet messaging implementation. Understand that most specifications are considered a minimum standard that a large group of vendors and standards bodies could agree upon, and that all vendors add additional functionality to these specs because that is what provides the value that customers need when evaluating products and building applications.

One discussion point with many customers new to WebSphere is as follows: embarking on a new platform or enterprise application requires a substantial investment in hardware, software, tools, education, and sometimes services. Usually, extensive due diligence was performed in picking the platform, and the investment is deemed to be long term. Switching platforms in the next two or three years would be a substantial loss of investment; most IT organizations would have a hard time convincing the business that a new investment is necessary (this is similar to the, "we have to upgrade" discussion). Additionally, many of the enhanced features of WebSphere products, such as caching and portlet messaging, contain very compelling functionality that would cost possibly hundreds of hours to design, develop, and maintain independently.

The one obvious caveat in this discussion is for third-party vendors and others who are actually building applications that are to be run on multiple platforms. These applications should probably degrade to the basic specification when necessary, but may also take advantage of enhanced features within different servers to provide improved performance, security, and manageability. Unfortunately, most of this functionality would need to be designed on a case-by-case basis; however, building a correctly layered and modularized architecture enables you to plug in capability when possible.

One Size Does Not Fit All

This look at IBM's reference architecture helps to set the stage for the product suite functionality and major layers that may exist within your environment. You can imagine that large organizations or complex environments have many if not all of these reference architecture components in place, or at least have them in the planning stages.

IBM's product suite contains a bewildering array of products and services, and the list continues to grow as IBM adopts new products to fill gaps in its portfolio. Sometimes major overlap occurs in functionality from one product to the next and determining which feature to use can be overwhelming. Just remember that IBM does not build products in a one-size-fits-all manner. The customer base ranges across every conceivable size and industry; enabling customers to shape and squeeze these products into their environment is a top priority.

If all this has you confused, don't worry; you find out more about some of these options throughout the book.

Building Blocks of Application Architecture

Now that much of the groundwork is out of the way, how do you actually start designing the application? With distributed applications the obvious starting point is to look at the basic n-tiered architecture and understand how a layered architecture can be expanded to fit within this model. Figure 1.5 shows a classic three-layered architecture you might see in any application. In fact, you should see it in most applications. These layers could easily map to different tiers within the infrastructure, but they could just as easily all reside within the same tier; that is, a single application server that provides some type of web application to end users.

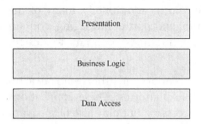

Figure 1.5   Separation of concerns

One of the goals of software engineering is to separate different types of application functionality into logical areas of concern. These three layers are often called by different names, although the presentation layer title often is consistent:

- Presentation layer: Sometimes also called the user interface layer, it defines the visual elements used to lay out applets and views, to navigate, and to make selections via buttons and check boxes.
- Business logic layer: This layer contains entities such as business objects, business components, integration objects, and business services.
- Data access layer: This layer is often also called the persistence layer. It provides a logical representation of the underlying physical database and is independent of the installed relational database management system. The data access layer does not always have to access a database, and may sometimes be broken up into the enterprise access layer or service access layer to provide communication with other systems and applications within the enterprise.

One thing to be careful of during discussion is to fully identify what these layers represent. For example, does the data access layer actually represent the database and DBMS, or is it really a software persistence layer that then communicates to the actual database on a separate tier within the infrastructure? Often infrastructure tiers and software layers are intermingled in these diagrams and it is important to distinguish between the two. For this reason, you need to ensure that you consistently name the layers to account for their purpose within the architecture.

Many applications can be designed just using these three layers; however, there is often a need to create more separation for complex applications. A simple extension shown in Figure 1.6 illustrates how this separation might look within the context of a single, simple web application. The layers, although very logically defined, can still be packaged and deployed within the same Web Archive (WAR) file. This chapter covers packaging and deployment options later on so don't think that this is a final recommendation by any means.

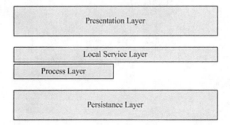

Figure 1.6 A simple layered architecture

In Figure 1.6 the top layers are as follows:

- Notice that the business layer has been broken down into additional layers that encompass specific functionality.
- The local service layer has replaced the business logic layer as the main middle tier and provides access to all back-end services for the presentation layer. Coming from a mostly portal background where multiple applications are being developed for a shared environment, the local service layer becomes a point of control to any external systems. You will see the benefit of this local service layer in later chapters, but for now it just illustrates how to break down layers into additional layered components.
- The data access layer has been replaced by the persistence layer. This is a naming convention that has taken hold within the industry, but there will be differences within each organization in how layers are defined.

As additional layers are flushed out within the architecture a common question to ask yourself is when to stop. This question is not as hard to answer as it sounds, although it is an "it depends" type of question. Using layers to group "types" of functionality makes sense. Thinking about our first try at creating a logical model we could view types of functionality as presentation, business, data access, and so on, but this is probably too high a level for many projects to be the final state. A good guiding principle is to keep it simple when possible. Do you have a business process layer in place or plan to in the near future?

Detail in Layering

At some point you need to choose the amount of detail that should be outlined within the layered architecture. Figure 1.7 shows the presentation layer broken into two separate layers: the presentation view and the presentation controller layers. This type of distinction may or may not be necessary within your environment.

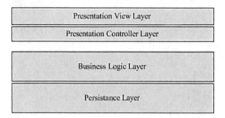

Figure 1.7   Breaking down the presentation layer

For example, if you have designed a custom presentation controller framework using a page controller or front controller pattern, then making this distinction and providing appropriate examples may be necessary to ensure that the development team can continue to follow this approach. However, if you are using a canned framework for presentation, such as Struts or JavaServer Faces, then making this distinction may not be necessary unless you want to provide specific guidance to the developers.

A Complete Example

Figure 1.8 may look more like what you think of as a layered architecture.

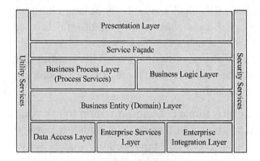

Figure 1.8   Complete layered architecture

The layers provide better detail than the original three layer approach and are as follows:

- Service façade: The service façade is based on the original service pattern from the Gang-of-Four, Design Patterns book published in 1995 (Gamma et al., 1994). The idea is to encapsulate business behavior behind a thin layer to hide the underlying complexity of the system. In this example this concept is apparent in several different ways: The local service layer (LSL) and the business logic layer (BLL) both provide the functionality of a façade to the presentation layer.
- Business logic and business process layers: While some overlap may occur between the components, depending upon your use, this can be two distinct yet complementary layers. The business logic layer is commonly where the presentation layer requests some business data or transaction to occur. This layer is generally custom-developed code that interacts with the domain layer and data access layer. The business process layer acts at a different level and is designed as an interface for applications to either start or interact with short- or long-running business processes. This layer is responsible for managing the overall execution of the business process.
- Business entity or domain layer: The domain layer is composed of objects that represent components in your business domain and the relationships between them. For example, domain objects may represent customers, orders, employees, or insurance policies.
- Data Access and Enterprise Services Layers: Data and services access encapsulates the mechanics of storing and retrieving information from the backend. These types of transactions are usually messy with transactional awareness, connection management and pooling, and specific communication protocols for each system being accessed.
- Security services: These services provide the necessary security for all levels within your architecture and may be provided already by the application server itself. Your organization may also require custom services, such as when you have an external authorization engine that is used to determine access rights to different components and information within your organization based on job title and role.
- Utility services: Utility services provide all of those general things necessary across all layers of the application. Logging is probably the most obvious example; however, additional services may include caching, monitoring, or even XML parsing.

Are All These Layers Really Necessary?

Interestingly, many of these layers may appear to merge at times, or fail to provide a clean separation. It seems at times that the domain layer and data access layer need to be tightly coupled to work together. This is probably true in the implementation space and in many cases may not be a problem within your architecture.

You can easily make a case for having too many layers. However, I often question myself when making the claim that a clean separation allows for modifications without affecting the rest of the system. In theory this approach is correct; however, in practice it is almost never the case. Imagine your house—you can easily replace the roof or even replace the exterior of your house with siding. It illustrates a clean separation between the plumbing and electrical with the outside façade of your home. Replacing the foundation of your home, however, is significantly more work and can in extreme circumstances require digging up or lifting and moving the entire structure The main concerns that we need to take into account are illustrated in Figure 1.9.

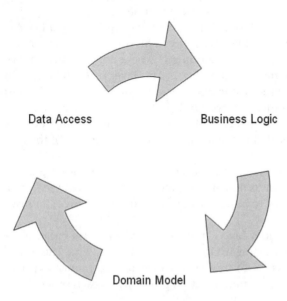

Figure 1.9   Logical Separation of concerns

However, the point of layering your architecture serves more than one purpose. It is about the following:

- Controlling the flow of the application and the actions of the development team
- Reusing the components that fully represents your business requirements, and if they don't then extending them to provide a more complete representation
- Enforcing standards and codes on the structure to ensure that it is built correctly and will perform adequately in production

Separation of concerns is also about reducing code duplication within your application. If every presentation component needed to access data, but each in a slightly different way, then you would have a lot of trouble when it came time to deploy, test, or maintain the code. However, by separating the application into layers where each layer can focus on a specific functional area, you can focus on specific aspects of the application and keep some of your sanity in this complex world.

Adding Flexibility into Your Layering Structure

In my opinion the structure shown earlier in Figure 1.8 is too imposing. It illustrates a heavily layered architecture in which the components at the very top have to wind their way through many layers to get to functions at the very bottom. In some cases this structure is fine, and if the interfaces are built correctly, what is going on behind any façade should not be apparent, but your goal is slightly different. You want a flexible architecture that can be put into place in any number of applications of any size. As such you don't want to impose such a rigid architecture on your projects. Figure 1.10 illustrates a provision for increased communication between layers, sometimes allowing upper layers to go directly to some of the persistence functionality.

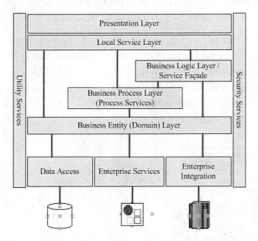

Figure 1.10   Communication between layers

Suppose a small piece of the screen has to display some data, such as an alert, a message from the CEO, or perhaps even the cafeteria menu for the day. Forcing the application or servlet to traverse 6+ layers to get this data may be overkill. In these cases going directly to the persistence layer or perhaps the domain layer may make sense.

Skipping layers can have some major disadvantages so some discussion about what any feature really does will be necessary, but notice that enforcement still exists within the layering. Again the local service layer (LSL) comes into place. For the example of the cafeteria menu, you only want to access the back end datasource once a day and not once for every user or every request. In this example the LSL would probably provide some caching capability or an interface for several presentation components to access the same data. The main issue at hand in this case would be scalability and manageability, so skipping layers is allowed without any formal discussion. Always remind your team to use rigid software engineering practices while still maintaining flexibility.

Layers Versus Tiers

I tend to use the terms layers and tiers in very distinct ways. For me the distinction between them is one of logical versus physical separation. This keeps the idea of layers versus tiers very simple and lets me visualize the application structure at a high level. Of course, real life or production environments are never that simple. What is meant by a physical separation? Is it a separate Java Virtual Machine (JVM) or application server instance, or is it a physically separate machine, or set of machines, within the infrastructure?

One of the core ideas behind layers is that they allow for a logical separation, which in turn provides the opportunity for physical separation. A tier is usually a separate physical layer or set of layers within the application, while a layer itself does not necessarily exist on a separate tier. Several or even all layers may exist on the same tier or physical machine.

Figure 1.11 illustrates in a very simple manner the idea of how logical layers can be separated into physical tiers. Designing your architecture in layers, modules, or some other type of grouping or encapsulation enables you to distribute layers at a later date. Is all of this discussion overkill? Probably, but hopefully you can see the value in keeping the terminology straight and understanding the implications of your architecture. Any misunderstanding in the architecture will lead to mistakes and possibly future problems.

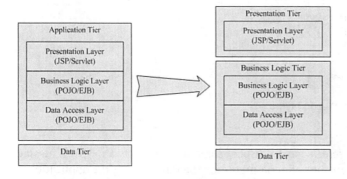

Figure 1.11   Layers versus tiers

Whether you will need to make the separation of layers to different tiers at a later date depends upon your organization and the demands on your application. Adding additional tiers after a system goes live is much harder than doing it upfront. For example, hardware and operations costs must be considered if an additional tier is to be added to an environment. These estimates are usually provided at the beginning of a project, and hardware is ordered long before any testing is conducted. The implications involved in adding tiers are not something to forward to near the end of the project. Will the business be willing to provide funds for a mistake made in estimation by IT? Additionally, moving layers to separate tiers puts your application design and development to the test. Did the developers follow the architecture correctly to allow this move to happen smoothly? Did the design account for remoteability of layers?

Figure 1.11 shows some technologies applied to some of the layers. Later chapters cover more of the options available and offer some guidelines for how to choose an implementation approach.

Figure 1.12 shows an example where it appears some layers are simply not needed within the application. The reality is that the three prerequisite layers are still there; they are just hidden within some new terminology. For smaller applications this approach is entirely reasonable. For large applications this approach might be impossible. The goal is to find what is right for your project and for projects within your organization.

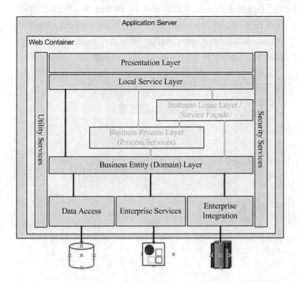

Figure 1.12   Non-distributed use of layers

Martin Fowler in his book, *Patterns of Enterprise Application Architecture* (Fowler 2003) states, "The First Law of Distributed Object Design: Don't distribute your objects!" You should probably take this statement to heart during the lifetime of the project. Listening to customers talk about building web services everywhere and distributing business logic across multiple tiers can be disorienting. Unless IT realizes the repercussions of distributing objects across a multitiered environment and understands the responsibility involved in building these types of applications, you shouldn't rest easy. This awareness of repercussions usually occurs right after a problematic Go-Live. Then the proverbial light bulb moment occurs for everyone.

Deployment Patterns for a Layered Architecture

There are many benefits to the idea of separation of concerns. Even in a single web app solution, this separation is important. Figure 1.13 illustrates the combination of a layered architecture with a deployable component or application. This example shows a single web application packaged within a web archive or WAR file. This deployment package is common for many applications today.

Because every application is different a need exists for flexibility within the layers to account for any number of different applications within your environment. Chapter 2, "Setting a Standard" addresses more about project and organizational standards; however, it is important to understand that the architecture you design today should be similar to the one that you design for the next application or project, assuming of course, you are part of an organizational IT shop, and not an external consultant with multiple customers.

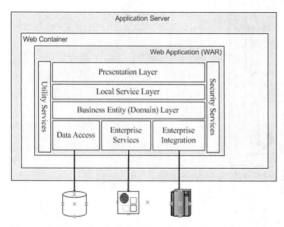

Figure 1.13   Single WAR file deployment

Although Figure 1.13 illustrates the simplest case, it is by far not the only case. One of the main goals when designing an overarching architecture is the reuse of services. Many web applications access the same set of services or data store. In other cases changes made in one part of the application may need to be reflected in another part. Figure 1.14 shows an example where multiple web apps can take advantage of shared tiers within the environment.

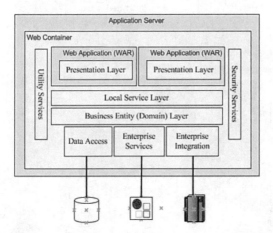

Figure 1.14 Architecting for multiple web apps

Notice that we are still not really distributed although we can take advantage of the scalability features of WebSphere and expand this tier as necessary. For many applications this will be the core of your environment; you can imagine that many of the services that you access through your enterprise services module are created using a similar architecture to the one in Figure 1.14. This approach offers a flexible architecture that you can duplicate across your environment and adapt to the needs of that specific service or application.

Figure 1.15 is probably closer to what you might imagine when you think about application architecture, but it is only an expansion of the cases discussed so far. Distributing your layers within the EJB container and perhaps to a separate tier within the environment should happen on a case-by-case basis. Don't automatically conclude that EJBs are required within your application. The same goes for web services, JMS, and other distributed technologies until some analysis is performed on your requirements.

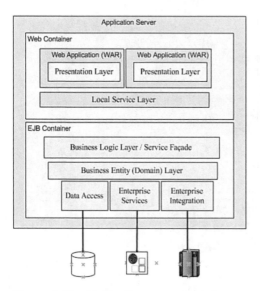

Figure 1.15   Distribution across containers

In his follow-up book, *J2EE Development without EJB*, Rod Johnson (Johnson & Hoeller, 2004) makes a strong case against the use of EJBs in J2EE applications. In many cases I think his analysis is right on, having seen firsthand the trouble that development teams can get into on complex projects. However, with some recent specification releases, including EJB 3.0, the Java Persistence API, and even the Service Data Objects 2.1 specification release, some of this effort becomes less complex. You can take advantage of distributed environments more easily, but still focus on the primary goals of performance, scalability, and correctness.

Think about Common Cases, Not Every Possible Contingency

I remember a case about "keeping it simple" from a few years back. I was leading an effort as part of the infrastructure/deployment team to move from a legacy source code management system to a new system that would fit better within our WebSphere-based environment. The choices were between Concurrent Versions System (CVS) and another popular version control system, which I'll call SystemX. Because of our requirements, the small size of the team, and so on, my recommendation was to use CVS and build a continuous integration environment around it. When discussing this approach with the development team lead and the project manager I explained the options and the reasons behind my recommendation. The discussion immediately launched into versioning scenarios, with each example becoming more complicated than the last. I explained that we were accommodating the majority of cases, and would have to worry about these extreme examples as they occurred. These things had never occurred in the past mind you, but this team was convinced that they had to account for every possible contingency.

Soon after this I left this project (for different reasons), but one of my close friends and a colleague took over as project lead and kept me informed of the team's progress. The project team did go ahead and implement SystemX against my initial recommendations, and after several months and a host of problems, the team eventually reverted to CVS as their final system.

This example is not meant to argue against any particular system, only to express the notion that every product, architecture, and design has its place. Overarchitecturing a solution can be as much a concern as under architecturing the solution.

Layers Versus Modules

One topic not discussed yet is the idea that layers are more of an abstract separation of the types of functionality that you often encounter within distributed applications. The names typically given to different layers identify the type: presentation, business logic, domain model, and so on; however, the components that actually populate each layer are highly dependent upon your business and the type of application you are designing.

Modules, also sometimes called components, are usually developed within each layer that provides the actual functionality that you are expecting. The use of modules allows you to expand or change functionality within each layer as required, and the modules are as varied as the many aspects of an organization and the services that IT provides. No good way exists for an organization to be able to identify every module that it may need all at one time. Additionally, as discussed previously about deployment options for layers, you may have noticed that not every application makes use of all layers. The same holds true for modules, allowing some flexibility for project architects to make design decisions and still stay within the overall guiding framework. Identifying layers upfront provides the guiding framework for each project or program; however, the next level of identifying new or existing modules within each layer should be performed during the functional analysis or design phases of a project.

Identifying Modules

Every diagram can be different, but in this book I have adopted a simple style to identify major and when appropriate minor modules within a system, as shown in Figure 1.16. A simple box with the major identifying functionality is sufficient. Indicating whether the

interface of that module is external or internal to that layer is also important. Doing so identifies to the development team which components are available for use by other layers
within the system and provides some guidance on how the internal structure may be
defined when building a set of modules.

External modules are identified here as nodes that extend outside the confines of the layer
itself. Internal modules have nodes that do not extend outside, but rather are contained
completely within the module itself.

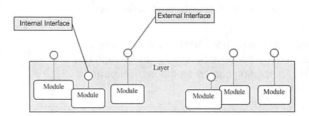

Figure 1.16   Types of modules

As you can see the nomenclature is quite simple, yet it provides enough information to
identify major functionality within each layer and does not force the team to try to identify
all functional modules at once.

Defining Modules

Module definition is an effort in itself. Whereas layers are relatively simple to define as types
of functionality, modules are components of the functionality itself and therefore dependent upon your environment or application. Figure 1.17 shows a set of different modules that
you may define within your system.

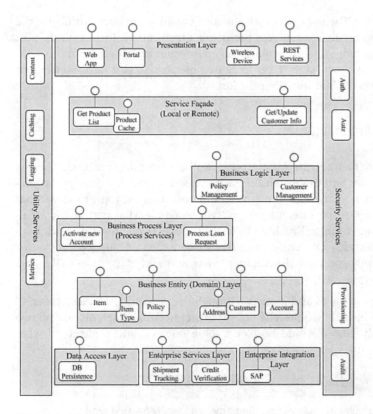

Figure 1.17   Modules within each layer

This module list is not exclusive, nor does it attempt to show every possibility. In reality there is often not a single design approach. For example, REST services may exist in other layers as opposed to only in the presentation layer. There is a strong trend toward reusing code and services within an IT organization. The goal has always been there, but reaching it has eluded many development teams. This is especially true once you are beyond the confines of a single team or project and trying to reach an enterprise. This approach, and this book, can help with that effort if you take the time to do it right. Under pressure many teams forget the less glamorous things such as maintaining a clean separation between layers and fully documenting and cataloging components and features for potential reuse.

One of the reasons Service Oriented Architecture (SOA) is gaining such popularity in IT organizations today is because it allows greater code reuse through greater abstraction of the different services that are necessary in many applications today. The penalties, or should I say challenges, is performance, security, and governance around the creation and use of SOA services. Development teams need to ensure they understand the challenges and the benefits of any approach they use. The use of SOA within your organization does not negate the benefit of good application architecture across the whole organization. In fact, to do SOA properly you need to spend more time on application architecture than ever before, as your services may be used in ways you haven't yet imagined or have Service Level Agreement (SLA) requirements that you did not initially plan for.

A View Perspective on Architecture

Trying to look at the entire architecture for a project can be a daunting position. There is often simply too much to try and understand. I have focused heavily on one type of diagram for most of this chapter. Many books on architecture touch on the topic of views; that is, looking at the application from different perspectives based on what part of the architecture you are interested in. Phillippe Kruchten in his 1995 paper (Kruchten 1995) first popularized the idea of the 4+1 view of architecture. The set consisted of four separate views: logical view, process view, physical view, development view, and a set of use cases that brings all the views together.

This book isn't so hung up on views and models. Through my years in IT as a developer, IT manager, and consultant I have drawn literally dozens of architectural diagrams and no two have looked the same. My advice would be to do some research and understand what options are available, then use what makes sense for your application.

Be Mindful of Colors

Whenever I use color in architecture diagrams, especially layered type diagrams, people are immediately aware of it within the image. I get asked the question more often than I should, "what do the colors signify?" Whenever this happens I have to think about whether I did intend to use color to signify items within the diagram. More often than not, I was looking for a way to make the diagram more pleasing to my viewers and/or to distinguish between different artifacts within the diagram.

But what happens when a drawing is copied in black and white, which is often the case during architecture reviews? Any use of color is immediately lost. The same can hold true for those among us who might be color blind, or in the case of this book, where images are purposely printed in grayscale to reduce printing costs. In some cases the use of color is warranted, such as to identify security interactions versus data flow. However, even it can fall prey to a world where color is still expensive to reproduce.

Conclusion

Face it. Why do we really care about all this anyway? Because we want software that works well; is easy to maintain; is fast, scalable, and secure; and fits the needs of the business or end users. That's a tall order by any stretch. Think about traditional architecture and building a house. Architects and contractors often have lots of experience and they don't always get everything right. My wife and I often comment that in our next house we are going to have this feature or that, or comment on design decisions that don't really agree with the way we live. That is not to say the next owners or tenants won't love these features that we sometimes find a little bit lacking.

In the same way, software architects have to deal with these issues, and make decisions that future users or architects may or may not agree with. Development teams (or contractors) may use substandard materials or cut a corner here and there that can result in problems or brittle software. Do I want the laundry room next to the kitchen, or upstairs closer to the kids who seem to generate all that laundry? If it's not in the right place, can I live with it? The same types of questions apply when building software.

The approach put forth in this chapter and in much of the book is about decomposing your application into layers and then deciding where those layers fit within the infrastructure. Other architectural approaches such as a service-oriented approach still apply, but at a higher level. The definition of services and the development of those services can be approached separately and have their own requirements and constraints within the organization. The focus here is at the application level and to provide enough detail to building something that meets the overall goals and requirements of that system.

Links to developerWorks Articles

A1.1 WebSphere at developerWorks: http://www.ibm.com/developerworks/websphere/

A1.2 WebSphere Application Server Zone: http://www.ibm.com/developerworks/websphere/zones/was/

References

Gamma, Erich, Richard Helm, Ralph Johnson, and John M. Vlissides (November 10, 1994). *Design Patterns: Elements of Reusable Object-Oriented Software*. Addison-Wesley Professional Computing Series.

Fowler, M. (2003). Distribution Strategies. In *Patterns of Enterprise Application Architecture* (p. 89). Boston: Pearson Education, Inc.

Johnson, Rod, and Juergen Hoeller   (2004). *J2EE Development without EJB*. Indianapolis, Indiana: Wiley Publishing, Inc.

Kruchten, Philippe (November 1995) "The 4+1 View Model of Architecture," *IEEE Software*, vol. 12, no. 6, pp. 42–50.

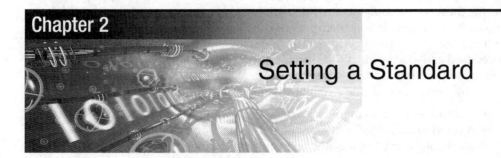

Chapter 2

Setting a Standard

Standards are an important concept, but achieving them is probably one of the most overlooked opportunities to improve the quality of software applications. On the surface, standards may seem like a trivial concept, but good application architecture starts with them. You often hear sports analogies about getting back to the basics; in software development these standards are the basics. This chapter covers standards and how to set the right ones for your organization or project and offers some recommendations and ideas for you to build upon with your own standards documentation.

Organizational Standards and Conventions

I have noticed over the last few years that some topics come in cycles. This may be a result of an ever-changing industry but standards are one of those topic areas that seem to come around every few years for a new set of discussions. Why do we need them? To quote myself in an article that was published in IBM developerWorks in 2007:

A2.1

> "Basically, things that are shared require that everyone who uses them gets along and plays nicely. Convincing organizations that this is a good idea seems to be a constant struggle. We are all bounded by the daily responsibilities of our jobs and the goal of getting projects finished, but it is everyone's responsibility to promote the idea that rules are a good thing. Rules help to promote cooperation, prevent mishaps and misunderstandings, enhance accountability, and enable recovery. That is, assuming we get things right in the first place. . . ."

The industry recognizes that for any development effort, standards are very important, but achieving them is something we rarely do well. Following well-designed programming standards can result in greater consistency within the delivered code, better quality code, and code that is easier for other developers to understand and maintain. Additional benefits of well-designed and -documented code include a reduced cost of long-term maintenance and the ability to transition artifacts to another team member or team. Before we get too deep in the weeds here, let me define a couple of terms:

- A **standard** is a minimum set of rules for the way something has to be done.
- A **convention** is a suggestion for how you might do something. It is the way things are usually done, but it is not necessarily set in stone.

Be careful how you define these terms to your development team. Often we use terms like naming conventions within a set of standards. Obviously you cannot put together a list for naming components that may be developed over the foreseeable future; however, this does not mean that the suggestions you put in place are optional, either. Sometimes these terms are used interchangeably and mean the same thing to the team. This is fine as long as everyone understands the meaning.

Everyone agrees that standards are important, but why devote an entire chapter to them? Because many organizations struggle with coming up with a comprehensive set of standards that can be implemented and, more importantly, enforced by the development side of the organization. If you don't write them down, then standards do not really exist, and you can't realistically expect developers to follow them. You also cannot expect to write them after the fact and have developers change their code to match what you have decided, especially if they are in the middle of a coding cycle. Doing so is not fair to anyone and is definitely not a good use of allocated company funds.

Putting the "Engineering" in Software Engineering

Sometime last year, I heard a well-respected colleague, Tom Alcott, use the phrase, "the use of rigorous software engineering principles" during a presentation of his I was attending. This struck a chord with me because it succinctly described a concept that I had been struggling with for a long time. It seems that day after day, I and others keep chanting this mantra of, "rigorous software engineering principles," looking for the nirvana of software engineering, when the reality is that reaching perfection in application development is as hard as it is in the metaphysical world.

So how do you reach it? You reach it the same way that other engineering disciplines ensure that things are built and perform correctly—by putting in place standards, codes, and conventions and ensuring that people follow those rules and guidelines as much as possible. Then you physically inspect to be sure things are done right, making changes in the standards as necessary.

You might assume that the recommendation is for architects to actually look at the code that the development team has delivered. If you are thinking this then you are absolutely right. Later in this chapter I talk about the code review process; however, for now understand that this process is not as intimidating as you might expect, but it is something that is non-negotiable. Think of it this way: You wouldn't buy a house without an inspection would you? Then why accept mission-critical software without an inspection?

More often than not, the software you are building costs more than your house, or at least more than mine cost, yet it is almost always accepted on faith that it will run reliably. Maybe it's because the developer's own money isn't the money being spent. I often think that if they did consider it as their own money, IT shops would run quite differently.

Many reasons exist for promoting this type of standardization within your development team. Working on large or even small project teams, we've all been in situations where looking over or even modifying the code of another team member has been necessary. Testing, reviewing, and debugging code that doesn't follow any standards (or your standards) can be a daunting task, even for the best of programmers. How many times has a piece of code been scrapped and rewritten for lack of understanding? I have to admit that I have done this more often than not on projects or with particularity complex APIs.

Because each project is different with widely varying requirements, separating standards from environmental factors and creating a separate document for the development environment setup and configuration is necessary. The types of documents of the most interest are

- **Coding standards and conventions:** This is the core of the discussion within this chapter—to list out organizational standards and guidelines that can be followed across multiple projects.
- **Development environment and setup:** Setting up the developer's desktop is usually separate from the initial standards. Each project may have its own set of rules so this document may be specialized for larger projects. Usually there will be a standard set of processes for the setup and use of things like version control.
- **Component completion and review process:** This area may be part of the initial standards document; however, there is a lot of room here for customization on some projects. Review processes may be more rigorous on those projects that have higher visibility or that have more riding on their success. The team may make a conscious decision to reduce or increase flexibility within the review process.
- **Specialized documents:** Specialized documents may be created by different teams within the organization. For example, the security team should create a set of documents that outlines good and bad security programming practices. They may want you to test and review for cross-side scripting attacks within your web pages. Accessibility and usability standards may be put into place by HR or UI teams. Ensuring that all web-based applications are useable by screen readers and other tools is important in today's working environment.

Many organizations will have additional documentation standards for their projects. These additional requirements usually revolve around how the project fits within the physical environment, so they are beyond the scope of this book; however, you should make an attempt to fit these recommendations into your own environmental standards.

Standards Documentation

Standards documentation should consist of enough information that developers don't have to struggle to understand how to use the standard; however, the documentation cannot be so rigid that it tries to encompass every possible situation. Although there is much that can be included, a simple list should include the following topics:

- Naming standards and conventions
- Internal documentation
- Logging and tracing
- Exception and error handling
- Project and packaging file structure
- Use of external libraries
- General design guidelines
- Unit testing requirements
- Code completion and review process requirements

This chapter focuses on these topics and provides some guidance on how to handle them. Notice that this list should be geared toward your specific project or organization. Many industry- and language-specific standards should be incorporated into your projects. These can be listed or referenced into your standards whenever necessary, but you don't need to reinvent the wheel. Basic Java best practices and conventions such as the use of string concatenation, or putting more than one command on a single line, are tasks that should be handled during the code review process. They can be documented in an extension document or better yet on a Wiki so that they can continue to evolve with your organization. Take care however, this area could potentially grow to be unwieldy if not managed appropriately and any documented standards then lose their potential do to good.

Naming Standards and Conventions

I don't like to go overboard on any standards, but naming standards are something that can be well defined across an entire organization. For the most part these standards follow the Java standards issued by Sun for Java development. Many of the examples in this book follow the usual Java standard conventions. Common Java naming standards should be followed wherever possible. Of all these types of standards, I think that package names are the most important and will have the most impact on your development effort later in the project. Naming standards are an example of a convention, where some guidance is given, but flexibility is also required in how the convention is put into use within the project.

Packages

Package naming is something that should be well defined across your entire organization. If you have never seen a project where no standards were put in place, then you are lucky. Usually you will just end up with naming structures all over the place, with many developers using the defaults that were provided by the tooling or whatever code they copied their initial program from. When naming a package for classes within your application you might begin with the following structure:

```
Model: com.<domain>.<department | team>.<appname>.model
Data Access: com.<domain>.<department | team>.<appname>.dao
Business Function: com.<domain>.<department|team>.<appname>.<function area>
Servlets: com. <domain>.<department | team>.<appname>.servlets
Portlets: com. <domain>.<department | team>.<appname>.portlets
Test Classes: com. <domain>.<department | team>.<appname>.test
```

You can really use whatever structure makes sense for your app. Additional objects may follow a similar naming structure when necessary:

```
com. <domain>.<department | team>.<appname>.beans
com. <domain>.<department | team>.<appname>.util
com. <domain>.<department | team>.<appname>.objectmanager
```

JSPs should also follow a package or folder structure within the Web Archive file. This structure would usually be something similar to

```
com. <domain>.<department | team>.<appname>.jsp
```

I think it is easy to go either too short or too long on package names, so keep your eye on what developers are trying to do within their structure. You can also add subpackages as you deem necessary. For example, in some of my code I may add a subpackage to determine what type of presentation this object is representing, such as

```
com. <domain>.<department | team>.<web | portal | mobile><appname>
```

The main point here is to put some guidelines in place before any code starts to be developed. After a package structure is laid down it is very difficult to refactor your code libraries to adhere to a new structure. A well defined package naming structure also helps in monitoring and trace components at runtime.

Many of these standards are a mixture of what I have found works in projects and the classic Sun Java standards available at http://java.sun.com/docs/codeconv/. Most standards do not go into this level of detail with identifying package names, but specifically for your organizational standards you should for the sake of consistency across teams and projects.

Classes and Interfaces

Class and interface names should be nouns, in mixed case with the first letter of each word capitalized. For example

```
class MyUniqueClass
```

Some general guidelines for class naming include the following:

- Keep class names simple and descriptive.
- Use whole words.
- Avoid acronyms and abbreviations (unless the abbreviation is much more widely used than the long form, such as URL or HTML).

Functions and Methods

Methods names usually describe some action taking place. As such they should be written as verbs describing what action they are going to perform. Methods are written in mixed case with the first letter of the first word in lowercase and the first letter of each additional word capitalized.

```
calculateInterest();

registerAccount();

getCustomerList();
```

Variables and Constants

Like methods, all variables should be in mixed case with a lowercase first letter.

```
int     startPosition;

char    middleInitial;

String accountNumber;
```

Variable names should not start with underscore or dollar sign characters in most cases. Sometimes underscores are allowed for internal uses, or if a code generator is used, such as the JET engine (sometimes known as JET2), within the eclipse framework.

Constants should be written as all uppercase with the words separated by an underscore.

```
static final String LDAP_HOST_NAME = "myldap.ibm.com";

static final String LDAP_HOST_PORT = 389;
```

Variable names should be as short as possible yet still be meaningful to the use of the variable. One character variables, except for simple counters or very temporary variables, may be considered, but even then a more descriptive name of what the counter is for may be necessary.

Java Server Pages

JSP page names should follow the same standard as class names using a mixed-case approach with the first letter of each word capitalized.

```
ViewCustomerList.jsp

UpdateCustomer.jsp

TransferAccountBalance.jsp
```

You should adapt a strategy for the initial JSP for any particular application if it is necessary. For example, if your application has a specific JSP that is always shown first, then that JSP should be named `Main.jsp` or `Index.jsp`, or something equally descriptive to assist with identification. JSP names should be kept as simple as possible, but again keeping the description to something that is recognizable to the casual observer.

Internal Documentation

Internal documentation refers to comments that are actually embedded within your code. This type of documentation serves several purposes. It typifies good programming practices. Being forced to write comments means you have to think about what your code is doing and how to describe it to your fellow programmers or consumers of your code components. It also helps in code reviews or when others have to make a change to code that you originally developed.

Internal documentation is almost always an afterthought, right alongside removing all the `System.out` lines from your code. Often what comes to mind toward the end of the project is to add comments for the generation of Javadoc for your application or system layer. But internal documentation is way more than just an abstract set of HTML documentation files. Many of the tools available today can leverage these comments within the environment to assist other developers who may be using your components or middleware libraries Figure 2.1 shows how your documentation can be displayed within Rational Application Developer.

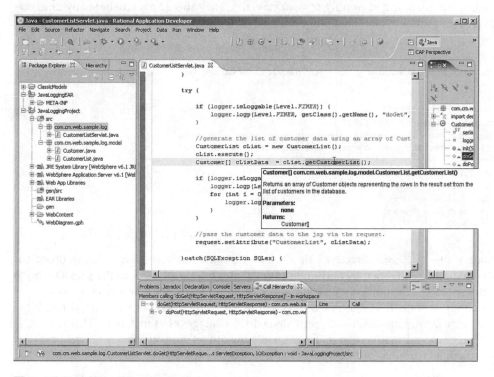

Figure 2.1   Internal documentation

You can imagine the benefit this could bring to a layered architecture where the upper layers are fully dependent upon lower layers to access data and systems. Being able to access the API documentation would be of great benefit.

The information published by Sun about using Javadoc can be extensive, outlining how to place your comments within the code. There may be a need to ensure that some development teams go to an extreme especially when a team is creating an API that will be used by other projects and teams. Many tools are available that can do an analysis on comments and recommend changes; as programmers are forced to redo some of their comments they will become more experienced in inserting documentation on the fly. For example, class specifications should include an executive summary, state information, OS hardware dependencies, allowed implementation variances, and security constraints.

Other sections may also be useful to users of this class. For example, when a method can accept null values, it should be explicitly documented so that others understand how to use it effectively. This level of detail would definitely be useful to any teams using this class.

For our purposes we are sticking to some of the basics. Rigid software engineering standards aside, I think honestly if we can get this level of detail we should consider ourselves lucky.

Class Header Information

Class headers are at the beginning of your class file. They should also include any `include` sections listed within your class. The comments should outline the use of the class without being too verbose.

```
/**
 * Servlet implementation class for Servlet: JavaLogging
 *
 * @web.servlet
 * name="JavaLogging"
 * display-name="JavaLogging"
 * description="This servlet displays some sample data and
 * illustrates the Java Logging API use within WebSphere"
 * <p>
 * @web.servlet-mapping
 * url-pattern="/JavaLogging"
 * <p>
 * @author Joey Bernal
 * @version 1.0
 **/
```

Including the `@author` directive can allow some static analysis tools to break down the errors that are found down by author, but it may also tell people new to the project who to ask if they have questions about some piece of code. Many frameworks need to provide information on how to instantiate a class within the framework. For example, through the use of some factory method that is provided which manages class instances. This seemingly trivial piece of information can make or break how others use your library classes or if they avoid them all together.

Class Methods

For methods, a minimum set of information should be included in the documentation. This includes

- A description of the method
- What parameters the method takes
- Any exceptions that are thrown
- What the method returns

```
/**
 * Returns an array of Customer objects representing the rows in the
 * result set from the list of customers in the database.
 * <p>
 * @param          none
 * @return         Customer[]
 */
public Customer[] getCustomerList() {
```

You might also include additional information like known bugs, or any pre- or post-conditions that may be necessary for this method.

Getters and Setters

Getters and setters are specific, single-use functions that allow you to store and access data within your value objects or domain classes. As such they require similar documentation to what you would provide for functions and methods.

```
/**
 * Returns the value of column CUSTOMERS_CONTACTLASTNAME.
 * in the row represented by this object.
 *
 * @return         Object
 * @throws         SQLException
 */
public Object getCUSTOMERS_CONTACTLASTNAME() throws SQLException {
 return select.getCacheValueAt(rowNumber, 3);
}
```

Inline Comments

The mention of inline comments probably brings to mind commenting all the constants and variables within the class file, which is correct. Every variable declaration within your code should have a comment.

Guidelines are available for using inline comments (//) as opposed to using C-style comments.

```
/*
 * This is what I mean by C style comments
 *
 */
```

You should research these guidelines and determine how important keeping to them is to your effort and how much detail is necessary.

You can use inline comments to document the why as well as the how certain things are done a specific way. In development you can make an infinite number of choices. Understanding why a specific choice is made is very important in understanding the whole component or application. Of particular importance are areas that would be tricky for another reader to understand. This scenario is often difficult for the developer to judge, but think about times you have gone back to your own code and tried to understand what you were trying to do. Anytime you use a control structure such as a loop, `if`, or `try` statement is a good time to consider putting in a comment about that structure and its use.

Remember that for commenting to work you have to remove some ego from the situation. During a code review, discussion may occur about a particular approach. This should be an honest discussion with possible debate, but developers should not feel that their every move is being questioned. This will cause more problems later in the project as developers become more resistant to the code review process.

Another school of thought proposes that when inline comments are used to explain some tricky piece of code, that the code itself should be simplified or refactored in some way. This is a valid concern during code review, especially when a particularly nasty set of code is uncovered and becomes indecipherable, even with embedded comments. Decisions have to be made regarding the manageability of that section of code versus the delivery of the over-all project.

Logging and Tracing

Logging and tracing is an area of great debate in today's applications. Many different approaches and flavors of logging are available and even more opinions exist as to which approach is the best. Again you should take a one-size-does-not-fit-all approach and understand that different projects require different approaches.

I believe that simpler is better; here are a few key items to look for in a logging approach:

- The approach should be as easy as possible. Developers need to be as verbose as possible with their trace messages, so ease of use is of primary importance.
- You need a good set of different logging levels. Twenty different levels aren't needed; a half dozen will probably do. Again, the goal is to minimize confusion or indecision with any of the developers.
- There needs to be an easy way to change logging levels at runtime. This factor is important because in case of a problem you don't want to have to restart the server, which may make the problem go away.

Wrappers have always been the popular approach when putting together a logging strategy, even to the extent that development teams try and wrapper industry standard logging packages to simplify the approach for their team. I haven't understood this logic completely; our developers are expected to understand complex libraries, such as Spring, Hibernate, JavaServer

Faces, and so on, yet people think they might struggle with log4J? I make light of the situation but you can see how misguided the effort can become.

I have to admit that I have changed approaches over the years and have looked at the pros and cons of log4J, WebSphere's JRAS, Apache Commons Logging, and others. Logging in the WebSphere environment can get complicated, with class loading conflicts being at the forefront of problems that people encounter. Luckily logging can be simplified to a short set of guidelines that can be distributed and enforced across all your WebSphere projects. Starting with WebSphere version 6, the JDK 1.4 version of the logging API is being used within the environment. This approach makes use of the java.util.logging package, which allows consistency and, of course, simplicity in your applications. Another benefit is that there are no additional jar files that are usually sprinkled throughout your packages. Interestingly enough, I sometimes review code that has not one, but two different logging libraries sitting in the lib directory. Often neither is used very effectively.

System.out

I cannot stress enough that `System.out` messages are not to be tolerated within any code deployed to WebSphere Application server. I would like to be more open minded about its use, but have found that there is no good place to draw the line as to when it would be appropriate or not to use. Developers will always use the `System.out` log just to get some quick information about a running application; however, the logging approach recommended here is just as quick and can help avoid many of the problems that sometimes creep into production.

I have to admit that as a developer I am guilty of using and leaving `System.out` messages within my code. When I put on my administrator hat, however, I am merciless about making developers remove any last vestige of this type of logging and instead opt for clean logs that are more easily read by operations. `System.out` logs are not easy to manage. You can't remove items from the log to make them easier to read, without just turning off the entire log. Also, the `System.out` log may not be buffered, which could impact performance if you are doing a lot of logging within your application.

Using the Logger

Accessing the logger within your class is simple. Importing the java.util.logging packages provides the access you need to create and use a logger within your class.

...

```
import java.util.logging.Level;
import java.util.logging.Logger;
```

...

```
public class CustomerListServlet extends javax.servlet.http.HttpServlet {
```

...

```
private Logger logger =
```

```
Logger.getLogger("com.cm.web.sample.logging.CustomerListServlet");

...
```

In this case I use the package and class name of the class where I am using the logger. I prefer this approach across my entire application. The reason behind using this approach will become apparent later when I talk about the admin console and show how to turn on logging.

You can log using the logp method. Multiple ways exist to log messages, including several convenience methods; however, logp is the approach recommended by WebSphere.

```
public void logp( Level level,

  String sourceClass,
  String sourceMethod,
  String msg,

  Object param1)
```

Log a message, specifying source class and method, with a single object parameter to the log message. If the logger is currently enabled for the given message level then a corresponding LogRecord is created and forwarded to all the registered output Handler objects.

The parameters are as follow:

level	One of the message-level identifiers; for example, SEVERE
sourceClass	Name of class that issued the logging request
sourceMethod	Name of method that issued the logging request
msg	The string message (or a key in the message catalog)
param1	Parameter to the log message

The primary advantage of using logp is that it allows the use of WSLevel logging levels within your application. It also allows message substitution parameters, and class and method names in the log entry, which are important for knowing where the problems may be occurring within your code. You can actually log a message with the following:

```
if (logger.isLoggable(Level.SEVERE)) {
  String str = "This is a SERVRE message";
  logger.logp(Level.SEVERE, getClass().getName(), "doGet", str);

}
```

Performing a check to see whether the logging level is enabled using the isLoggable method is also recommended. Doing so helps to avoid generating logging data that will not be used. In this case you avoid generating a String object that will never be used, but that will have to be garbage collected, possibly degrading system performance.

Logging Levels

The Java Logging API provides several levels for outputting different types of information to your logs. WebSphere Application Server provides a couple of additional levels on top of these levels. In total there are 10 logging levels in addition to the management levels OFF and ALL. These management levels would not normally be levels that the development team would have to worry about. The WebSphere InfoCenter gives some definitions for each of these levels and what they would be used for:

OFF   No events are logged.

By default the following log levels are output to the System.out file:

Level	Type	Description
FATAL	WsLevel	Task cannot continue and component cannot function
SEVERE	Level	Task cannot continue, but component can still function
WARNING	Level	Potential error or impending error
AUDIT	WsLevel	Significant event affecting server state or resources
INFO	Level	General information outlining overall task progress
CONFIG	Level	Configuration change or status
DETAIL	WsLevel	General information detailing subtask progress

By default the following log levels are output to the trace.log file:

Level	Type	Description
FINE	Level	Trace information: General trace plus method entry / exit / return values
FINER	Level	Trace information: Detailed trace
FINEST	Level	Trace information: An even more detailed trace; includes all the detail that is needed to debug problems
	ALL	All events are logged. If you create custom levels, ALL includes your custom levels and can provide a more detailed trace than FINEST.

You can decide for yourself which levels make the most sense for your team or project. The preceding list may include too many levels for most developers to follow appropriately without either their having a lot of experience, or having several examples of different logging levels available so they can choose the right level to use. I suggest narrowing down the levels to something more reasonable. The following list defines a reasonable set of logging levels that can be described with concrete examples:

```
Level.SEVERE

Level.WARNING

Level.INFO

Level.CONFIG

Level.FINE

Level.FINER

Level.FINEST
```

By default WebSphere usually sets all loggers to the INFO setting. Because any level includes messages that are at a higher level this will also include messages of type WARNING and SEVERE. Generally you want this type of information to display anyway so you can be informed of something bad happening within your system.

Logging of type SEVERE is reserved for big problems within the application. These would generally be exceptions that are thrown within the application. Exception handling is covered in the next section, but the actual logging of exceptions is one of the most common uses of a logging framework.

```
}catch(SQLException SQLex) {

if (logger.isLoggable(Level.SEVERE)) {

logger.logp(Level.SEVERE, getClass().getName(), "doGet", "Servlet failed: " +
SQLex.getMessage());
logger.logp(Level.SEVERE, getClass().getName(), "doGet",
SQLex.getStackTrace().toString());

}

//something bad happened, so display error jsp.
nextJSP = "WEB-INF/com.cm.web.sample.log.jsp/Error.jsp";

}
```

The preceding example not only logs the exception but also provides the end user with an error page that allows the user to continue with the application or try again later.

Logging of type INFO is generally simple. As an example it can be used to tell you that an object has been instantiated or initialized. The INFO level could also be used to show progress on long-running tasks or processes. This level does not generally need to be a type of problem, but can track progress within the application or system.

```
if (logger.isLoggable(Level.INFO)) {

logger.logp(Level.INFO, getClass().getName(), "init", "initalized");


}
```

You can specifically set the CONFIG logging level to see whether any parameters are set incorrectly within your application. Usually external systems such as databases or data sources, LDAP, or web services are different for each environment. It is not unheard of for parameters to not be changed as an application is moved through the deployment chain from development to QA to Stage and finally to production.

```
if (logger.isLoggable(Level.CONFIG)) {

logger.logp(Level.CONFIG, getClass().getName(), "initializer", "DataSource Name",
dsName);


}
```

Providing specific logging for these parameters can be very useful in situations where you are not sure that something is set correctly.

Method-Level Timers

Trace-level logging should include some level of timing data, at least at the method level. Complex parsing or calls to remote or external data sources should also include their own timing data. Is this extra work? You bet! Is it worth it in the long run? Absolutely! I can't count the number of times I wish I had this type of data. Take a little care to ensure that this data is only calculated when a very detailed level of tracing is turned on, otherwise you are building slow production performance into your system.

Generally you should use a tracing level of FINE for this level of logging. You can make good use of the tracing levels FINE, FINER, and FINEST, depending on the problem that you are facing. Timing traces are an example of FINE level tracing. Timing traces are used to see how fast requests are processing through the application. At the start of each method you can initiate some values and output the fact that the process has entered the method.

```
long start = 0;
if (logger.isLoggable(Level.FINE)) {

start = java.lang.System.currentTimeMillis();
logger.logp(Level.FINE, getClass().getName(), "init", "Entering: " +
NumberFormat.getNumberInstance().format( start ));


}
```

This trace would be output to the `trace.log` and would look something like the following:

```
[12/16/07        15:16:39:515        EST]        0000002b        CustomerListS        1
com.cm.web.sample.log.CustomerListServlet doGet Entering: 1,197,836,199,515
```

At the end of each method a follow-up entry would calculate and display the result of timing data.

```
if (logger.isLoggable(Level.FINE)) {

 long finish = java.lang.System.currentTimeMillis();
 long total = finish - start;
 logger.logp(Level.FINE, getClass().getName(), "init", "Exited: " +
 NumberFormat.getNumberInstance().format( finish ));
 logger.logp(Level.FINE, getClass().getName(), "init", "Time spent: " +
 NumberFormat.getNumberInstance().format( total ) + "milliseconds");


}
```

This code would display data in the `trace.log` similar to the following:

```
[12/16/07 15:16:39:750 EST] 0000002b CustomerListS 1
com.cm.web.sample.log.CustomerListServlet doGet Exited: 1,197,836,199,750
[12/16/07 15:16:39:750 EST] 0000002b CustomerListS 1
com.cm.web.sample.log.CustomerListServlet doGet Time spent: 235 milliseconds
```

You have lots of opportunities to improve the set of standards your organization requires. For example, you may want to build auditing functionality into your applications. This feature may provide for an AUDIT level message to output to the logs whenever a process or method takes longer than some set threshold. This is especially important when you are dependent on a back-end system such as a database or web service. You can log the event along with the query itself to understand when and where some problem took place. I don't recommend using this approach everywhere because just generating the time values and performing the comparisons could become expensive if used too extensively. However, this approach may be good for potential hot-spots within the application where you may expect some performance issues, and will certainly help when your project moves into performance testing.

Working with Logging and Tracing

This type of logging offers several benefits, one of which is the ability to configure logging from within the admin console. Loggers are automatically displayed within the admin console Diagnostic Trace Service (see Figure 2.2) settings area. Using a package name approach can greatly increase the ability to turn on and off loggers at the right scope.

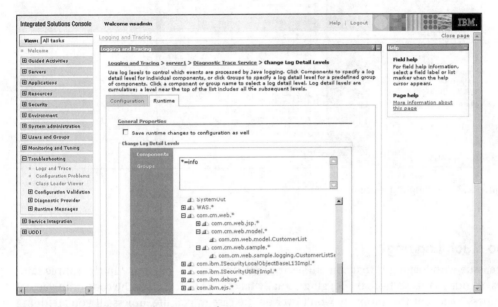

Figure 2.2 Admin console trace services

Turning on too much logging (see Figure 2.3) can cause an avalanche of information into the logs that will quickly overwhelm anyone trying to get usable information about a problem. The better approach is to selectively turn on logging for the potential problem area or to turn it on more generally at higher levels until you narrow down the problem area and can turn on full tracing to a deep analysis.

You can change logging levels on the fly using the admin screen. Click on the package you want to examine to set the appropriate levels. This approach is invaluable when diagnosing a problem in a running environment where you suspect that a restart would mask the problem, or make it go away for a while.

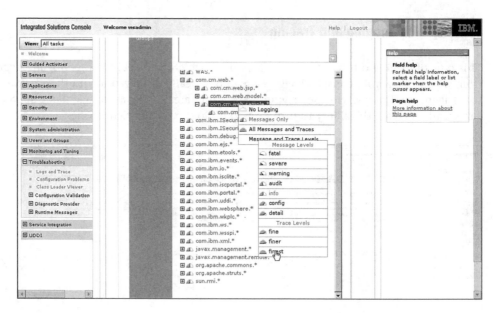

Figure 2.3   Setting log levels

Too Much Logging?

One issue with logging is that sometimes it can be too much—or can it? In the simple samples of code in this section, the logging actually takes more effort than the code doing actual business logic. But this probably won't ever be the case in real life, unless all you are doing is displaying table data and nothing else. But the reality is being verbose with your code should be a good thing. If the code is well formatted and the internal documentation is verbose enough, then code becomes more readable and maintainable, both during development and at runtime.

Good logging standards should be one of the basic building blocks in the framework of your architecture. Imagine if you were building a house and instead of putting a stud up every 12 or 16 inches, the builder decided to only put them up every once in a while? Luckily, people build houses better than we build software, because otherwise your house would never pass inspection and never be allowed to go beyond the framing stage. Some developers are naturally more verbose than others, but there has to be some minimum standards, or building codes if you will, to ensure your application can withstand the high winds and rain that we have to plan for.

Why Not Use Aspects?

Aspect-oriented programming is a development approach that attempts to separate many of the routing and repeating parts of development into their own set of objects. AOP specifically focuses on topics of a cross-cutting concern, or those items that cut across the entire development effort. Logging is one of those cross-cutting concerns. It is something that we do everywhere and not specific to any one part of the code. Whenever the discussion starts to focus on aspects the discussion always turns to logging, mainly because it is the most obvious example of a cross-cutting concern with any application. While this is interesting I don't believe I can get the same type of detail needed by relegating logging to a different set of layers. I believe that logging and tracing have to be built into the system to get the maximum detail.

Unless you have been at the back end of a project that is having trouble in production, understanding how important this standard really is may be difficult. Aspects can play another role in instrumentation of code that can be very powerful.

Exception and Error Handling

Exception handling is a topic that is probably even more controversial than some of the other topics discussed in this chapter. I don't have any silver bullet solutions regarding this topic, but I can offer guidance for some decisions for this part of your project. Much of the debate and discussion around exception handling revolves around two specific areas—handling exceptions where they occur, or throwing them up through the call stack.

Checked Versus Unchecked Exceptions

More often than not I agree with the idea that unchecked or runtime exceptions should never be caught. If you are not sure of the difference between checked and unchecked exceptions then you need to open a programming book and dig in. The general idea is that unchecked exceptions are things you should be looking for in your code anyway, such as a null pointer or an array out of bounds. Checked exceptions are things you can't really do anything about, such as an out-of-memory error

So with these basic definitions in mind, you should only throw checked exceptions within your code, and only those things that you can reasonably expect the calling code to handle—Of couse any errors that the calling method might expect from your code should be documented.

I do not like the idea of building large custom exception libraries within your application. This technique has always seemed counterintuitive to me when trying to reduce the bulk and complexity of an application. Each layer should only worry about the calling layer and what it might be able to do with a thrown exception. Letting upper layers determine whether the calling layer can reasonably handle an exception or will need to re-throw it is beyond the scope of the lower layer designers. From there is the calling layer's responsibility to determine whether it can actually handle the exception or needs to throw it higher up the stack.

Think about what the calling method may be looking for. If a method passes a null parameter and gets back a null result then it should be expecting to handle that exception and do
some internal value checking. If you are within a middle layer it might be your responsibility to notify the calling program that it has passed you a null when you know that will cause
problems.

You have probably heard it before but it is worth saying again, because I see it time and
again when I do code reviews for customers:

Never hide an exception!

Hiding exceptions is asking for trouble, and then not wanting to know about it. If you do
not know what I mean by exception hiding take a look at the following code example:

```
} catch (SQLException SQLex) {
 //Do nothing here.

}
```

In this case I caught the exception, a `SQLException`, and then did nothing, just kept running my program. Undoubtedly something is going to crash during this request and more
than likely it will end with an ugly-looking error message to the end user requesting this
data. Don't catch `java.lang.Exception` except in the presentation layer of the application.

```
} catch (Exception ex) {
```

Many people will disagree and say not to catch general exceptions at all, but I think that in
the presentation layer you have a responsibility to ensure that your end users receive generic
error messages, rather than a stack trace on their screens, even if the prettier message is fairly
useless.

The next point about handling exceptions, especially in the upper layers of your code, is to
do something responsible with them.

```
}catch(SQLException SQLex) {
if (logger.isLoggable(Level.SEVERE)) {

logger.logp(Level.SEVERE, getClass().getName(), "doGet", "Servlet failed: " +
SQLex.getMessage());
logger.logp(Level.SEVERE, getClass().getName(), "doGet",
SQLex.getStackTrace().toString());
}

//something bad happened, so display error jsp.
nextJSP = "WEB-INF/com.cm.web.sample.log.jsp/Error.jsp";

}
```

Notice in the preceding code snippet the `catch` block changes the display JSP to provide an
error message to the end user. More than likely when something bad happens we don't get
any returned data and the JSP would end up with an empty data set for display. An alternative approach is to add some handling code in the display JSP to handle an empty data set.

The possibility exists that the logging code itself may throw an exception. Additional wrapping of a `try/catch` may be necessary to avoid this problem.

```
}catch(SQLException SQLex) {

try{
if (logger.isLoggable(Level.SEVERE)) {

logger.logp(Level.SEVERE, getClass().getName(), "doGet", "Servlet failed: " +
SQLex.getMessage());
logger.logp(Level.SEVERE, getClass().getName(), "doGet",
SQLex.getStackTrace().toString());
}

//something bad happened, so display error jsp.
nextJSP = "WEB-INF/com.cm.web.sample.log.jsp/Error.jsp";

} catch(…) {


}
```

This is especially true when you are trying to close resources such as a data connection. This may seem like overkill, but it has happened time and again. The approach you use depends upon your level of comfort, your timeline, and the skill of your development team.

Project and Packaging File Structure

Some basic guidelines for packaging structure are necessary for ensuring consistency across multiple applications and projects within the organization. Without these initial guidelines, everyone will do his or her own thing. Deployment teams within large organizations indicate that often every single application has its own deployment quirks because the teams all took different approaches to packaging.

Actually listing out the directory structure for how applications will be packaged within your environments might be useful. This list would include JAR, WAR, and EAR files to ensure a standard for everyone to follow. In addition, be sure to document specific requirements; for example, the location of JSP files within the Web Archive. The following are some guidelines for project packaging:

- JSP files should reside in a folder that maintains the package naming structure of the application.
- JSP folders should reside within the WEB-INF folder in the WAR file for security purposes.
- The EJB JAR modules and Web WAR modules comprising an application should be packaged together in the same EAR module.
- Utility classes used by a single Web module should be placed within its WEB-INF/lib folder.

- Utility classes used by multiple modules within an application should be placed at the root of the EAR file.

- Utility classes used by multiple applications can be placed on a directory referenced via a shared library definition.

Many teams are looking for additional guidance in how to design applications for proper packaging. I recommend looking to the development team to see how they are doing things now, and how they can be changed for the better. The more you involve the people who actually perform this function the better off your projects will be.

Using External Libraries

The use of third-party and open source libraries must be handled a little differently from other standards within your organization. The main challenge is that trying to guess at all the requirements your development teams may encounter is simply too hard. As such listing all the libraries they may need is difficult. The two schools of thought on the matter are as follow:

- Option 1: Let the application developers package their third-party libraries within the archive file for deployment.

- Option 2: Try to build out shared libraries that everyone can use and depend on.

The reality is probably somewhere in the middle, but personally I like to know what the developers are using and why, even if it does end up packaged in a WAR or EAR file. Logging APIs is a perfect example. Without a little oversight more logging libraries and copies of the same set of libraries will sneak into your system, causing you to lose the control you so nicely put in place earlier in this chapter and possibly causing unexpected class loading conflicts.

One cause of this proliferation of libraries may be the developers' lack of knowledge or misunderstanding of what features are already available either through WebSphere itself or currently deployed shared libraries within the system. WebSphere shared libraries (see Figure 2.4) help reduce the number of libraries within a system by allowing multiple applications to use them.

Versions of specific libraries should be standardized once they are used within the system. You don't need every team using a different version of some function. Occasionally, a team may need to use a specific version of an API, but it is probably not the case for all your teams. Special approval can be made on a case-by-case basis to package a particular version with the application if necessary. The key point is to be aware of what libraries are being used by your applications. Understand and document what is being used and why, so you are not surprised when problems occur.

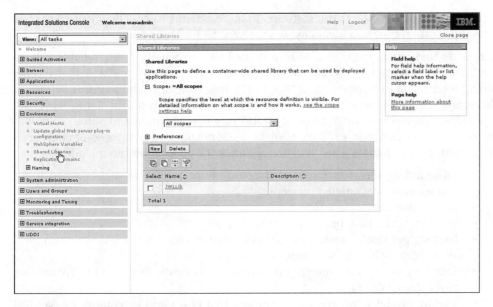

Figure 2.4 WebSphere shared libraries

When a team makes a request to use a library, the architecture or governance team should be ready to respond quickly. Development teams do not have time to waste—time is of the essence. Remember you are there to serve the development team, not the other way around, so a quick response, discussion, or approval will ensure that the next request follows the same channels and the development team does not try and circumvent the system.

Unit Testing Requirements

Unit tests are one of those line items I see on every project plan, but that rarely get performed, mostly because they are ill defined by the industry as a whole. We like to talk about unit testing. Often unit testing is described as that magical thing that developers do right before the code moves to another stage in the project, like Q/A or UAT. Because we continue to discuss unit tests (real or imagined) in our projects, it must mean that we think it is an important topic, an important line item that we can use to improve the quality and reliability of our code. If only we knew the half of it!

A2.2

Most people who are involved with software projects of any type understand the need for good testing at all levels. Heck, for that matter, any user who has ever had to deal with a buggy piece of software can understand the need. Testing is designed to catch problems before software ships or a system goes live. In some cases releasing buggy software can annoy the user and may result in your being labeled a bad programmer or your company identified as one who produces bad software. In more extreme cases, a buggy piece of code can result in lost revenue to a company, or may even be life threatening.

You need to understand what unit testing is used for—to remove bugs. What is a bug? Sometimes this definition is difficult to pin down. In general, any function that returns incorrect results could be considered a bug. But in most software products, this definition includes any action or inaction that does not comply with known requirements. Rarely are the product requirements written to incorporate every possible input and output combination, so in many cases developers have to make do. Some obvious and not-so-obvious cases that developers try to handle when building a part of the application can include

- Not returning incorrect results that could be interpreted as correct when input parameters are not entered correctly.
- Null or blank entries in a form.
- Incorrect entries in a form.
- Handling purposeful, malicious entries in a form. This form of security testing will not specifically be discussed here.
- Testing a piece of functionality many times with similar input data to ensure that results are consistent.
- Entering invalid input and data to ensure that errors and exceptions are handled gracefully and explanations are useful to the user.

Many of these types of tests are not enumerated within the requirements or test scenarios and are often something that the developer just assumes he or she must do. In addition, nonfunctional tests must often be performed, which includes making sure the results of a test are not only accurate for one user, but returns consistently accurate results as many users access the same code, or that the results displayed to each user of the system are correct for that user only. Developing an application that works correctly at this level can be a difficult task. For example, consider the following:

In order to improve performance of an application the team decides it will cache the data being used as much as possible, which results in the ability of the application to handle more users as load and scalability tests are performed. However, some users get the wrong results on their screen. Perhaps they are seeing the results from the user before them. This may be disastrous, for example, in the case of payroll forms or personal information.

You see from this simple example that a balance needs to be achieved between performance and functional correctness; however, without testing this balance can never happen.

Many types of testing can be performed within software development. Figure 2.5 illustrates a realistic view of the types of testing generally defined as necessary on a development project.

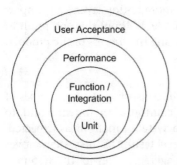

Figure 2.5   Levels of development testing

Different project teams often put a different emphasis on some areas. Many projects focus more on performance while others may not give performance a second thought, at least not until the site is live. Chapter 8, "Catching and Performance," focuses on performance testing. Most of the layers you should readily understand, but for clarity's sake I enumerate them here:

- **Unit testing:** You can think of a unit as the most basic structural element of a system. This general definition is the one mostly followed in this book. In many languages a unit could be defined as a function or a method, but it also may be thought of as a bit broader, such as a unit of functionality or behavior.
- **Function/integration testing:** Functional testing, sometimes called black-box or closed-box testing, evaluates the results or data derived by a system without regard to how the system is built. For most web-based applications, functional testing assumes that a user enters data into a page and evaluates the returned results. While on the surface this testing is similar to unit testing, the scope is normally set at a business function level. Integration testing means testing combined components in a single environment, such as hardware and software components, including different pieces of an application that are designed to work together. These two types of testing often work hand in hand and so are together in this circle.
- **Performance testing:** Performance testing is not so much about a single user's results as the ability to provide the correct results to many users within a given time period. Ensuring speed and minimizing system overhead leads directly to the ability of a system to handle a large number of users. This characteristic is commonly known as system scalability. Performance testing and tuning is a fine and sometimes dark art and requires skills both in development and infrastructure to achieve good results.
- **User acceptance testing:** User acceptance testing means ensuring that the system meets or exceeds end user expectations. Even the most finely tuned or best-working system is worthless if it doesn't do what the user expects or is too hard to use. Ideally, test scripts are built based on the original requirements of the system to see whether the end product matches what was originally defined.

Whether you perform all of these types of tests, or even add more testing layers, it is important to know what you are expecting to gain from a testing cycle. Without this end result in mind you are wasting time and money and possibly jeopardizing the success of the product.

What Is a Unit?

You can typically consider a unit as the first link in the chain consisting of several types of tests. This testing provides a way for developers, within the comfort of their own world, to assure themselves that the smallest unit or component of a system functions as expected. This assurance also provides the base for additional higher-level testing as the system moves away from the center circle in Figure 2.5 to a broader, more aggregate view of the system.

A simple definition of unit testing is the ability to test the smallest unit or component of code as possible. While it is the essence of what you want to accomplish, it can be a little misleading. Most of the testing that occurs within a project, if testing occurs at all, happens in large chunks at the functional or user acceptance level. Looking behind the glass one can rationalize using more fine-grained ways to validate the behavior of code. If assurance can be gotten that the behavior of individual components is correct, then it stands to reason that as those components are brought together, or integrated, then they will function correctly at the higher level.

So unit testing can actually make code better and ensure that a component behaves as expected. But there is more to it than that. A pleasant side-effect of creating and running unit tests on a continuous basis is that it can help ensure that ongoing changes made to code don't have the unexpected effect of breaking earlier working pieces.

On some projects I have developers write out manually the list of tests that their code should be tested with, before they start coding. This step is the minimum developers should do for any piece of functionality they are coding. It also helps ensure that the developer understands the requirements correctly, and the list can feed into later QA or UAT type test scenarios.

Realistically, our components are too modular to be considered a single unit. However, going to the other extreme and testing at the method level may be too fine grained. The approach walks a fine line in trying to determine what to test, and how to get valid results.

The Trouble with Web Testing

Before the web and server-side programming, the definition of unit testing was not as difficult to pin down. Most applications had a main() method of some type that could be run on the command line. Building unit tests that had knowledge of what the application was trying to do was a simple matter of building test classes that ran the program, with the distinct advantage of being able to see inside the code. With the advent of the web and J2EE programming, components now run inside a container that creates or instantiates classes and then calls specific methods as required. In addition the container provides objects of its own as parameters to methods that contain the input and output values for processing.

Writing tests for web application code from within a `main()` method is often worthwhile. Much of the business logic within a web application can still be called from outside the web container. Much time can be saved by testing as much as possible outside the container or using a mock framework of some sort to test these components. You can also leverage in-container testing frameworks like Cactus to help you accomplish your goals.

Agile Approaches

Agile developers are some of the biggest proponents of unit testing and as such many support the idea of test-first development. Test-first development is a great way to ensure that a developer fully understands what he or she is creating before actually coding it. Generally, this testing process can be automated using a testing framework such as JUnit. Of course, all this testing can come at a price.

Not all testing frameworks are created alike, so developer training or some system configuration may be necessary before test-first development becomes seamless within your environment. Also, if the development effort is taking advantage of an application framework such as a portal or e-commerce server, the testing framework may not integrate well within the environment. Finally, to effectively conduct test-based development the entire team needs to be skilled enough to design and code appropriately.

Many developers or architects when initially confronted with the idea of unit testing and JUnit are convinced that it is the way to go. I know that I have spent many hours looking for the right approach to unit and in-container testing. While these strategies are valid, one person learning a new approach versus trying to get an entire team to adopt a strategy and perform it correctly are two different things. Be cautious in this area and be sure that what you propose is doable and will add value to the project.

Code Completion and Review Process Requirements

The best way to ensure that quality components are being created is to perform a peer review on the code. This is also a time and place for your manager or team lead to understand the work and be confident that this code is ready to deploy. The steps involved in declaring code complete is brief: Before a developer declares code complete, usually he or she checks the code in and tells the project manager or team lead that the code is finished. The PM then checks that component as complete on his or her list and the developer moves on to another function.

What is interesting to me is that we wonder why we have problems. Really, in what other job can we get away with declaring the job finished without someone checking our work or questioning how we might have performed some actions? This chapter provides some guidelines for setting up standards and rules for development, but more important is checking that these standards are being followed.

I personally am not a big fan of checklists. You may not believe me because of my focus on standards, but documentation for documentation's sake is never fun or productive. Rather than checklists I suggest guidelines. These are things that a developer can do a follow-up check with to ensure that they won't get flagged during a code review. Performing a code review, by the way, is the first thing the PM or team lead should ask to do on the completed code. Here is a list of potential guidelines:

- The code is really complete. No stubs, No partial have-to-do's like removing `System.out` lines or adding comments.
- Some initial static analysis has been done, obvious things are taken care of such as hard-coded properties, and exceptions are handled appropriately.
- Third-party and open source libraries have been disclosed and approved for use within your application.
- The code has been compiled, unit tested, and deployed to a test server for some basic and documented functional tests, depending upon your team approach.

Your team should feel free to come up with a more robust set of completion requirements that outline in detail the tasks that should be accomplished; however, the actual code review process will flag most of those items. Having a documented list of requirements could potentially save time during the review process if the code that is presented has a lot of problems. You will have to weigh the effort involved in enforcing a set of requirements against the skill-level of your development team.

Code Reviews

Code review is a dirty word for many of today's development teams. I'm sure it has to do with the word *review*. Being reviewed and having others point out your shortcomings is never a pleasant experience. We should change this name to something that is more acceptable to people. Or maybe we should just get over it and embrace the idea that reviews are about the quality of the product, not the quality of the developer.

Many engineering roles have different levels of experience, usually an apprentice and a journeyman or licensed status. The same is true of software engineers: Some developers are more experienced or more productive than others. Code reviews help with the process of becoming a better developer, not only in the standards category, but through discussion about different approaches within the code. Developers should look at the code review process as a learning process, not a judgment on his or her ability. It is a chance for more experienced members of the team to pass on their experience or suggestions and a chance for everyone to learn from the group experience and build their skills.

Ideally code reviews are scheduled throughout the development cycle. Early code reviews should be scheduled after a developer has a working model of the code, and then, of course, a final review should be scheduled before the code is signed off on. This initial early feedback enables good communication between team members and enables the team lead or architect to understand how architectural decisions are being implemented. It also enables some feedback for previously made architectural decisions as well as clarifications if something is not well understood.

I often leave it to the developers to schedule code reviews during the development cycle. I will suggest that they should schedule a review in the next week or so to make sure their approach is fully understood. PMs can shoulder this burden to ensure it gets built into the project plan. The one deadly sin is blowing off the reviews because of lack of time. Any time spent now will multiply the time saved later. This concept has been proven again and again and so should not be a topic for debate. Developers are notorious for putting off code reviews as long as possible, asking for a little more time to just finish this one section.

The Danger of Putting Off a Review

On a previous project I took over as technical lead during the switch from the design to the development phase. One particular individual on the team was very difficult to get along with. As lead it was within my rights to remove this person and find a replacement, but I was young and thought that action would be extreme. I had been a team and squad leader in the army so I figured I could handle my share of problem team members. My solution was to give this person a small but important piece of the application where he could work in some isolation without bothering the rest of the team.

From time to time I would check on how things were going, always getting back the right response that everything was moving along nicely. Close to the end of this phase I started to dig a little deeper and some warning flags started going off that all was not as it should be. I suggested we do a code review, which was received very negatively. After a bit of a struggle I was able to force a code review with this individual and some of the leads of the team to discover disastrous results.

The majority of the reviews agreed that the code was nowhere ready to run and some parts had to be completely redesigned. I was forced to take a senior programmer off another piece of functionality and have him work with this person to rewrite the code. This example actually illustrates two wrong moves:

- Moving a problem developer out to a side feature without facing the problem head on

- Not reviewing everyone's progress

Like I said, I was young! I personally prefer the brown bag approach where a scheduled lunch hour is used to perform the review. The truth is one hour is never long enough, so schedule several hours and let people leave early if necessary rather than try to extend a meeting that is going long. Providing food such as pizza or takeout is usually enough of an incentive to get everyone who is required to attend to show up on time.

You Don't Have to Know Java for a Code Review

Okay, so the preceding statement is only slightly true—but you don't have to be an expert. Undoubtedly, you have Java experts on your team who can provide the expertise to uncover any problems. However, everyone learns a little something at group code reviews. Embarrassment should never be the focus of a review for anyone; that is, if you ever expect to have more than one review for that developer.

The idea of a code review is to let the specific developer walk you through the code process step by step. Start with gaining an understanding of what he is trying to accomplish, then look at code files to understand how he has implemented this functionality. You might make several passes through the application, first for general understanding and then to review more mundane items like adherence to standards, handling of exceptions, logging, and so on.

One item to determine is who should actually attend the code reviews. My approach is that this is part of the technical team's development process, not a step-out review. Management should not generally attend unless they are involved at that level. Having them there only puts pressure on the person who is being reviewed and side-tracks the conversation to other topics. PMs might attend for some of the review but not generally be involved in the technical part of the discussion. Business analysts might also be involved in some part of the review to ensure that the initial requirements were understood and followed within the application.

Communicating the Vision the Wiki Way

Coming up with a reasonable way to socialize, communicate, educate, maintain, and enforce the standards you define within your organization is not usually a problem for small teams. However, within the context of a large organization these tasks can be difficult. Socializing the message to development teams is just the first step. The next part of the process is project enforcement and incorporating a feedback loop to incorporate improvements and additions.

One way to accomplish all these goals are through wikis. They are becoming increasingly popular to accomplish the goal of creating a community around standards. This approach enables you to publish and then maintain standards in a readily consumable manner. PortalPatterns.org (see Figure 2.6) is publicly available and can be used as an example site.

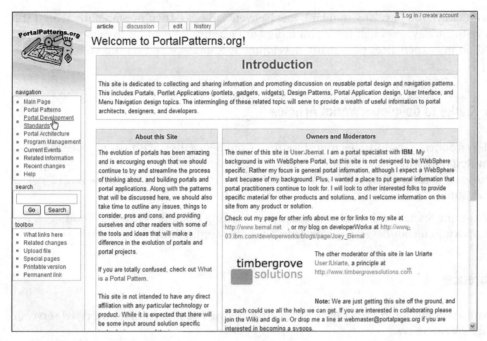

Figure 2.6   PortalPatterns.org

This site's goal is to build community and agreement on standards as well as provide examples for organizations looking to build their own set of standards.

Conclusion

This chapter outlined the importance of setting standards within your organization or project. I am not able to provide complete answers to every nuance of what you might need, but the general flavor and type of standards that you need to be successful have been outlined in this chapter. This book just scratches the surface of what you need for many projects within your organization.

If you are asked to put together standards for your organization, I believe it would take a small team of three or four people several weeks of part-time work to come up with a solid, comprehensive set of standards. This is a minimum effort; a comprehensive set will take longer.

As for any of the discussion within this chapter if you disagree with any of my advice, then feel free to call me an idiot and do your own thing. I have always made the point

I would rather you have any standard, maybe even bad ones, then no standards at all. I still believe this today, although more and more I am learning to commit to recommendations based on my experiences with many development teams working on the WebSphere platform.

Links to developerWorks Articles

A2.1 WebSphere Developer Technical Journal: Comment Lines, With Great Power comes Great Responsibility:
http://www.ibm.com/developerworks/websphere/techjournal/0712_col_bernal/0712_col_bernal.html

A2.2 Getting Started with Unit and Component testing using IBM Rational Tools:
http://www.ibm.com/developerworks/edu/ws-dw-ws-testing.html

Reference

WebSphere Application Server InfoCenter: http://www-306.ibm.com/software/webservers/appserv/was/library/

Portal Patterns: http://www.portalpatterns.org

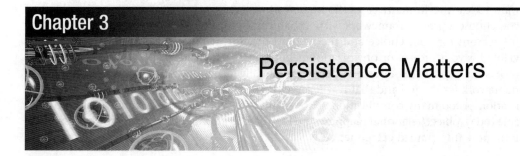

Chapter 3

Persistence Matters

The Persistence layer is covered early in this book for two reasons:

- Persistence, data storage, and Object/Relational (O/R) mapping components can provide a base for many applications. In a traditional bottom-up design, this area may be designed first within the architecture.
- Persistence is where many applications go wrong and where you might first look when they start to have trouble. That trouble could be performance, security, or functionality related. Data drives many applications, so you might focus on this particular aspect of the application.

I mentioned in earlier chapters that organizations expect the development team to be experts on new technology even as they continue to add new requirements for the system and new frameworks become available to the development community. Make no mistake, however; application architecture is hard. As we look at different layers of the architecture we need to understand several different technologies. We are really just scratching the surface of what you will have to do in a real enterprise application. I hope, however, you can extrapolate much of what I discuss to your own environment and application architecture.

Types of Persistence Frameworks

Thankfully, several popular persistence frameworks are available to developers today. This is a huge leap from just a few years ago when developers were still struggling with custom JDBC code. However, even with using a framework much potential still exists for things to go wrong. Overloading a database with queries is still very possible, and some thought is required in the database design.

A3.1

I want to warn against picking a framework because you think it is popular or because you want to learn it. In many cases the framework you choose probably won't be a problem, if you choose a proven framework with a solid community or vendor behind it. Think about the reasons for your choice and the amount of effort it might take to make a framework viable for your project or organization. Choosing a framework just because you think it is cool is not a good use of business dollars. Some diligence is necessary to ensure it is the right framework for the job and that it will serve the needs of the business without undue modification or too many complications. Essentially, two types of popular frameworks are available today, object/relational mapping and SQL based, although these could be broken down into more fine-grained categories.

Object/Relational Mapping

Object/relational mapping is the ability to persist Java objects to a relational database or set of tables. The idea is to actually transform data into the two different formats. Relational tables and object-oriented classes each use a different structure so the ability for a developer to "think" in terms of objects and not be concerned with how the relational tables are designed is considered a huge advantage.

In the O/R mapping category, Hibernate is arguably one of the most popular persistence frameworks available today. The growth has been pretty steady over the last several years as more projects try to leverage industry experience rather than try to build their own framework. Other products in this category include Oracle's TopLink and the Java Persistence API, which are discussed later in this chapter.

SQL-Based Frameworks

SQL-based frameworks seek to provide a robust JDBC type of framework where your domain objects or Java beans are mapped to specific SQL statements. This approach can be simpler and more familiar to many programmers, yet still reduce many of the issues that you would face by creating your own persistence framework. The difference is the ability and flexibility in which you can use custom SQL statements in your application. I'm not claiming that the decision between roll your own and an available framework is that cut-and-dried, but you get the general idea. In this category are frameworks like iBATIS and Spring JDBC. We could probably add plain JDBC to this category as well.

Why Not Roll Your Own Framework?

One could very easily make a case for a roll-your-own framework; however, at this point in time doing so does not seem reasonable except for very simple cases, and even then it is a stretch. With all the robust and popular frameworks readily available, building your own is hardly necessary, if not another bad use of project dollars. You can hardly build a framework that is as robust or complete as many of the currently available frameworks. In the case you are looking at a custom approach, an argument could be made that the ramp-up time for the team to learn a new framework would work against them; that is, the "not invented here" syndrome. Although this may be partly true, using a good layered approach can help isolate much of the team from having to learn the custom framework right away, instead depending on one small subteam to provide them with the DAO layer and Entity objects required by the application.

WebSphere Data Source Resource Reference

I will make a quick point upfront about resource references within WebSphere for data source access. While a data source provides the access point to a specific database, there is another level of abstraction that is recommended to acquire and use a data source.

Resource manager connection factories are actually defined by the J2EE specification, and are used to create resource connections. In this case the resource manager connection factory would be the javax.sql.DataSource interface.

In Appendix A, "Setting Up the Data Sample," I provide an example of setting up a data source for the Classic Models database. Throughout this book the data source name will be something like jdbc/CModelsDS or jdbc/cmDS. This name identifies it as a JDBC data source when performing the datasource lookup. One school of thought considers this name to be not enough redirection when performing a data source lookup. The general thinking is that using this name in the lookup ties the server to providing this value to the data source. This could result in security or configuration problems because you are essentially hardcoding the data source name within your application. Accessing a data source using the provided DS name has been deprecated in WebSphere, and using this approach you are likely to see the following error in your `SystemOut.log`.

```
 [12/1/07 16:27:27:234 EST] 0000002b ConnectionFac W   J2CA0294W: Deprecated usage of
direct JNDI lookup of resource jdbc/CModelsDS.  The following default values are
used: [Resource-ref settings]

    res-auth:                   1 (APPLICATION)
    res-isolation-level:        0 (TRANSACTION_NONE)
    res-sharing-scope:          true (SHAREABLE)
    loginConfigurationName:     null
    loginConfigProperties:      null
[Other attributes]

    res-resolution-control:     999 (undefined)
    res ref or CMP bean name:   null
    Database pool properties:   null
    primeID:                    0
isCMP1_x:                   false (not CMP1.x)
isJMS:                      false (not JMS)
```

The way to avoid this warning is to include a resource reference within your application that allows your application to use a specific value for the lookup, but also gives the WebSphere administrator or deployment manager the ability to change the data source name on the deployed server.

The main way to set up this reference is to use a `ResourceRefBinding` in the `ibm-web-bnd.xmi` file that is contained within the project WAR file. `ResourceRefBindings` can be used on JNDI resources such as JDBC or queue references that are set up by the WebSphere administrator. Actually, two files have to be modified. One is the `ibm-web-bnd.xmi` file that was mentioned earlier, and the second is the project `web.xml` file.

ibm-web.bnd.xmi

```
<resRefBindings xmi:id="ResourceRefBinding_1196545201031" jndiName="jdbc/CModelsDS">
    <bindingResourceRef href="WEB-INF/web.xml#ResourceRef_1196545201031"/>
  </resRefBindings>
```

Once the reference is complete you can set up a `resource-ref` element within the `web.xml` file of your application.

web.xml

```
<resource-ref id="ResourceRef_1196545201031">
    <description>Classic Models DS Reference</description>
    <res-ref-name>jdbc/CModelsDSRef</res-ref-name>
    <res-type>javax.sql.DataSource</res-type>
    <res-auth>Container</res-auth>
    <res-sharing-scope>Shareable</res-sharing-scope>
</resource-ref>
```

If you are new to WebSphere this may seem like over-abstraction, but the goal is to provide good flexibility and abstraction between roles within your organization. Removing this warning can reduce log bloat and make log files easier to read. It can also make your code more portable because not using this approach is deprecated and susceptible to being changed in future versions of WebSphere.

iBATIS Framework

The iBATIS framework is designed to provide a simple approach to providing database access to your application (see Figure 3.1). *Simple* is a relative term; every new technology requires some knowledge building, but aside from very simple custom JDBC frameworks iBATIS is one of the simplest and more robust I have found. iBATIS has actually been around for about five years now; you can find the code at http://ibatis.apache.org. As of this writing some discussion is going on for starting work on version 3 of the iBATIS framework.

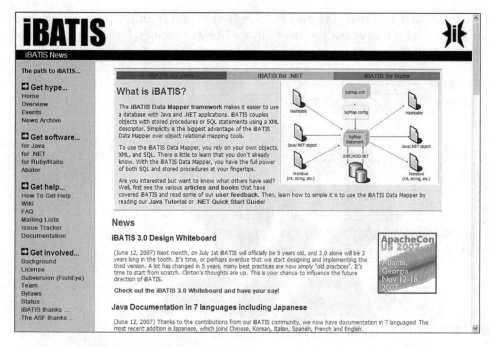

Figure 3.1   iBATIS data mapper framework

iBATIS uses a full SQL approach and works by mapping complete SQL to the classes that compose your domain model. The key word here is *SQL*, which you can generate or modify to allow for custom mapping specific to your application.

iBATIS comes with different features; the Data Mapping, or SQL Mapping Framework, is one part. A DAO framework included with iBATIS has been deprecated in favor of using the Spring DAO framework. Spring has full support for iBATIS built into the latest versions. Even though I emphasized the word *simple* when speaking about iBATIS, the entire package is very full featured and more than can be discussed in a single chapter.

Figure 3.2 illustrates a layered example of how everything fits together. This example does not use a business logic layer, but you can easily see how the business logic layer can fit into the overall architecture.

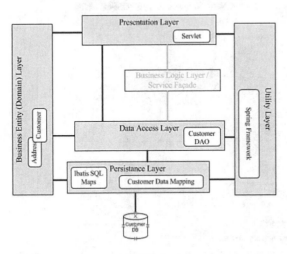

Figure 3.2   Layered iBATIS-Spring architecture

You can see a variety of classes within this diagram. Several seem to make sense, but a couple of them are new. It is not a stretch to imagine that you could custom code some of the new objects to provide similar functionality; however, your goal is to leverage best practices and frameworks where possible, without trying to squeeze in every feature known to man. This architecture strikes a nice balance for simple applications. Let's start with implementing iBATIS and look at the Spring components later on. To work with iBATIS, you need to create two key configuration files:

- `SqlMapConfig.xml`. There is one main `SqlMapConfig.xml` for each application. This file contains information such as the data source that iBATIS should be using and a list of the SQL map resources (`SqlMap.xml` files) that need to be used to manage the database interaction.
- `SqlMap.xml` file(s). For each set of SQL queries there is generally a related `SqlMap.xml` file. Often it is broken down by domain objects. For example, you might have a `CUSTOMER_SqlMap.xml` and an `ORDERS_Sql_Map.xml` file. In some instances you could have many more of these files. `SqlMap` files contain the actual SQL and the mappings for managing your database interaction.

The mapping statements that are contained within each DOMAINOBJECT_SqlMap.xml file are used to perform the actual data interaction. Figure 3.3 provides an overview of how these files fit together within the iBATIS framework. The input and outputs of each mapping statement are provided by the domain classes and the DAO classes that allow use of the specific mapping statements.

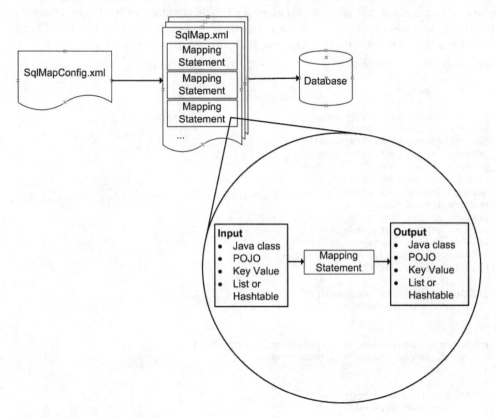

Figure 3.3 iBATIS mapping overview

iBATIS mapping statements work with a variety of data types such as classes, primitives, lists, and hash tables. You can call a mapping statement with a single parameter such as a key value and it can return a complete object populated with the data represented by that key value. Before getting too far along in this discussion, let's implement the model so you understand how the mapping will occur.

Implementing the Customer Class and Customer SQL Mapping

Probably the most important part of implementing any persistence architecture is the design of the domain model—that is, the classes that actually make up the objects within the provided domain. In this case those classes will map pretty closely to the tables that are provided within the sample database. We have very common objects such as customers, employees, orders, and products. `Customer.java` is a standard POJO (Plain Old Java Object) hat you would expect to see in any application. In fact, it is so standard that I have to make the additional point that nothing special is needed for using this class with iBATIS.

```java
package com.ibmpress.cm.model;

public class Customer {

    private Short customernumber;
    private String customername;
    private String contactlastname;
    private String contactfirstname;
    private String phone;
    private String addressline1;
    private String addressline2;
    private String city;
    private String state;
    private String postalcode;
    private String country;
    private Short salesrepemployeenumber;
    private Double creditlimit;

    public Short getCustomernumber() {
        return customernumber;
    }

    public void setCustomernumber(Short customernumber) {
        this.customernumber = customernumber;
    }

    public String getCustomername() {
        return customername;
    }
...
```

I have left off some of the getters and setters for brevity, but the example provides every-thing else you would see in the rest of this class. Interestingly, this class would be very similar to the class we would use in the EJB3 example later in this chapter, except with the necessary annotations.

Mapping the Customer Model

The `SqlMap.xml` file consists of two main parts: a result map, which is used to map to the `Customer.java` file; and the mapping statements themselves, of which there can be many. Result maps can be simple or complicated, but they are mainly used to map the values of each field to a field in your class. The following is an example of the `DB2Admin_Customer_SqlMap.xml` file.

```
<?xml version="1.0" encoding="UTF-8"?>
<!DOCTYPE sqlMap PUBLIC "-//ibatis.apache.org//DTD SQL Map 2.0//EN"
"http://ibatis.apache.org/dtd/sql-map-2.dtd">
<sqlMap>

<resultMap class="com.ibmpress.cm.model.Customer" id="CustomerResult">

        <result column="CUSTOMERNUMBER" jdbcType="SMALLINT"
        property="customernumber"/>
        <result column="CUSTOMERNAME" jdbcType="VARCHAR" property="customername"/>
        <result column="CONTACTLASTNAME" jdbcType="VARCHAR"
        property="contactlastname"/>
        <result column="CONTACTFIRSTNAME" jdbcType="VARCHAR"
        property="contactfirstname"/>
        <result column="PHONE" jdbcType="VARCHAR" property="phone"/>
        <result column="ADDRESSLINE1" jdbcType="VARCHAR" property="addressline1"/>
        <result column="ADDRESSLINE2" jdbcType="VARCHAR" property="addressline2"/>
        <result column="CITY" jdbcType="VARCHAR" property="city"/>
        <result column="STATE" jdbcType="VARCHAR" property="state"/>
        <result column="POSTALCODE" jdbcType="VARCHAR" property="postalcode"/>
        <result column="COUNTRY" jdbcType="VARCHAR" property="country"/>
        <result column="SALESREPEMPLOYEENUMBER" jdbcType="SMALLINT"
        property="salesrepemployeenumber"/>
        <result column="CREDITLIMIT" jdbcType="DOUBLE" property="creditlimit"/>

</resultMap>
```

The result map class contains the location of your result class and an id that will be used to reference this map in the mapping statements for each query. For each field in the table you identify that field name and map it to a property in the customer class along with the data type of that field. Having the result map in place now makes creating the mapping statements that do most of the work needed for the persistence model easy. The following selectCustomerByPrimaryKey is an example of a <select> mapping statement. There are about eight mapping statement types in all, including <select>, <insert>, <update>, <delete>, and others that allow you to perform more custom actions. The <select> mapping statement is probably the simplest and most used of all the mapping statements. The following is a Select statement mapping from the DB2Admin_Customers_SqlMap.xml file.

```
<select id="DB2ADMIN_CUSTOMERS.selectCustomerByPrimaryKey"
parameterClass="com.ibmpress.cm.model.Customer" resultMap="CustomerResult">
select CUSTOMERNUMBER, CUSTOMERNAME, CONTACTLASTNAME, CONTACTFIRSTNAME, PHONE,
ADDRESSLINE1, ADDRESSLINE2, CITY, STATE, POSTALCODE, COUNTRY, SALESREPEMPLOYEENUMBER,
CREDITLIMIT from DB2ADMIN.CUSTOMERS where CUSTOMERNUMBER = #customernumber:SMALLINT#
</select>
```

The statement provides both an input set as a parameterClass and an output set in the form of a resultMap (defined earlier). The query is pretty close to what you might find in a standard JDBC call with the addition of an inline # (pound sign) parameter to provide the criteria you need for this selection. Calling this statement from the CustomerDAO.java class you could provide the following method.

```
public Customer selectCustomerByPrimaryKey(Short customernumber) {
        Customer key = new Customer();
        key.setCustomernumber(customernumber);
        Customer record = (Customer)
        getSqlMapClientTemplate().queryForObject("DB2ADMIN_CUSTOMERS.selectCustomerBy
        PrimaryKey", key);
        return record;
}
```

Notice that you can use the Customer class as both the input and output for this statement; however, they are actually two different instances of the class. You could actually do away with the `parameterClass` in this instance and just pass in a primitive to complete the `where` clause; however, an example class often can be very useful if you want to create very dynamic queries.

Additionally, having a consistent approach can also be important for ensuring that your layer within the application is used consistently and for providing type safety within application usage. Another example of a mapping statement using the `<update>` command shows how consistent the statements can be within the `DB2Admin.Customers.SqlMap.xml`.

```
<update id="DB2ADMIN_CUSTOMERS.updateCustomerByPrimaryKey"
parameterClass="com.ibmpress.cm.model.Customer">

        update DB2ADMIN.CUSTOMERS
        set CUSTOMERNAME = #customername:VARCHAR#,
        CONTACTLASTNAME = #contactlastname:VARCHAR#,
        CONTACTFIRSTNAME = #contactfirstname:VARCHAR#,
        PHONE = #phone:VARCHAR#,
        ADDRESSLINE1 = #addressline1:VARCHAR#,
        ADDRESSLINE2 = #addressline2:VARCHAR#,
        CITY = #city:VARCHAR#,
        STATE = #state:VARCHAR#,
        POSTALCODE = #postalcode:VARCHAR#,
        COUNTRY = #country:VARCHAR#,
        SALESREPEMPLOYEENUMBER = #salesrepemployeenumber:SMALLINT#,
        CREDITLIMIT = #creditlimit:DOUBLE#
        where CUSTOMERNUMBER = #customernumber:SMALLINT#
    </update>
```

The `<update>` statement does not have a return result map; rather, it returns an integer representing the number of rows that have been updated.

Configurating iBATIS

After the `sqlMap` is complete you need to configure iBATIS to recognize the data source and the SQL maps that are required. The `sqlMapConfig.xml` file is used to identify this information. This section shows how you might configure this file if you were going to write your own DAO class around iBATIS; later you find out how to configure it with Spring.

The basic `sqlMapConfig.xml` is composed of several parts. The header identifies the start of the XML document and some of the initial settings that are possible within iBATIS.

```
<?xml version="1.0" encoding="UTF-8" ?>
<!DOCTYPE sqlMapConfig PUBLIC "-//iBATIS.com//DTD SQL Map Config 2.0//EN"
"http://www.ibatis.com/dtd/sql-map-config-2.dtd">

<sqlMapConfig>

<settings cacheModelsEnabled="true" enhancementEnabled="true" maxSessions="64"
maxTransactions="8" maxRequests="128" />
```

The `settings` element allows specific settings to be enabled within your iBATIS models. You can configure several settings, but you need to take care to understand how they might impact your application. For example, the `cacheModelsEnabled` option allows iBATIS to use cache models within mapped statements; however, you must create those models before they are used in the application. You should also know where you want caching to occur—at this level or higher within the application layers. An architect should understand this level of detail to help make the best decisions. An architect not understanding something of this detail may lead to future problems, because the development team may not raise the issue until it is too late.

The `transactionManager` and the `dataSource` element allow you to configure the data source and type of transaction management you will use within your application. In this case I have configured the `dataSource` element to work directly with the database and provide all the necessary information to make a connection.

```
<!-- transactionManager type="JDBC" -->
<!-- dataSource type="SIMPLE" -->
<!-- property value="COM.ibm.db2.jdbc.app.DB2Driver" name="JDBC.Driver" / -->
<!-- property value="jdbc:db2:CMODELS" name="JDBC.ConnectionURL" / -->
<!-- property value="db2admin" name="JDBC.Username" /-->
<!-- property value="db2admin" name="JDBC.Password" / -->
<!-- property value="15" name="Pool.MaximumActiveConnections" / -->
<!-- property value="15" name="Pool.MaximumIdleConnections" / -->
<!-- property value="1000" name="Pool.MaximumWait" / -->
<!-- /dataSource -->
<!-- /transactionManager -->
```

Notice, however, that those settings are commented out because I would rather use the WebSphere data source that is created in Appendix A:

```
<transactionManager type="JDBC">
        <dataSource type="JNDI">
                <property name="DataSource" value="jdbc/CModelsDS" />
        </dataSource>
</transactionManager>
```

Finally, the `config` file should identify all the `sqlMap` files that are needed for this application. In this simple example there is only one file; however, in more complex cases you could have several `<sqlMap>` elements within the `config` file.

```
<sqlMap resource="com/ibmpress/cm/sqlmap/DB2ADMIN_ORDERS_SqlMap.xml" />

</sqlMapConfig>
```

Notice that you have actually written some SQL for use within the persistence framework. Using SQL provides great control over how the data is manipulated, yet removes much of the mundane JDBC programming from the application. You also continue to leverage WAS data sources and take advantage of shared data connection pools.

Adding the Spring DAO Framework

The best approach when exploring iBATIS within your environment is to understand how to use the iBATIS framework independently of other frameworks. In this chapter you have used the iBATIS SqlMaps to interact with a data source directly; however, the iBATIS project has deprecated the DAO framework component that comes packaged with the download and has recommended that developers use the Spring DAO framework instead. Luckily for us, it is a good match, and Spring comes with full iBATIS support built in.

Spring has become pretty popular over the last couple of years and we have to give credit to Rod Johnson and the Spring team for filling a much-needed hole around business object management. For the most part, Spring should be a framework that you need to consider in almost any application; however, I think that you need to impose limitations and areas exist where Spring may not be the best fit. You find out more about Spring in Chapter 4, "Designing the Middle Tiers," in the context of the business logic layer. For now, you learn how to use it in this application.

In this example, you use Spring in the simplest sense of this application—to function as a factory for DAO beans that you need to create. For the most part, you simply extend some built-in Spring support for iBATIS to accomplish this goal.

The data access object needed for this application is a very simple case. First you create the CustomerDAO.java interface to define the method signatures needed:

```
package com.ibmpress.cm.dao;

import java.util.List;
import com.ibmpress.cm.model.Customer;

public interface CustomerDAO {

    void insertCustomer(Customer record);
    int updateCustomerByPrimaryKey(Customer record);
    List getCustomers();
    Customer selectCustomerByPrimaryKey(Short customernumber);
    int deleteCustomerByPrimaryKey(Short customernumber);
}
```

Five methods are defined within the interface. You can implement these methods in the CustomerDAOImpl class. This implementation class extends the Spring SqlMapClientDao Support class that is available as part of the iBATIS support within the Spring libraries. This support includes all the helper classes and methods that are needed to use the SQL maps that were created earlier. The entire CustomerDAOImpl.java class is here for your viewing. Going through the provided methods and seeing how they interact with the Spring-iBATIS framework should be educational.

```
package com.ibmpress.cm.dao;

import java.util.List;
import org.springframework.orm.ibatis.support.SqlMapClientDaoSupport;
import com.ibmpress.cm.model.Customer;

public class CustomerDAOImpl extends SqlMapClientDaoSupport implements
CustomerDAO {

        public CustomerDAOImpl() {
        super();
    }

    public void insertCustomer(Customer record) {
        getSqlMapClientTemplate().insert("DB2ADMIN_CUSTOMERS.insertCustomer",
        record);
    }

    public int updateCustomerByPrimaryKey(Customer record) {
        int rows =
        getSqlMapClientTemplate().update("DB2ADMIN_CUSTOMERS.updateCustomerByPrimaryK
        ey", record);
        return rows;
    }

    public List getCustomers() {
        List list =
        getSqlMapClientTemplate().queryForList("DB2ADMIN_CUSTOMERS.getCustomerList");
        return list;
    }

    public Customer selectCustomerByPrimaryKey(Short customernumber) {
        Customer key = new Customer();
        key.setCustomernumber(customernumber);
            Customer record = (Customer)
        getSqlMapClientTemplate().queryForObject("DB2ADMIN_CUSTOMERS.selectCustomerBy
        PrimaryKey", key);
        return record;
    }

    public int deleteCustomerByPrimaryKey(Short customernumber) {
        Customer key = new Customer();
        key.setCustomernumber(customernumber);
        int rows =
        getSqlMapClientTemplate().delete("DB2ADMIN_CUSTOMERS.deleteCustomerByPrimaryK
        ey", key);
        return rows;
    }

}
```

The class diagram for this application shows a different view of how the pieces fit together (see Figure 3.4). The client application will initiate the web context and get an instance of the CustomerDAO.java file.

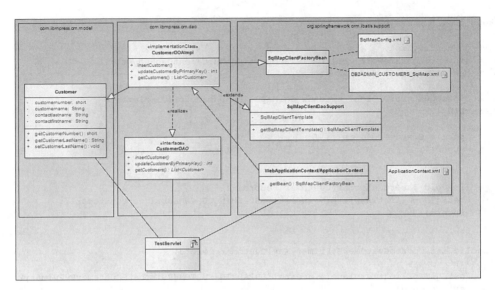

Figure 3.4   iBATIS-Spring class diagram

By default Spring provides objects as singletons unless you configure it to provide objects in one of the other modes that have recently become available. You could have created a custom DAO as a singleton and used it directly. In fact, in my previous book, *Programming Portlets Second Edition,* I do just this and provide an iBATIS DAO framework as an independent singleton. Managing objects is one of the strengths of Spring, and using a factory to look up objects simplifies some of the development interdependencies. Try using the introspection available within some tooling on a singleton to get an idea of what I am talking about. Being able to look up the DAO through the Spring context and using the dependency injection function to set up the SQL map configuration are very useful.

The final step is to wire up the Spring components so everything can work together. You use the `applicationContext.xml` file to pull all the dependencies together.

```
<?xml version="1.0" encoding="UTF-8"?>
<!DOCTYPE beans PUBLIC "-//SPRING//DTD BEAN//EN"
"http://www.springframework.org/dtd/spring-beans.dtd">

<beans>

<!-- Data source bean -->
<bean id="testDataSource" class="org.apache.commons.dbcp.BasicDataSource" destroy-
method="close">
        <property name="driverClassName">
                <value>COM.ibm.db2.jdbc.app.DB2Driver</value>
        </property>
        <property name="url">
                <value>jdbc:db2:CMODELS</value>
        </property>
        <property name="username">
```

```
                <value>db2admin</value>
        </property>
        <property name="password">
                <value>db2admin</value>
        </property>
</bean>
```

Note two data sources are configured within this file: the `testDataSource` and the `prodDataSource`. This configuration provides an easy way to switch between the two and allow persistence functionality testing both inside and outside the WebSphere container. The `prodDataSource` uses the WebSphere data source that has been set up within the application server while the `testDataSource` uses a direct connection to the database.

```
        <bean id="prodDataSource"
class="org.springframework.jndi.JndiObjectFactoryBean">
        <property name="jndiName"
                value="java:comp/env/jdbc/CModelsDSRef"/>
        <property name="lookupOnStartup"
                value="false"/>
        <property name="cache"
                value="true"/>
        <property name="proxyInterface"
                value="javax.sql.DataSource"/>

        </bean>
```

Next are some setup prerequisites for using iBATIS. You use `SqlMapClientFactoryBean` to load `sqlMapConfig.xml` and all the SQL maps so they can be provided to the DAO class via dependency injection. Don't worry if you don't understand dependency injection just yet; Chapter 4 goes into more detail about it.

```
<!— Web SqlMap setup for iBATIS Database Layer —>
<bean id="customerSqlMapConfig"
class="org.springframework.orm.ibatis.SqlMapClientFactoryBean">
        <property name="configLocation">
                <value>/WEB-INF/sqlMapConfig.xml</value>
        </property>
</bean>
```

Finally, the DAO bean is configured with the correct data source and the SQL map configuration bean. These properties are injected into the DAO bean or provided upon initialization.

```
<!— Customer DAO Bean —>
<bean id="customerDAO" class="com.ibmpress.cm.dao.CustomerDAOImpl">
        <property name="dataSource">
                <ref local="prodDataSource"/>
        </property>
        <property name="sqlMapClient">
                <ref local="customerSqlMapConfig"/>
        </property>
</bean>

</beans>
```

The `bean id` is important because that is what the client will use to look up the DAO at runtime. Because you have moved the data source information to Spring you can remove it from the iBATIS configuration file. The `sqlMapConfig.xml` file is now reduced to effectively one line at this point as shown here:

```
<?xml version="1.0" encoding="UTF-8" ?>
<!DOCTYPE sqlMapConfig PUBLIC "-//iBATIS.com//DTD SQL Map Config 2.0//EN"
"http://www.ibatis.com/dtd/sql-map-config-2.dtd">

<sqlMapConfig>
<sqlMap
resource="com/ibmpress/cm/sqlmap/DB2ADMIN_CUSTOMERS_SqlMap.xml" />
</sqlMapConfig>
```

That's pretty much it for building a complete, robust, albeit simple, persistence framework for your application.

Running a Test

I will not go into too much detail on testing your framework. The provided sample code has examples that can be run both outside and inside the WebSphere application server container. The main difference between the two is the data source and the Spring application context that is used. The IbatisSpringDAOTestServlet walks through some of the methods and simply outputs the values to the browser.

```
package com.ibmpress.cm.web.ibatisdao;

imports …

import org.springframework.web.context.WebApplicationContext;
import org.springframework.web.context.support.WebApplicationContextUtils;

import com.ibmpress.cm.dao.CustomerDAO;
import com.ibmpress.cm.model.Customer;

public class IbatisSpringDAOTestServlet extends HttpServlet {

        CustomerDAO customerDAO;
```

The servlet defines an instance variable of type `CustomerDAO`. Generally instance variables are not considered good programming practice, so its use should definitely raise some flags during a code review. A good discussion of why it is being used should occur and be internally documented with a comment for future reference.

In the servlet `init()` method you can get a handle to the DAO and then store it locally for reference throughout the lifecycle of the servlet. The Spring `WebApplicationContext` is used to look up the DAO using the `getBean()` method.

```
 public void init(ServletConfig config ) throws ServletException {

super.init();

// Load Spring framework Web context
```

```
WebApplicationContext wac =
WebApplicationContextUtils.getRequiredWebApplicationContext(
config.getServletContext() );

//get customer data access object
customerDAO = (CustomerDAO)wac.getBean("customerDAO");


}
```

In the doGet() method of the servlet is where all the action happens. This method exercises many of the methods contained within the DAO. In the first part a new Customer object is created and then inserted into the database. I have removed some of the print writer statements for clarity.

```
protected void doGet(HttpServletRequest request, HttpServletResponse
response) throws ServletException, IOException {

                PrintWriter writer =response.getWriter();

                short custNum = 9999;
                Customer myCustomer = new Customer();
                myCustomer.setCustomernumber(custNum);
                myCustomer.setCustomername("mynew customer");
                myCustomer.setContactfirstname("Bernal");
                myCustomer.setContactlastname("Joey");
                myCustomer.setCountry("US");
                myCustomer.setPhone("123-456-7890");
                myCustomer.setCreditlimit(999999.99);

                customerDAO.insertCustomer(myCustomer);
```

Another section in the method is a lookup on all Customer objects in the table. This section gets a complete list of customers and then iterates through the data, outputting some basic information about each customer.

```
                List custList = customerDAO.getCustomers();
                Customer cust;
                Iterator it = custList.iterator();
                while (it.hasNext()) {

                        cust = (Customer) it.next();

                        writer.println(cust.getCustomernumber() + " " +
                        cust.getCustomername() + "<br>");
                }
```

This complete example is about as simple as I could make it while still providing a reference to how you might approach a persistence layer within your application. Keep in mind that even though it is a fairly simple example, there is still a lot to do; many decisions need to be made and many things considered before it can be called a production-ready application. The next section describes another approach using the EJB V3 specification and the Java Persistence API.

Transactional Thinking

For many applications built for WebSphere today, the impact of transactional interactions is not at the top of the list. Many applications are read only, or have light traffic and updates, and simply don't require robust transactional capability. However, other applications do require this capability but it is not taken into consideration during the design phase of the project. The ACID (Atomicity, Consistency, Isolation, and Durability) test is not designed simply for computer science students to learn and then forget! It is designed to provide a simple way to determine whether your data interaction requires transactional consideration.

You can find many references on ACID and how to manage and use transactions within your application, but you can keep a couple of key questions in mind to determine whether this capability is necessary within your application:

- A transaction is some amount of work that often consists of several discrete operations or steps. Do you have scenarios where multiple tables need to be updated, or several queries need to be run in succession? Are the events dependent upon one another—that is, if one fails, should they all roll back to the initial state?
- Transactions usually need to be isolated from each other. Do you have situations where multiple users are dependent upon or are updating the same set of data—for example, account information?
- Completed transactions should be in a state where they cannot be undone. If the user is notified that a transaction is complete, the system should guarantee it has completed successfully.

Keep in mind that adding transaction capability also adds complexity to your application, resulting in possible longer development and additional testing. These are not bad things, but they should be accounted for in your project estimates and not taken for granted as just part of the development routine.

For iBATIS some transactional support is already provided. Each single SQL statement is run within its own transaction; no demarcation is required. But many times you want to run local transactions that consist of two or more statements. iBATIS provides the ability natively to start and stop transactions, but unfortunately, it is difficult to use now that the DAO is wrapped with Spring. Spring assumes that you want to take advantage of its capabilities such as data source management and transaction support. You can wire up a transaction manager in Spring such as the `org.springframework.transaction.interceptor.TransactionProxyFactoryBean` and manage transactions at the Spring level.

If you do need to worry about transactions within your application then look closely at the technologies you are choosing and understand how mixing technologies can impact your choices. Traditionally EJB technology has been the choice for heavy transactional applications; the latest release of EJB specification 3 has become easier to use and more flexible by incorporating some of the best features of newer persistence frameworks. The discussion now moves to helping you understand how to use EJB3 within your application framework.

EJB 3 and the Java Persistence API

Many years ago during the dot-com boom I was involved in a major real estate portal project. We used the term *portal* more generically back then as portal application software was
not widely available, but the architecture was a standard three-tier approach using EJBs,
servlets, and JSPs. Using this approach was the hot trend during those times and technically
the fit was correct for this particular application. The results, however, were a little less than
stellar. Take 40 hot young programmers who could barely spell Java, mix in several complex
new technologies and a list of requirements gathered from weeks of user sessions, and you
can imagine the results. In the years since then I have worked on several projects using different versions of the EJB spec, but I always seemed to encounter the same complexity problems.

EJBs have gotten a mixed response across the industry over the years. For a long time no real
alternative existed although development teams made do by simplifying their applications—even to the point of people trying to retrieve data directly from within their JSPs,
which continues to amaze me. The fact that libraries like the Java Standard Tag Library
include this capability is quite confusing, but fortunately, JSTL is complex enough to learn
that it hasn't appeared to exacerbate the problem.

More recently alternatives to EJBs for building service and persistence layers have become
more readily available. Persistence frameworks like iBATIS and Hibernate, and lightweight
containers like Spring, have been able to fill the gap and allow development teams to build
robust, layered applications without EJBs. I would have predicted a few years ago that this
was going to be the death knell for EJBs, although I might have been a bit hesitant to say so
publicly. But the EJB gods fought back and performed powerful magic. EJB3 and the Java
Persistence API draw upon the best ideas from persistence technologies such as Hibernate,
TopLink, and JDO as well as a light framework, POJO development, and dependency injection. Customers now no longer face the choice between incompatible non-standard persistence models for object/relational mapping. In addition, the Java Persistence API (JPA) is
usable both within Java SE environments as well as within Java EE, allowing many more
developers to take advantage of a standard persistence API.

EJB 3 offers so many new and exciting features that I don't even know where to start.
Dependency injection with POJO development, annotations, JPA, and the fact that it is a
Java EE standard technology all combine to make it a serious option for application devel-
opment. Two key points to keep in mind within this example are the greatly simplified pro-
gramming model for creating session EJBs, and creating a persistence layer with annotated
POJOs.

One thing to remember about JPA is that it is a standards-based persistence framework, as
opposed to many of the other approaches that have been discussed in this chapter. iBATIS,
while heavily adopted by development teams in many organizations, is not a Java standard.
Adopting a standards-based approach at all layers can be an important part of your architecture strategy if you choose to go that route.

A3.2

Understanding the Approach

With the iBATIS example discussed earlier you saw how the code fit within a layered architecture. This example follows a very similar approach that can be layered in several ways.
Figure 3.5 shows the class diagram for the example in this section. As usual the sample code
will be downloadable for examination. Download information and complete descriptions of
the examples are available in Appendix B, "Running the Examples."

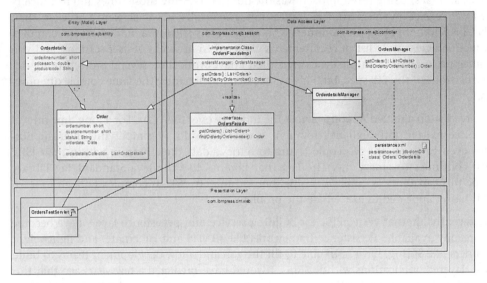

Figure 3.5   JPA layered approach

The entity layer contains the domain model that emulates the objects within our business
domain. In this case are the Order object and the Orderdetails object. Notice that they
are related in a one-to-many relationship; that is, one or more Orderdetails for every
Order object. In the data access layer are two sets of components. One set is the session
bean façade that is used by clients to access and use the persistence layer. The other set of
components are the OrderManager components that actually perform the persistence interaction necessary for the entities involved.

Depending on where the functionality that is embedded within the session façade, one
could classify the façade as the DAO layer or a business logic layer. My inclination in a simple project is to embed business logic within that façade; however, in this example there is
not real logic so I have to classify it as a DAO layer that can be accessed by both local and
remote application clients.

Entities with POJOs and Annotations

Annotations were introduced in Java 5 as part of the metadata spec, which was defined
within JSR 175 in 2004. It is from this spec that the awesome power of annotations within

EJB 3 and JPA has evolved. Honestly I wasn't that impressed with the idea of annotations until I started using them and realized how much code they could actually save. With your entity beans, annotations offer two powerful advantages:

- The ability to use these beans outside of this application as pure POJOs because the annotations will simply be ignored
- They save you a lot of code and deployment descriptor configurations that you would normally have to do to configure this EJB-based application

The best way to understand how annotations work is to walk through an example, as follows. The `Orders.java` entity starts as any other class; however, after the `import` statements you include the `@Entity` annotation.

```
package com.ibmpress.cm.ejb.entities;

import static javax.persistence.FetchType.EAGER;
import static javax.persistence.TemporalType.TIMESTAMP;
import …

@Entity
```

This annotation identifies the class as a persistent domain object. When the class is deployed the container will recognize it and will expect additional annotations within the entity.

JPA uses a variation of SQL called the Java Programming Query Language (JPQL) to manage interaction with the database. JPQL looks very similar to SQL; however, you need to understand the syntax and context to create the right queries. Static queries are usually defined within a `@NamedQuery` or `@NamedQueries` block, and the queries are executed by the EntityManager. You find out how to use the Entity Manager later in this section.

```
@NamedQueries({

    @NamedQuery(name="getOrders", query="SELECT o FROM Orders o"),

    @NamedQuery(name="getOrdersByOrderdate", query = "SELECT o FROM Orders o
WHERE o.orderdate = :orderdate"),

    @NamedQuery(name="getOrdersByShippeddate", query = "SELECT o FROM Orders o
WHERE o.shippeddate = :shippeddate"),

    @NamedQuery(name="getOrdersByCustomernumber", query = "SELECT o FROM Orders o
WHERE o.customernumber = :customernumber"),

    @NamedQuery(name="getOrdersByRequireddate", query = "SELECT o FROM Orders o
WHERE o.requireddate = :requireddate"),

    @NamedQuery(name="getOrdersByStatus", query = "SELECT o FROM Orders o WHERE
o.status = :status")

})
```

This example has five named queries that are statically defined. All are SELECT queries that work with different query parameters so that you can query an entity in different ways. JPQL actually supports <SELECT>, <UPDATE>, and <DELETE> statements even though I have only used the <SELECT> statement within this example. Also note that all the query names have to be unique within this deployment module.

The next part of the class is the same as any other bean with several additional annotations embedded within the code. The @Id annotation identifies this instance variable as the identity for this entity. This normally equates to the primary key that is in the matching table for this entity. The @Lob annotation is used for large fields within the database such as CLOBs, BLOBs, or large character fields. Additionally you use the @Temporal annotation to identify how you want to map Date or Calendar types to the database.

```
public class Orders implements Serializable {

        @Id
        private short ordernumber;

        @Lob
        private String comments;

        private short customernumber;
        private String status;

        @Temporal(TIMESTAMP)
        private Date orderdate;

        @Temporal(TIMESTAMP)
        private Date shippeddate;

        @Temporal(TIMESTAMP)
        private Date requireddate;

        @OneToMany(mappedBy="ordernumber",fetch=EAGER)
        private List<Orderdetails> orderdetailsCollection;
```

Because Orderdetails are a related entity you can prefetch all the detail of your order when you load an order. With the @OneToMany annotation you can define a parameterized list of Orderdetails entity objects within the Order. Using the mappedBy attribute you can define the relationship column of the Order entity with the @Id of the Orderdetails entity. Also note that I used EAGER as the fetch attribute to define how this list is loaded. The @OnetoMany annotation actually defaults to LAZY loading; however, in this case I believe that an Order without the details is of little use except in a few cases. By contrast the @ManytoOne annotation actually defaults to EAGER fetch so it is important to understand the impact of these annotations and perhaps even comment on the results within your source files.

The rest of the class is pretty standard with getters and setters for all the private variables that represent class attributes.

```
        public Orders() {
                super();
        }

        public short getOrdernumber() {
                return this.ordernumber;
        }

        public void setOrderdate(Date orderdate) {
                this.orderdate = orderdate;
        }

        ...

        public void setOrderdetailsCollection(
                        List<Orderdetails> orderdetailsCollection) {
                this.orderdetailsCollection = orderdetailsCollection;
        }

}
```

Overall you can see this is not a complicated setup. It can, however, quickly become complicated to the novice trying to build complex functionality within a new framework. A quick look at the Orderdetails class shows that it is very similar in design:

```
@Entity
@NamedQueries({

        @NamedQuery(name="getOrderdetails", query="SELECT o FROM
Orderdetails o"),

        @NamedQuery(name="getOrderdetailsOrdered", query = "SELECT o FROM
Orderdetails o ORDER BY o.orderlinenumber"),

        @NamedQuery(name="getOrderdetailsByProductcode", query = "SELECT o
FROM Orderdetails o WHERE o.productcode = :productcode")})

public class Orderdetails implements Serializable {

        @Id
        private short orderlinenumber;

        private double priceeach;

        private short quantityordered;

        private String productcode;

        @ManyToOne
        @JoinColumn(name="ORDERNUMBER")
        private Orders ordernumber;
```

I have to admit this is what might be called an anemic domain model. It is called that because it maps nearly directly to the data tables where the database field equals an attribute within the class. A richer domain model would likely include some behavior within the objects themselves. The beauty of a POJO-based entity model is that you have that flexibility within your application to add more functionality with very little effort.

Entity Managers

The entities are now in place but you need a way to manage them in a consistent manner. The Entity Manager is what controls the persistence of the entities that you have defined. The entities would really be of little use without the Entity Manager to control the CRUD (Create, Read, Update, Delete) functionality of the entity data. The OrdersManager uses the EntityManager API to perform the required persistence functionality. The class is a standard class that takes advantage of the API and exposes a set of methods to interact with the Orders data.

Before you get into the EntityManager let's spend a moment on the `persistence.xml` file that is necessary to tie in the persistence metadata. The `persistence.xml` file defines the `persistence-unit` that you can use. The name of the persistence unit is a reference to when an entity manager instance is created. The persistence unit also defines the data source that is being used and a list of the entity classes that are needed with this application.

```
<?xml version="1.0" encoding="UTF-8"?>
<persistence version="1.0"
xmlns="http://java.sun.com/xml/ns/persistence"
xmlns:xsi="http://www.w3.org/2001/XMLSchema-instance"
xsi:schemaLocation="http://java.sun.com/xml/ns/persistence
http://java.sun.com/xml/ns/persistence/persistence_1_0.xsd">
        <persistence-unit name="ClassicModelsDataEJB">
                <jta-data-source>jdbc/cmDS</jta-data-source>
                <class>com.ibmpress.cm.ejb.entities.Orders</class>
                <class>com.ibmpress.cm.ejb.entities.Orderdetails</class>
        </persistence-unit>
</persistence>
```

Two main annotations are used in this class that assist with its identity. The `@JPAManager` annotation identifies the target entity for this manager class, and the `@SupressWarnings` annotation removes any complier warnings for unchecked exceptions that may occur in this class. This is a convenience annotation that you should use with care and carefully document.

```
package com.ibmpress.cm.ejb.controller;

import javax.persistence.EntityManager;
import javax.persistence.EntityManagerFactory;
import javax.persistence.Persistence;
import javax.persistence.Query;
import javax.persistence.TemporalType;
import com.ibm.jpa.web.Action;
import com.ibm.jpa.web.JPAManager;
import com.ibm.jpa.web.NamedQueryTarget;
import com.ibmpress.cm.ejb.entities.Orders;
```

...

```
@JPAManager(targetEntity=com.ibmpress.cm.ejb.entities.Orders.class)
@SuppressWarnings("unchecked")
public class OrdersManager {

        public OrdersManager() {}

        private EntityManager getEntityManager() {

                EntityManagerFactory emf = Persistence
                .createEntityManagerFactory("ClassicModelsDataEJB");

                return emf.createEntityManager();

        }
```

The `getEntityManager()` method returns an instance of the EntityManager to other methods within the `OrdersManager` class. This method references the `persistence.xml` file located within the project, or more specifically the `persistence-unit` that is defined within the `persistence.xml` file. In addition to the persistence context the EntityManager provides some transactional context for the entity components and exposes the lifecycle methods for each entity. I show a few examples of the `OrderManager` class to help illustrate how this occurs.

The `createOrders()` method provides the ability to create a new order within the database. Reviewing the code you can see how the interaction is wrapped heavily within the transaction methods `.begin` and `.commit` of the EntityManager API. This provides a clean way to ensure transaction stability within your persistence architecture, although you do have to code the methods, or rely on wizards to provide the proper context. The single method `em.persist` is used to create a new record in the database. My one concern here is that from the developer's perspective, we haven't reduced the complexity completely. One must still take care to ensure that coding errors do not occur within the application.

```
@Action(Action.ACTION_TYPE.CREATE)
public String createOrders(Orders orders) throws Exception {
        EntityManager em = getEntityManager();
        try {
                em.getTransaction().begin();
                em.persist(orders);
                em.getTransaction().commit();
        } catch (Exception ex) {
                try {
                        if (em.getTransaction().isActive()) {
                                em.getTransaction().rollback();
                        }
                } catch (Exception e) {
                        ex.printStackTrace();
                        throw e;
                }
```

```
            throw ex;
        } finally {
            em.close();
        }
        return "";
    }
```

The `deleteOrders` method is very similar to the createOrders method; however, it does contain a few subtle differences. For example, you call the `em.merge` method with the provided Orders object. This is because you have no idea where the Orders object that is passed into the method came from. It is the job of the EntityManager to manage entities, so a merge ensures that this bean data is synchronized with any other entity that might have been created. After that you can call the `remove` method and know you are removing the correct record in the database.

```
@Action(Action.ACTION_TYPE.DELETE)
public String deleteOrders(Orders orders) throws Exception {
        EntityManager em = getEntityManager();
        try {
                em.getTransaction().begin();
                orders = em.merge(orders);
                em.remove(orders);
                em.getTransaction().commit();
        } catch (Exception ex) {
                try {
                        if (em.getTransaction().isActive()) {
                                em.getTransaction().rollback();
                        }
                } catch (Exception e) {
                        ex.printStackTrace();
                        throw e;
                }
                throw ex;
        } finally {
                em.close();
        }
        return "";
    }
```

Notice two items of interest here. First in the preceding methods I am catching the generic Exception, a practice I spoke negatively about in Chapter 2, "Setting a Standard." Much of this code was generated by a wizard within Rational Application Developer version 7.5. This example illustrates nicely how you should always review generated code for correctness and for adherence to your organizational or team standards.

The other type of query that you can do with the `OrdersManager` class is a named query. This is accomplished via the `createNamedQuery` method.

```
@NamedQueryTarget("getOrders")
public List<Orders> getOrders() {

                EntityManager em = getEntityManager();
        List<Orders> results = null;
        try {
```

```
                     Query query = em.createNamedQuery("getOrders");
                     results = (List<Orders>) query.getResultList();
          } finally {
                     em.close();
          }
          return results;
  }
```

Before we get too far in the development let's take a look at how all this fits together as a set of projects. For this initial example I show how to package everything together as a single EAR file deployment package. This is typical of many applications that are locally hosted in a single application server instance.

Figure 3.6 shows a screenshot of my RAD 7.5 workspace for this example. You can see the final result actually contains four separate projects. Up to now you have only identified one of them. In reality it is not the focus of the book to work at this detailed level, but I think understanding how this example fits together in the project space helps you to visualize how the layers map to actual code. The entity beans and entity manager classes reside in the ClassicModelsDataEJB project in Figure 3.6, as well as the `persistence.xml` discussed earlier.

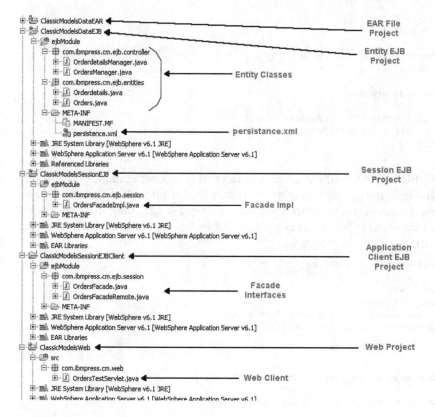

Figure 3.6   Project layout

Now the goal is to build out the rest of the application. The next step is to create the session façade, which will eventually provide both a local and remote interface for your applications. The `ClassicModelsSessionEJBClient` will contain the session façade interfaces, while the `ClassicModelsSessionEJB` will contain the implementation for the interfaces. Notice that there is only one implementation for both the local and the remove interface. Finally, the `ClassicModelsWeb` project will contain the servlet application for testing the entire application. You then break up different components of the application into different projects to remove any circular references that may occur when trying to include some of the components in other projects. For example, the web application requires a reference to both the session interfaces and the entity objects. Additionally, the session implementation requires a reference to the session bean interfaces and the entity objects. It can be confusing, but this is the best way to provide good encapsulation and reuse of the components.

The session interface for the persistence layer is actually quite simple. It is a standard interface with one annotation; the `@Local` annotation tells the container that this is a local interface for a session or message bean.

```
package com.ibmpress.cm.ejb.session;

import java.util.List;
import javax.ejb.Local;

import com.ibmpress.cm.ejb.entities.Orders;

@Local
public interface OrdersFacade {

        public List<Orders> getOrders();
        public Orders findOrdersByOrdernumber(short ordernumber);

}
```

In all other ways this interface is unremarkable. In fact this is another example of the beauty of the EJB 3 spec—that one simple annotation can turn the file into a local interface for an EJB. The implementation of this interface also contains only a single annotation, that being the `@Stateless` command. This command identifies in lieu of a deployment descriptor that this is, in fact, a stateless session bean.

```
package com.ibmpress.cm.ejb.session;

import java.util.List;
import javax.ejb.Stateless;
import com.ibmpress.cm.ejb.controller.OrdersManager;
import com.ibmpress.cm.ejb.entities.Orders;


@Stateless
public class OrdersFacadeImpl implements OrdersFacade {

        OrdersManager orderManager = new OrdersManager();
```

```
        public List<Orders> getOrders() {

                List<Orders> list = orderManager.getOrders();
                if (list == null) {
                        System.out.println("list is null");
                }
                return list;
        }


        public Orders findOrdersByOrdernumber(short ordernumber) {
                return orderManager.findOrdersByOrdernumber(ordernumber);
        }



}
```

That's it! The EJB section of the application is complete. It may look like a lot of code, but if you have done EJBs in the past you know this is not a lot of work. For your initial applications you can simplify everything a bit by reducing the number of methods and the amount of functionality you are providing.

Testing the Application

None of this effort is worthwhile unless it does something useful for your business. For this you need some kind of client interface, which allows useful work to be done. In this case you won't be doing any useful work for a while, but you can pretend. A separate web application can be built to test how this interaction will occur. You have the privilege of being able to take advantage of several new features and capabilities in the WebSphere EJB 3 Feature Pack. The first is that local references to EJBs happen automatically within the container. WebSphere recognizes the EJB you are referencing and can inject that EJB into your application on demand. The OrdersTestServlet contains a single annotation, @EJB, in the header. You define the instance variable within the servlet and preface it with the @EJB annotation to signify that this object is an EJB that lives somewhere within the container.

```
public class OrdersTestServlet extends HttpServlet {

@EJB
private OrdersFacade ordersFacade;

...

protected void doGet(HttpServletRequest request, HttpServletResponse
response) throws ServletException, IOException {

PrintWriter writer = response.getWriter();
response.setContentType("text/html");

Short orderid = 10100;

writer.println("OrderTestServlet using OrderFacade(Local) <br><br>");
```

```
Orders myOrder = ordersFacade.findOrdersByOrdernumber(orderid);
```

...

Later in the `doGet` method when you reference the `orderFacade` variable, it is simply there, having been injected into your class as a dependency that you defined earlier in the class. Chapter 4 discusses dependency injection in more detail. Running the example you can see that it pulls back the order number that you defined in the class and lists the order details information for that order (see Figure 3.7).

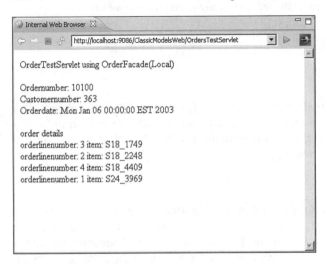

Figure 3.7   Test servlet using local interface

For good layer separation, however, everything in one EAR file is not good enough. You have to at least understand how persistence can be encapsulated into a separate deployable component and still be used by other developers working on their own areas.

Remote Clients

Figure 3.8 provides a view of the application similar to Figure 3.5. Most of the classes you will recognize as ones that you just defined and created encapsulated within different projects, but still deployed within the same EAR file. There is the possibility, however, that remote clients may want to use this persistence layer, so you should make some provisions for this approach.

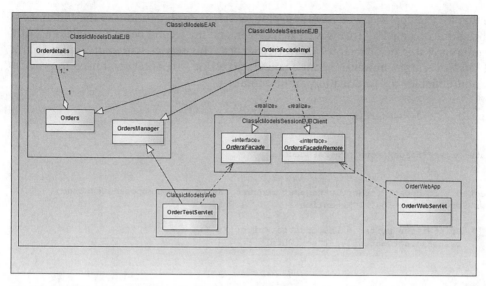

Figure 3.8   Local and remote deployment

You can accomplish this task quite easily after all the heavy lifting done earlier in this section. You just need to add a remote interface to the application and provide an implementation. OrdersFacadeRemote provides the remote interface via the @Remote annotation.

```
package com.ibmpress.cm.ejb.session;

import java.util.List;
import javax.ejb.Remote;

import com.ibmpress.cm.ejb.entities.Orders;

@Remote
public interface OrdersFacadeRemote {

        public List<Orders> getOrders();
        public Orders findOrdersByOrdernumber(short ordernumber);

}
```

An additional change that you need to make to the session bean implementation is to include the additional remote interface so that your remote client can access the same information.

```
@Stateless
public class OrdersFacadeImpl implementsOrdersFacade,

                                        OrdersFacadeRemote {
```

Note that for this approach you have to deploy two separate applications to the container—one being the original EAR that was created earlier, and the second being a standalone WAR file containing this new "remote" OrderWebServlet. This servlet starts out similar to the local servlet example; however, because you are accessing it remotely you need to provide some additional lookup information to the container.

```
public class OrderWebServlet extends HttpServlet {

@EJB
private OrdersFacadeRemote ordersFacade;


protected void doGet(HttpServletRequest request, HttpServletResponse response)
throws ServletException, IOException {

        PrintWriter writer = response.getWriter();
        response.setContentType("text/html");

        try {

                InitialContext ic = new InitialContext();

                OrdersFacadeRemote ordersFacade = (OrdersFacadeRemote)
                ic.lookup("com.ibmpress.cm.ejb.session.OrdersFacadeRemote");

                Short orderid = 10100;

                ...
```

The javax.naming.InitialContext has to be created to pass the JNDI name of the EJB that is required. The EJB container will provide JNDI binding for the EJBs that are deployed. Both a long and short binding are provided depending upon your need for strong type safety within the server. Here is an example for the two interfaces, both remote and local:

```
00000014 EJBContainerI I   CNTR0167I: The server is binding the
OrdersFacadeRemote interface of the OrdersFacadeImpl enterprise bean in the
ClassicModelsSessionEJB.jar module of the ClassicModelsDataEAR application.

The binding location is:
ejb/ClassicModelsDataEAR/ClassicModelsSessionEJB.jar/OrdersFacadeImpl#com.
ibmpress.cm.ejb.session.OrdersFacadeRemote

00000014 EJBContainerI I   CNTR0167I: The server is binding the
OrdersFacadeRemote interface of the OrdersFacadeImpl enterprise bean in
the ClassicModelsSessionEJB.jar module of the ClassicModelsDataEAR
application.

The binding location is: com.ibmpress.cm.ejb.session.OrdersFacadeRemote

00000014 EJBContainerI I   CNTR0167I: The server is binding the
OrdersFacade interface of the OrdersFacadeImpl enterprise bean in the
ClassicModelsSessionEJB.jar module of the
ClassicModelsDataEAR
application.
```

```
The binding location is:
ejblocal:ClassicModelsDataEAR/ClassicModelsSessionEJB.jar/OrdersFacadeImpl
#com.ibmpress.cm.ejb.session.OrdersFacade

00000014 EJBContainerI I   CNTR0167I: The server is binding the
OrdersFacade interface of the OrdersFacadeImpl enterprise bean in the
ClassicModelsSessionEJB.jar module of the
ClassicModelsDataEAR
application.

The binding location is:
ejblocal:com.ibmpress.cm.ejb.session.OrdersFacade
```

Remember that for the local interface you didn't need to use this binding; the server was able to identify the correct EJB and inject it for us. After you have the correct binding you can run the test servlet as shown in Figure 3.9.

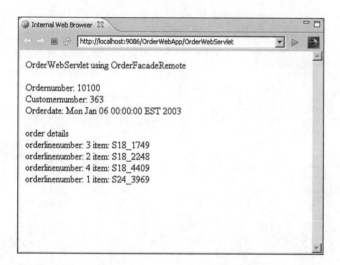

Figure 3.9   Test servlet using remote interface

Conclusion

Whew! This chapter covered a lot of material. Hopefully, it has provided the basis upon which you can start to define your own persistence strategy and how that fits into your overall architecture. Know that there is no rights or wrongs—well, actually, there are a lot of wrongs, but usually not until you get to implementation. At this point the fact that you are defining an approach that will get shared within your development team and across your organization is a big step in the right direction.

Links to developerWorks Articles

A3.1 DeveloperWorks Technical Journal
Tired of Hand Coding JDBC by Roland Barcia
http://www.ibm.com/developerworks/websphere/techjournal/0510_col_barcia/0510_col_
barcia.html

A3.2 Building EJB 3.0 Applications with WebSphere Application Server
Roland Barcia, Jeffrey Sampson
http://www.ibm.com/developerworks/websphere/techjournal/0712_barcia/0712_
barcia.html

Chapter 4

Designing the Middle Tiers

A rguably the middle tier and business layers are some of the more difficult layers to clearly define. Somewhere between the persistence and presentation layers are one or more layers that provide a continuum of cleanly separated yet reusable functionality, which is the goal, right? This is the nirvana that architects search for within their organization or domain. Unfortunately, nirvana is way beyond the scope of this book, and probably beyond the reach of many organizations. This chapter can help you to begin that search by outlining some of the options that are available for your application. It also talks about the specifics of deploying middle layers and dependent libraries within WebSphere Application Server for use by other layers and applications.

Business Logic

The issue begins with where exactly business logic should be placed within the code. Chapter 3, "Persistence Matters," touched briefly on the idea of a rich domain model where entity components contain internal logic as well as attribute storage. This muddies the waters a bit when an entity component can perform specific operations. For example, take the case of sales tax calculation. It would stand to reason that an order object that contained both the overall order data and a list of order items could in fact calculate for itself the sales tax and other receipt information for that order. In fact, storing that information within the order when it is complete may be wise. This persistence may be important in cases where the sales tax rate is subject to change from time to time. Take a look at Figure 4.1 to see what I mean.

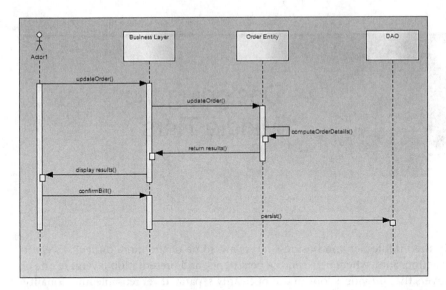

Figure 4.1   Rich domain model

In this example the Order Entity itself computes the details that are necessary to complete the order. This signifies a somewhat rich domain model in which the domain entities have some logic encapsulated within themselves to help make decisions. As I mentioned there is some sense in this approach because some of this information might need to be persisted.

On the other hand this type of computational logic could be contained within the business logic layer (see Figure 4.2) of the application, perhaps using the order date to determine the tax rate for orders over time. This approach actually puts more of the onus on the business layer, perhaps using this layer to perform additional tasks such as determination of other discounts that may be applied from time to time, such as buy two items get the third one free, or special discounts for specific types of orders.

In this case, the option exists that the Order Entity still needs to be updated to hold additional information. This information may be created by some calculated results of an operation.

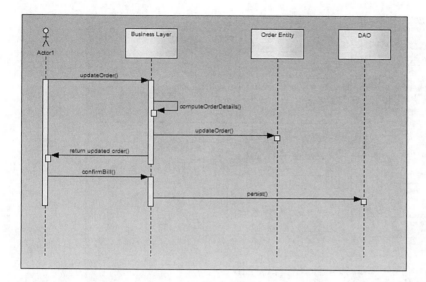

Figure 4.2 Business layer logic

Another HelloWorld Example

Okay, maybe this example isn't the simplest ever, but it is simple enough that everyone can relate to it. Using the classic Hello World example I show how you can design a business layer, and how you can use that business layer within your applications.

The example consists of one interface and an implementation class (see Figure 4.3) making up the business layer. An interface is probably not needed for this simple of an example, but it does allow me to separate the implementation of the business layer from the clients who use it.

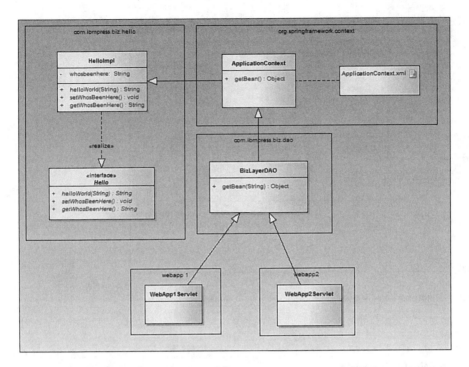

Figure 4.3 Business layer class model

The interface `Hello` really consists of one method, that being the `helloWorld()` method. It's not rocket science as far as examples go, but is simple enough to keep the focus on the design. I have added two additional methods that will make sense to you later in this chapter. They are designed to illustrate how a single layer may be shared across multiple applications within a single JVM. This concept is not always readily apparent unless you are used to working with multiple applications such as in a portal framework.

```
package com.ibmpress.biz.hello;

public interface Hello {

    public String helloWorld(String name);

    public void setWhosBeenHere(String value);
    public String getWhosBeenHere();

}
```

As expected the implementation for this interface is just as simple. I have created a single instance variable to hold some state information as different client applications use the service. The other methods simply echo parameters that are passed to them.

```
package com.ibmpress.biz.hello;

public class HelloImpl implements Hello {

   private String whos_been_here = "original value";

   public String helloWorld(String name) {
      return "Hello " + name;
   }
   public void setWhosBeenHere(String value) {
      whos_been_here = value;
   }

   public String getWhosBeenHere() {
      return whos_been_here;
   }
}
```

At this point I really have a number of choices for making my object visible to client applications and for making sure that I control the number of instances that are created within the environment. For this simple class I do not really care if multiple instances of this object are created, but if I were to use this object to access some backend, or manage a shared resource, I would definitely want to manage the creation of these objects. I could turn it into a session EJB like we used in Chapter 3 or perhaps add a `getInstance()` method and make the class into a singleton.

If you look back at Figure 4.3 you can see I have decided to use the Spring framework to control the creation of Hello beans. The Spring bean factory actually defaults to a singleton approach but provides a clean way of instantiating and accessing my objects. Defining the bean is as simple as declaring it within the `application.xml` file used by the Spring application context.

```
<?xml version="1.0" encoding="UTF-8"?>
<!DOCTYPE beans PUBLIC "-//SPRING//DTD BEAN//EN"
"http://www.springframework.org/dtd/spring-beans.dtd">

<beans>

   <!- HelloWorld Bean ->
   <bean id="helloBean" class="com.ibmpress.biz.hello.HelloImpl" />

</beans>
```

Making the Business Layer Accessible

There is a slight problem with using Spring in this context, that is, within a business layer. I could actually package this code within my enterprise application (EAR) file, or web application to ensure that I could access the application or web application context of Spring to access the beans, but what if I want to share this layer between different applications? Some decisions have to be made about the accessibility, deployment, and reuse of the business layer. In many cases making these decisions can be easy. A layered architecture can exist completely within the context of a single enterprise application or even web application.

A single deployable .ear file is not really the issue and may be the most common scenario within your organization. Applications rely on a logical separation within the JVM. This separation is part of the specification in many cases, such as not sharing session state between different applications. If you are wondering why I'm even bringing this up, think of portal-type situations where essentially separate applications share the same presentation space. Again the question arises: Why not make life easier by choosing a different distributed technology for this layer, such as EJBs or Web Services?

The reason is that every design decision has to be made with some trade-offs and limitations in mind. Distributing the layer comes at some cost, though initially that cost may not seem to be very big; however, requirements can sometimes grow. If I decided to locate the business layer on another tier I now have additional infrastructure to manage, with a total cost of ownership (TCO) of perhaps double what I initially considered. I have to make sure this tier is as robust as my original tier. This is in addition to any latency between system calls, which may or may not be acceptable based on application performance requirements.

So, in this case I am considering the least distributed approach where multiple layers live within the same application server, providing fast response and limiting overall ownership costs. Do not think there is only one approach worth taking. The point of this book is to show you how to design your architecture to take into account many different application requirements and constraints.

My goal in this example is to be able to share a Spring bean between multiple web applications. Doing so allows me to provide a single business layer interface that different applications can reuse as needed. Even as the business logic grows within this layer, updates can be made without affecting existing applications and without recoding or managing several instances of the same code base. We will talk in Chapter 10, "Managing Your Applications," about some of the governance issues and trade-offs with single versus multiple instances of your code base.

I have decided to go ahead and create a singleton, which can act as a wrapper around the Spring context. This simple class creates the Spring context and then passes to it any bean request that may come from client applications. This isolates the client from having to understand or use Spring, but allows the business layer to take advantage of cool features like dependency injection. Advantages may exist to having the client application work more closely with the Spring framework, but in terms of simplicity within my environment and limiting the possible amount of confusion with the development, this approach provides a very simple solution to what can be a very complicated problem.

`BizLayerDAO` is a very simple class that serves as a single entry point into any object within the business layer. The constructor creates the Spring context and stores it locally so that any object lookup uses the same context.

```
package com.ibmpress.biz.dao;

import org.springframework.context.ApplicationContext;
import
org.springframework.context.support.ClassPathXmlApplicationContext;

public class BizLayerDAO {

    static private BizLayerDAO _instance = null;
    static private ApplicationContext context;

    protected BizLayerDAO() {

            context = new
            ClassPathXmlApplicationContext("applicationContext.xml");

        }

    static public BizLayerDAO getInstance() {
      if(null == _instance) {
          _instance = new BizLayerDAO();
      }
      return _instance;
    }

    public Object getBean(String beanname){
        return context.getBean(beanname);
    }
}
```

The rest of the class is an out-of-the-box singleton implementation with a `getInstance()` method allowing client code to use the singleton. The `getBean()` method simply returns the object that is provided by the Spring context.

Getting Ready for Unit Testing

Testing within the development framework, in this case using Eclipse or Rational Application Developer, is fairly simple. Having my business layer consist of the Plain Old Java Object (POJO) approach allows me to keep things simple.

POJOs

Plain Old Java Objects is a design approach that uses simple Java classes that are not specifically tied to a framework and do not extend or implement an API. This technique allows for easier creation of your objects and business logic that you can then use with or without some type of container. The use of POJOs with Java Annotations is increasing, such as with EJB3 to allow a framework to manage the POJO appropriately.

I created a simple test class using JUnit to demonstrate the idea of building and running a set of unit tests. Then as I continue to build new functionality within my business layer I can add additional tests as needed. Notice that the test class has no real knowledge of Spring being used to provide the requested Hello object.

```
package com.ibmpress.biz.test;

import static org.junit.Assert.*;
import org.junit.Test;

import com.ibmpress.biz.dao.BizLayerDAO;
import com.ibmpress.biz.hello.Hello;
import com.ibmpress.biz.hello.HelloImpl;

public class HelloTest {

    public void testHelloWorld() {

    BizLayerDAO dao = BizLayerDAO.getInstance();
    Hello helloBean = (Hello) dao.getBean("helloBean");
    assertEquals("Result should append name to Hello",
                        "Hello Joey", helloBean.helloWorld("Joey"));

    }
}
```

Finally, let's take a quick look at the structure of this project (see Figure 4.4) within the development environment. Within Eclipse this project can be set up as a simple Java project. There are several dependencies within the project, including the Spring framework itself and some dependent libraries that Spring uses.

Figure 4.4 Project structure

The package structure is very straightforward and you can deploy the entire project as a JAR file within your application or environment. Notice that this layer is a simple POJO-based layer. The interface for each service and the implementation is in one package, and the data access point is in a separate package. Both are wrapped within the same project structure. Some testing classes have been added but they may not get packaged and deployed with the final code drop. One of the advantages of Spring is that you can get away with writing simple Java classes and wrapping them into a complete framework that will manage the objects and how they are accessed, as well as any dependencies the objects themselves might require.

WebSphere Shared Libraries

To support the use of third party frameworks and libraries you can leverage WebSphere Shared Libraries, which are designed to allow sharing of dependent JAR files across multiple applications. You can make shared libraries globally available across the entire JVM, or make them available to specific web applications only. This feature makes providing middle layer functionality encapsulated within JAR files to your applications easy. The process for the installation and configuration of shared libraries is not hard, but you must perform several steps to make these libraries available, as follow:

1. To set up a shared library you need to use the WebSphere administrative console or Network Deployment manager console. Click **Environment** and then **Shared Libraries**, as shown in Figure 4.5.

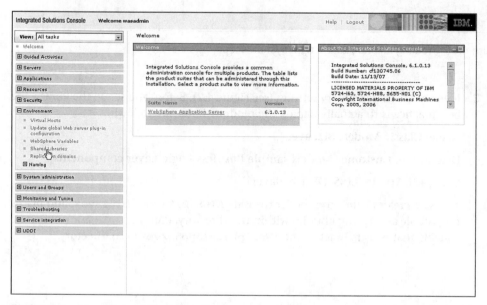

Figure 4.5 Creating a shared library

As with most everything in WebSphere Application Server, scope can be important in maintaining control of system resources. Limiting the visibility of resources to the system or set of systems that requires access helps maintain security reduced potential resource constraints. You can set some resources, like data sources, at multiple scopes. In these cases, some resource scopes have precedence over other scopes.

2. For this example, choose **Cell** scope, and click **New** to continue (see Figure 4.6).

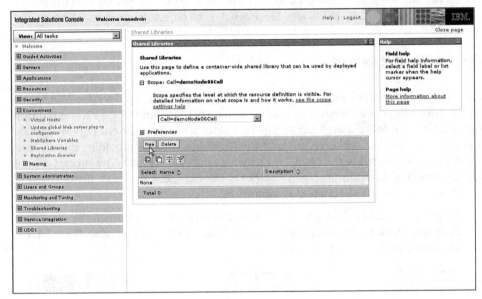

Figure 4.6   Creating a library at the right system scope

3. Identify the shared library settings (see Figure 4.7). Before you set up the library, the best practice is to actually deploy the module. Enter the following:

Name: **Classic Models BizLayer**

Description: **Customer Models sample Business Logic Layer components**

Classpath: **${WAS_LIBS_DIR}/bizlayer**

This step creates a directory under the WAS_LIBS_DIR called bizlayer, and places the JAR file and Spring libraries within this directory. WAS_LIB_DIR is a WebSphere variable that is usually set to the /WebSphere/AppServer/lib directory.

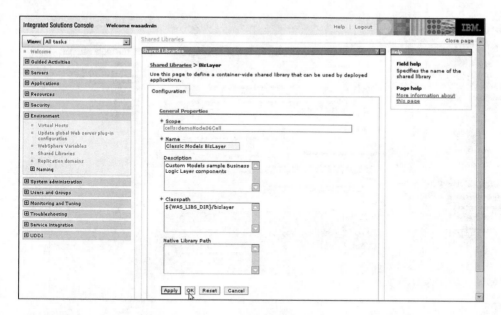

Figure 4.7 Library settings

4. Once the values are set up, click **OK** to create the shared library.

5. WebSphere Application Server settings are never complete until you save the settings to the Master configuration. Click the **Save** link (see Figure 4.8) to record your changes to the Master configuration. Notice that the shared library is now set up within the console.

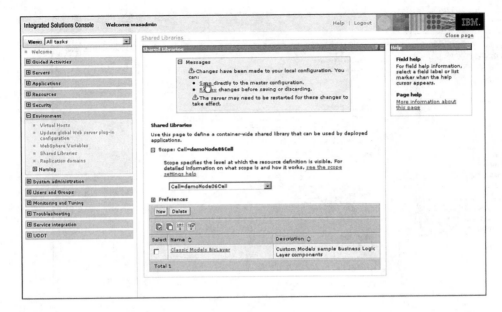

Figure 4.8   Save shared library settings

Making the Library Visible

Creating the shared library is only half the battle. Now you have to make the library visible to other applications within the environment. I mentioned earlier that you could do this at a server-wide level or for specific applications. For this example, you set the class loading at the server-wide level. Later in this chapter I show you how to make the library visible at an application level. To make the shared library visible at a server-wide level, follow these steps:

1. Click on **Servers, Application Servers, server1** (see Figure 4.9).

   The configuration screen for server1 appears. In your environment it might not actually be server1, but in many environments this is a default setup.

2. Under Server Infrastructure, click **Java** and **Process Management** then **Class loader** (see Figure 4.10).

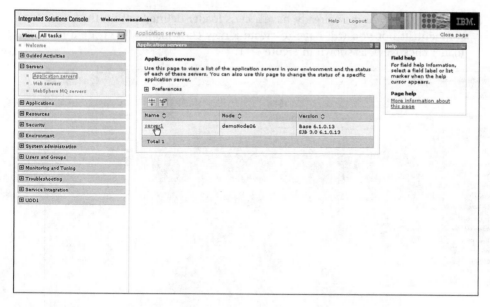

Figure 4.9   Choosing the server

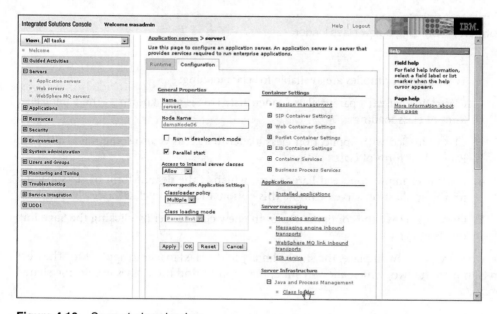

Figure 4.10   Server1 class loaders

3. In some cases you may already have a class loader defined within the server environment. If not you will have to create a new class loader. To create a new class loader click **New**, as shown in Figure 4.11.

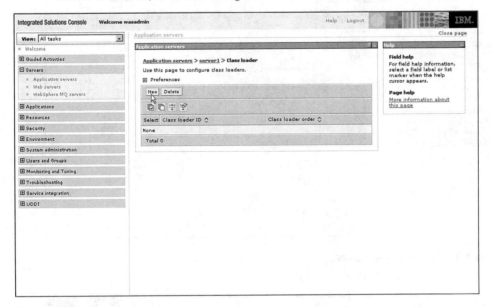

Figure 4.11   Creating a new class loader

Two options or modes are available for class loading:

Classes loaded with parent class loader first. This is also known as the Parent First form of class loading.

Classes loaded with application class loader first. This is also sometimes called the Parent Last form of class loading.

4. For this example you need Parent first, which is the default form of class loading for the application server. Choose this option and then click **OK** (see Figure 4.12).

5. Once again save the configuration of the new class loader by clicking the **Save** link (see Figure 4.13).

The two pieces are now in place: the shared library and a class loader to apply it to. The next step is to map the two, which allows your application to find the classes within the shared library.

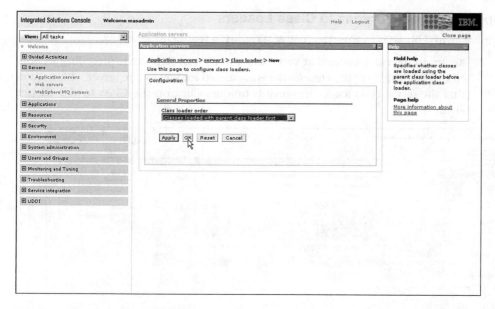

Figure 4.12   Parent first class loading

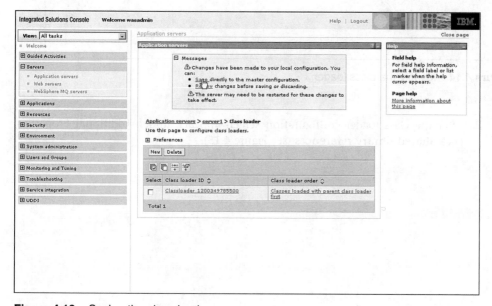

Figure 4.13   Saving the class loader

Mapping Shared Libraries to Class Loaders

Mapping shared libraries to the class loader takes just a few steps, as follow:

1. Return to the class loader that you created in the last step in the preceding section. Notice that the ID of the class loader was defined for you by the server. This ensures that the server class loader instance is unique. Click on the **Class loader ID** (see Figure 4.14).

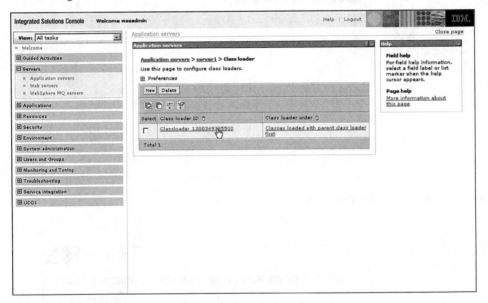

Figure 4.14   Identify the class loader

2. After the class loader configuration screen appears, under Additional Properties, click **Shared library references** (see Figure 4.15).

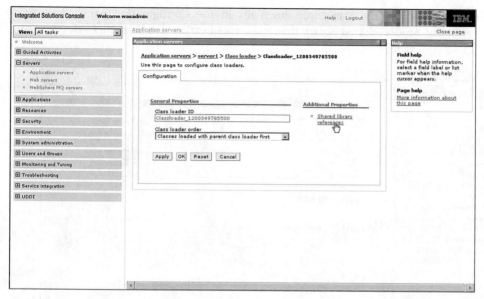

Figure 4.15   Reference shared libraries

3. In the screen that appears, click the **Add** button to create a new shared library reference (see Figure 4.16).

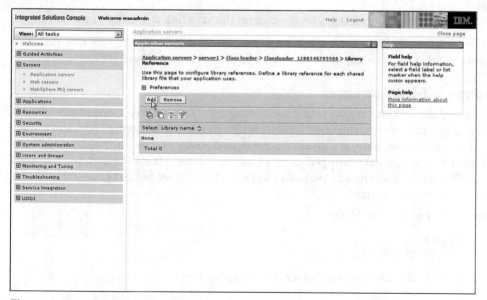

Figure 4.16   Add a new shared library

4. From the Library name drop-down list in the Configuration pane, choose the Classic Models shared library that you created earlier and then click **OK** (see Figure 4.17).

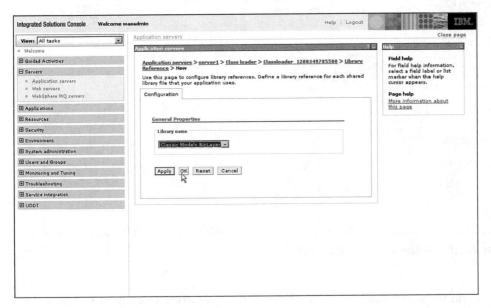

Figure 4.17   Choose Classic Models library

5. Finally, save your changes by clicking on the save link at the top of the screen.

That's it! I know it seems like a lot of steps but you can see how the different pieces fit together to provide you with a flexible way to provide access to shared libraries.

Testing the Business Layer

The whole point of this exercise is to provide a separate business layer that is accessible to the web application or presentation layer. With that in mind this chapter provides two separate web applications. Both of them access the shared library and use the `HelloWorld` service that it provides. I have stripped away much of the code from the BizLayerWebApp1 Servlet. This servlet uses the `BizLayerDAO` to get an instance of the `Hello` object and connect to the provided services.

```
package com.ibmpress.web.biztest1;

//import stuff
...

public class BizLayerWebApp1Servlet extends HttpServlet {
```

```
    protected void doGet(HttpServletRequest request, HttpServletResponse
    response) throws ServletException, IOException {

PrintWriter writer = response.getWriter();
response.setContentType("text/html");

writer.println("BizLayerWebApp1Servlet<BR>");

//get an instance of the singleton
BizLayerDAO dao = BizLayerDAO.getInstance();
//now request the helloBean that will be passed to Spring.
Hello helloBean = (Hello) dao.getBean("helloBean");

//exercise the methods in the helloBean.
writer.println(helloBean.helloWorld("Joey")+ "<BR>");

writer.println(helloBean.getWhosBeenHere()+"<BR>");

//let us know you used this instance.
helloBean.setWhosBeenHere("webapp1");

    }
}
```

Both of the web applications have the same set of code, but by switching between the two you can see that each servlet sets a new value in the `helloBean` to identify that it has used this bean.

Controlling Shared Libraries

I mentioned earlier that you can also set up shared libraries in the class loader of a specific web application. Understanding the order for class loading can be important in debugging application problems. The dreaded "class not found" error can be difficult to diagnose, especially when you are behind in a deliverable. WebSphere provides some additional information that can help in this matter. Clicking on **Troubleshooting, Class Loader Viewer** and then drilling down into a specific server can provide a view of the class loading hierarchy.

Figure 4.18 shows the structure for this example. Notice that the shared library JAR files are loaded by the WAS Jar Extension Class Loader while the web application is loaded by the WAS Module – Compound Class Loader. You have a clear view of where specific classes are exposed within the server.

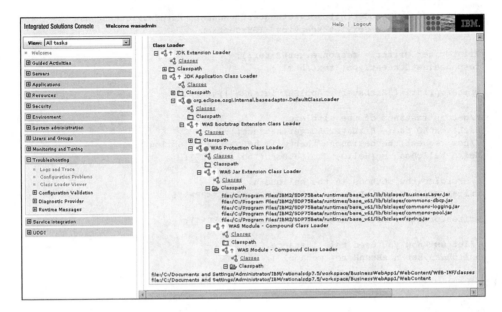

Figure 4.18   Class loader viewer

I don't talk a lot in this book about packaging your applications. I'm more worried about some of the larger design concepts. But it is important to point out that class loading troubles have caused a lot of problems with application deployments. This situation is especially true when conflicts occur between dependencies that are required for an application and similar libraries that are already available within the WebSphere runtime. Often a team declares that it needs a different version of a specific library because of required features within a new version. This question is one that your standards and governance model should address, having an exception process available if necessary. But in addition to having multiple versions of the same libraries strewn across your environment, it can become a very real class loading problem.

I mentioned earlier that you could also map shared libraries at the web application level rather than across the entire server. You do so via the configuration screen for the web application itself. Follow these steps:

1. Under **References** choose the **Shared library references** option (see Figure 4.19).

    You can map libraries at the application level or at the specific module level. For example, a single EAR file can contain several web modules, leading to mapping at the EAR level.

2. In the screen that appears, click the check box next to the level you require and then click the **Reference shared libraries** button (see Figure 4.20).

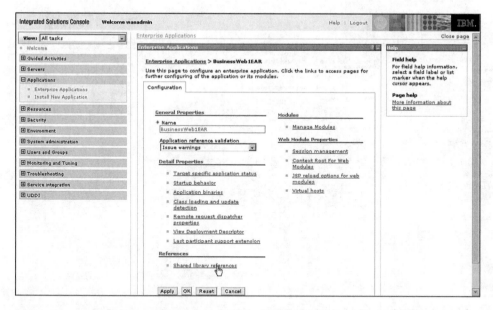

Figure 4.19   Application scope shared library references

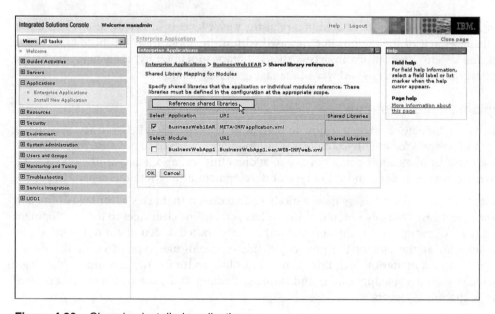

Figure 4.20   Choosing installed applications

3. The final step is to map the available shared libraries to the module. Select the right modules, and click **OK** (see Figure 4.21).

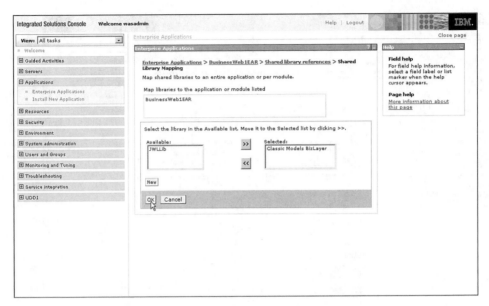

Figure 4.21   Mapping shared library references

In many cases mapping the shared library at the server level is sufficient, and it cuts down on management of the various libraries used within the application. In those cases where you don't want applications to access shared library functionality, then mapping at the application level is a very good way of managing those situations.

Implementation Options

One issue I have not discussed is how to determine the separation between the persistence layer and business logic. This example was purposefully contrived to not raise that question, but any real application is going to have to address this scenario. Many of the books available today on persistence and POJO type of development also ignore this separation.

Do we really care as long as we have a nicely crafted design that takes advantage of the best known practices? Probably not; but again, unless you outline clear rules to the development team (and follow up on the implementation) a nicely crafted design might not be what you end up with at the end of the project. In this enforced-rules type of effort the design becomes more a matter of discipline than of technical decisions. You determine what logic is needed within your application and business domain and how that logic is separated within appropriate layers.

The reality is this will probably never be perfect but if I can get you to consider this issue while designing your application then much of the battle will be won. The physical implementation of these layers helps to confuse the matter. Many of the frameworks that are used in persistence layers can also be used to provide business logic components: EJBs and Spring are two main culprits.

Another item that should be on your design agenda is whether to use Spring, as in the implementation of this example. I could have easily done without it, but I thought it was important to show some usage considering the growing popularity of Spring. Spring fills an obvious gap in the management of business objects within an application. Custom singleton and factory patterns can be difficult to create and manage, but Spring can provide this basic functionality in a robust framework. Now add in some true business object management value with dependency injection, aspects, and other features, and you begin to have an architecture that allows you to build business objects that are wrapped in a standard package.

Unfortunately one downside to using Spring is that it requires the development team to learn and understand more technology. In some cases there is no escaping this fact, but you are looking for a shared success, not to dazzle everyone with your technical brilliance. There is more to gain by delivering on time and under budget. Cases exist where development teams have dove headfirst into using Spring and encountered problems closer toward the release of the application. Spring can be doubly troublesome when coupled with a persistence framework such as Hibernate. The framework, the team, or the design is not to blame; it is simply the fact that the more complicated the design the higher the chance for problems.

Take a look at Figure 4.22 to get an idea of the potential complexity of Spring. Obviously the development team does not have to use all the packages available. In the last two chapters I have barely scratched the surface. But, do the development team members know which ones they can and can't use? Can you as the architect outline which packages are necessary and why you are requiring their use? All I request is that you look beyond the hype and understand the impact of the decisions you make in defining the architecture.

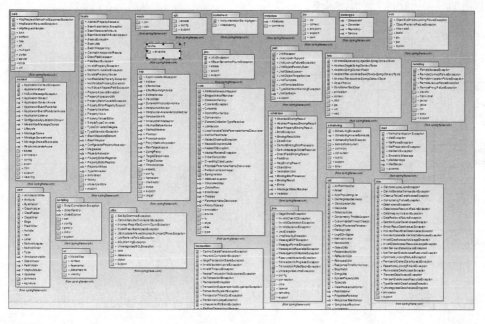

Figure 4.22 Spring framework

Business Process Layers

A4.1

Understand that as your application and organizational complexity grows so does the demand for managing and delivering advanced capability. In Chapter 1, "Application Architecture," I outlined business process layers in addition to or alongside business logic functionality. It can be fairly confusing trying to distinguish between business process, business logic, and persistence logic within your application.

Business process or rather, workflow, is the idea of taking tasks and bringing them together to perform some business function. These tasks are usually tied together using some type of language with the standard being the Business Process Execution Language (BPEL). BPEL allows you to formally define the relationship between tasks and the flow of data between them. You can see where things can quickly get complicated if you were trying to build a custom process engine yourself. Because of that your organization will probably decide to use an available process engine such as WebSphere Process Server for this effort.

So where does this fit within the overall architecture? Figure 4.23 gives you a good idea of one approach that an application might take when incorporating a process layer. I call this a process layer even though it sits within its own container on a separate tier. From a logical point of view it is still a layer within the application architecture, albeit a fully distributed layer, that should be incorporated much like the other layers are used.

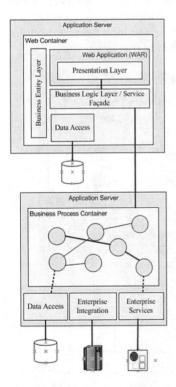

Figure 4.23   Business logic and process layers

Notice that there is still a local service layer or service façade to provide services to the presentation layer. There is still the possibility that this layer could service multiple enterprise or web applications. In the case of WebSphere Process Server, this local interface could be provided by the WPS client that can be installed on the client server, or a custom interface could be provided on top of this client to help drive the application design.

In either case you can see how complex the environment is about to become and hopefully you can understand my insistence on your trying to keep things as disciplined and as simple as possible, although in many cases neither goal is possible to achieve. This book focuses solely on building custom WebSphere applications and cannot begin to explain the workings of WebSphere Process Server in sufficient detail. Fortunately, there is a book that focuses on this layer called *WebSphere Business Integration Primer: Process Server, BPEL, SCA, and SOA* by IBM Press (1. Iyengar, et. al. 2008).

Conclusion

I admit we have just scratched the surface in this chapter. The options are numerous in determining which approach you want to take with the middle layers. Leveraging the EJB layer as was discussed in Chapter 3 is a viable option. If you are looking for something more local or perhaps lightweight, then the POJO model with or without a framework like Spring may be appropriate. This is especially true when layers are deployed within the same package structure and not on separate tiers of the infrastructure. The singleton model, while the subject of much debate, can still provide value when used correctly. In any case, hopefully you understand more of the options available to you. It's not just EJBs or servlets anymore; middle layers can be supported by frameworks or full-blown application servers such as WebSphere Process Server.

 ## Links to developerWorks Articles

A4.1 Designing the Business Service Layer - Jul 2004 by Nalla Senthilnathan
http://www.ibm.com/developerworks/web/library/wa-bsvlayer/

References

Iyengar, Ashok, Vinod Jessani, Michele Chilanti. (March 2008) *WebSphere Business Integration Primer: Process Server, BPEL, SCA, and SOA*. IBM Press.

Chapter 5

Presentation Frameworks

This chapter outlines some of the options available for developing the presentation layer. Abstracting business and back-end logic from the presentation layer can be difficult—specifically, in determining where the presentation layer ends and the rest of the application begins. This chapter helps to fill that gap through discussion of presentation frameworks and how they fit into the overall architecture of your application.

Choosing a Presentation Framework

In many ways, the presentation layer is where the rubber meets the road. By that I mean that the presentation layer is designed to interact with the end users and if you fail in this area, then all the work put in prior to this point will be useless. Obviously, some applications are more of a processing nature and may not interact with end users directly, but the reality is that most of the applications developed in web and application server space have some type of user interaction. This interface has to be fast and robust, it has to account for poor data entry by the user, or information that is missing from the back end, and above all it has to be pretty.

This is a tall order to an architect, and ensuring that it all takes place can consume much of your effort in the project. Ways exist to reduce this effort and enable your team to build a robust user interface in a consistent manner. In the past, Struts has probably been the prevailing framework; however, in recent years the trend has migrated to JavaServer Faces (JSF) as more teams move to adopt new technology. These are by far not the only presentation frameworks available, but they do require a hard look. Convincing yourself that this direction is worthwhile is not hard.

The word *framework* is probably as overloaded as many of the other words that are used in these types of books, and I like to use it in a couple of different ways. A particular language such as Java can be a framework for building applications. A single library can also be a framework, such as log4j, which is a framework for logging and tracing messages within your code. Additionally a product such as WebSphere Application Server or WebSphere Portal Server can be a framework that provides a robust environment in which to deliver your applications. Some of the features that a framework may provide include the following:

- Data Access
- Logging
- Event handling
- Caching
- Scheduling
- Messaging
- Examples, reference implementation
- Documentation
- Error handling

- Monitoring
- Performance
- Security
- Authentication
- Authorization
- Internationalization
- Support
- Standards compliance

At its root, the concept of a framework should make developing an application easier, but it can also present some challenges within the environment. Each additional framework, third-party library, or API that is incorporated into your environment can put additional demand on the developers of the application. Why? Because while each framework can add tremendous value to your specific project, developers need to learn the right application of the framework and understand the nuances and options for every choice they make.

Sometimes you might think that picking and choosing a set of known components will ensure your application's success; however, you can quickly overload a development team with new technologies that will slow development to a crawl, or worse, cause problems in production that are not well understood. Applying technologies to different layers should be done with care, and the right amount of education is necessary. Think about some of the current initiatives that you put in use today. If you were to pick a set of products such as JavaServer Faces (JSF), Spring, Hibernate, log4j, and so on, then layer on more complexity such as using WebSphere Portal for the presentation, this approach would be a challenge for any team to learn this much new technology, let alone deliver a robust application within a short timeframe, especially if any of these technologies are new to the team. Keep the level of experience of your developers in the front of your mind as you put the pieces together.

From an architect's viewpoint choosing the presentation framework can be a simple decision; that is, use JSF. The development team will take this mandate and happily go off and start building the application. Unfortunately, if you leave it at that you may not end up with the architecture you should have. Here is where you will walk another fine line between laying out the architecture and design, and digging in to the details of the implementation. I discussed the idea of a hands-on architect in Chapter 1, "Application Architecture," but how hands-on must you be to be able to provide a solid architectural direction to your team? The answer, of course, is that it depends, but a solid foundation is definitely necessary in whichever presentation framework you use. In this chapter we will determine where the separation of layers should occur, and leave some of the in layer details such as data validation to the developer on the ground.

JavaServer Faces

As of this writing, JSF is the anointed framework within the industry. I do not mean this in any negative way, I mean simply that most of the industry seems to have approved the specification and many new applications are being developed within this framework. Java has never been a one-size-fits-all type of language, so many other frameworks are available that have some amount of following. But JSF is one of those frameworks where it is way easier to make the decision to use the framework, than it is to actually use it for building your application.

A5.1

Why is that? Because learning JSF is hard. Customers love it when I say this because it lets them know they are not complete idiots who are the only ones struggling to understand JSF. Everyone struggles in the beginning, whether they admit it or not, but that struggle reflects the power of the framework and the features and nuances that are available. With that said, one of the most common questions I get from organizations who decided to adopt the framework is, "What is the best way to learn it?" My advice is always that once you understand the lifecycle then a lot of the concepts drop into place. Gaining this understanding is easier said than done in many cases, but the example outlined in this chapter might help to make it clearer.

This chapter examines JSF from an architect's point of view, which means understanding the high-level framework and how it fits into the overall architecture. Any more detail on the many features of JSF will require a reference book that is devoted more specifically to the details of JavaServer Faces development.

One example of this type of confusion is the debate over the Front Controller Pattern versus the Page Controller Pattern. Martin Fowler in his book, *Patterns of Enterprise Application Architecture* (Fowler), goes into some detail on the differences between these patterns. In terms of JavaServer Faces there has been much debate as to whether JSF is actually a Page Controller or a Front Controller framework. There is even suggestion that it is a Front Controller framework that offers the benefits of a Page Controller. While this makes for some interesting reading, the reality is you shouldn't care too much about this type of detail in the grand scheme of things. There are many reasons why you might or might not choose to use JSF within your organization or project; this is not one of them.

One of the core advantages of JSF is the idea of component-based development. That is, you can use JSF page components or widgets to build up the layout and data on your page. This powerful concept allows for the separation of concerns or duties that everyone has been striving for since the beginning of application development—that is, allowing inexperienced developers to work as assemblers who drag and drop components onto the page, while more experienced developers actually create the components and connect to the back end. Unfortunately, in JSF, while this abstraction has been somewhat achieved it is often referred to as leaky abstraction because though in theory it does provide a separation of concerns, doing so in practice is much harder to accomplish without knowing a lot about the underlying technology and system.

Before we go too far it is important to understand the JSF lifecycle. The lifecycle is the key to understanding how JSF actually works "under the hood," so this chapter spends some time helping you understanding this first. The JSF lifecycle is complex compared to the simple lifecycle events of, for example, servlets. This lifecycle may seem confusing to someone who is new to JSF, even if he or she has done a lot of Java programming previously. The key point to keep in mind is that every request/response cycle goes through some portion of this lifecycle (see Figure 5.1).

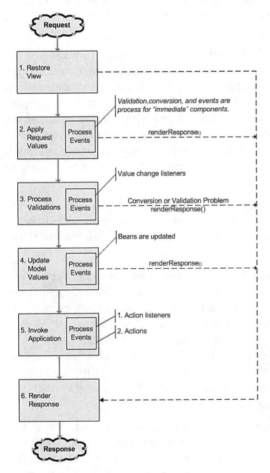

Figure 5.1   JSF lifecycle

I say *portion* because you can see there are many bail-out points throughout the lifecycle phases, so not every request will proceed through all six phases. In fact, having a request proceed through all six phases may be the rarer case.

Okay, saying this case is rare may be a bit of an exaggeration but you will see in the following examples where a full lifecycle is the best case. Before we get too far some explanation of the phases shown in Figure 5.1 is in order:

1. **Restore View:** This view is called whenever a request for a JSF page is made. This could be an initial request or the result of a button or link being clicked on a page that is being displayed. JSF will build a view or component tree of the page that contains all the components that are being displayed on the page along with event handlers and validators. This view will be blank for new pages and is stored in the Faces Context for subsequent requests. This is a good point at which to ensure that data provided is valid for the field type of each component.

2. **Apply Request Values:** The request parameters are decoded from the request and used to populate the component tree that was built in phase 1. Population of the tree may result in conversion or validation errors, which will trigger an error message to be placed on the error queue. Event listeners can be used to call a `renderResponse,` which will allow the process to proceed directly to phase 6 and display any error messages.

   If any components have the `immediate` attribute set to true then validation, conversion, and other events will be processed during this phase.

3. **Process Validations:** A process validation is designed to process any validators that are registered for components. If the validator fails then an error is added to the message queue, and the process advances directly to phase 6 of the lifecycle.

4. **Update Model Values:** At this point all the data should be considered valid and the model or backing beans that are tied to the components can be updated with the new values. Local data types should be able to be converted to the types defined within the bean properties. If any conversion fails when trying to set the model properties, then an error is added to the message queue, and the process advances directly to phase 6 of the lifecycle.

5. **Invoke Application:** With an updated model, application events can be called to perform actions on the updated data. This can be handled through action listeners defined on components, such as the button component. The navigation handler is also invoked and listens to the outcome of any action listeners to determine the next step in the navigation sequence. For navigation changes, control is passed to a new page.

6. Render Response: This phase displays the page and any errors that have occurred. This phase also saves the state of the page that is rendered so that it can be restored in phase 1 of the next request.

This lifecycle probably still is confusing, but I did mention there is a learning curve? The best advice I can give is to build your own application, following along with the example, and use components, such as the Phase Listener discussed later, to watch the process in the context of your own environment.

Lifecycle Phase Listener

The best way that I know of to really understand what is going on within your JSF application is to watch which phases and events occur during each request. A phase listener is an easy way to debug this process and help understand what is actually going on within your application. You can implement a phase listener with very little code. The following example is a simple phase listener that simply logs a before and after event.

```
package com.ibmpress.jsf;

import java.util.logging.Level;
import java.util.logging.Logger;

import javax.faces.event.PhaseEvent;
import javax.faces.event.PhaseId;
import javax.faces.event.PhaseListener;

public class MyPhaseListener implements PhaseListener {

    private Logger logger =
    Logger.getLogger("com.ibmpress.jsf.PhaseListenerImpl");

    public void beforePhase(PhaseEvent arg0) {
        logger.logp(Level.INFO, getClass().getName(), "beforePhase",
        arg0.getPhaseId().toString());
    }

    public PhaseId getPhaseId() {
        return PhaseId.ANY_PHASE;
    }

    public void afterPhase(PhaseEvent arg0) {
        logger.logp(Level.INFO, getClass().getName(), "afterPhase",
        arg0.getPhaseId().toString());
    }

}
```

Implement the listener as a Java class within your application or maybe as a library of utility class that can be included in all of your applications to make debugging easier during runtime. The phase listener has to be included within the `faces-config.xml` of your application as the following:

```
<lifecycle>
        <phase-listener>com.ibmpress.jsf.MyPhaseListener</phase-listener>
</lifecycle>
```

With the listener installed and your application reinitialized you will start to see messages in the log file during every request/response of the application. For example, when the application initially loads you will see log messages similar to the following:

```
PhaseListener I MyPhaseListener beforePhase RESTORE_VIEW 1
PhaseListener I MyPhaseListener afterPhase RESTORE_VIEW 1
PhaseListener I MyPhaseListener beforePhase RENDER_RESPONSE 6
PhaseListener I MyPhaseListener afterPhase RENDER_RESPONSE 6
```

Because this is an initial load the component tree contains no values and the process skips directly to phase 6 for rendering. My second piece of advice for learning JSF: Log everything! Not only is it good practice for debugging what is going on within your application, but also it is a great learning tool for understanding how the application is being called. Even when you begin to understand how things are working, logging is a practice and discipline that you need to acquire and follow. Chapter 2, "Setting a Standard," discusses logging in great detail.

About the Sample Application

The sample application that is provided in this chapter is as simple as I could make it while still providing some educational value. Really I needed to be able to illustrate how JSF ties into the overall architecture, and also show a few of the architectural features of JSF to those who may not be doing the actual development. The application consists of three JSP pages, which I use to show how data can be validated and saved within the context of a larger application. The pages are:

- **Create Profile:** This page brings up a blank form that allows the user to enter some basic profile information. This page has a `valueChangedListener` on the `customerID` value that lets you check or validate the value of the customer ID being provided.
- **Review Profile:** This page displays after the initial Create Profile page is submitted. The action that is set on the Save button provides a place for some additional validation and to persist the model to the back-end data store.
- **Profile Saved:** This page simply displays the end result of the data being stored and serves as verification for the user.

Navigation between the pages is relatively simple, providing a way to move back and forth, as you can see in Figure 5.2.

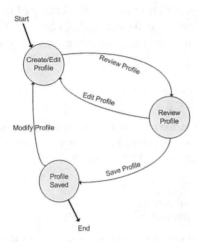

Figure 5.2   Sample JSF application

JSF Navigation

You can better understand the navigation model by looking through the the `faces-config.xml`   file. Each page is set up with some navigation information. The `ReviewProfile.jsp` page has a specific navigation rule that is applied to that page. This rule examines the return result from the `doSaveProfileAction`. If the action is 'profilesaved' then the rule will navigate to the `ProfileSaved.jsp` page.

```
<navigation-rule>
    <from-view-id>/ReviewProfile.jsp</from-view-id>
    <navigation-case>
      <from-action>
      #{pc_PageReviewProfile.doSaveProfileAction}</from-action>
      <from-outcome>profilesaved</from-outcome>
      <to-view-id>/ProfileSaved.jsp</to-view-id>
    </navigation-case>
</navigation-rule>
```

The `CreateProfile.jsp` page also has a specific navigation rule applied. This rule examines the outcome of the `doCreateProfileAction` and looks for the value of 'complete'. When this occurs the rule will navigate to the `ReviewProfile.jsp` page.

```
<navigation-rule>
    <from-view-id>/CreateProfile.jsp</from-view-id>
    <navigation-case>
      <from-action>
      #{pc_PageCreateProfile.doCreateProfileAction}</from-action>
      <from-outcome>complete</from-outcome>
      <to-view-id>/ReviewProfile.jsp</to-view-id>
    </navigation-case>
</navigation-rule>
```

This next section is a more generic rule that applies to the entire application, that is, if any navigation outcome is 'editprofile' then go to the CreateProfile.jsp page.

```
<navigation-rule>
  <navigation-case>
    <from-outcome>editprofile</from-outcome>
    <to-view-id>/CreateProfile.jsp</to-view-id>
  </navigation-case>
</navigation-rule>
```

Through these examples you can see how navigation can be tied to specific actions or events, or left open for use by any page within the application. Depending on the amount of detail within your design, these events and values should be defined during design for implementation by the development team.

JSF within the Overall Architecture

JSF introduces a number of concepts that may be new to people who are learning the framework. The idea of backing beans is a concept that often gets muddled within the architecture. Backing beans are model- and application-based Java classes that can be tied directly to components and actions. JSF provides for the addition of user interface–based beans that provide UI-based functionality directly to the JSP. These UI or PageCode beans often provide a convenient location for application functionality, but you should take care to ensure that developers do not dump all the application logic into these classes.

I find it helpful to map out where services and data access should exist within the architecture and then provide or stub out those components during development. When designing these layers, one general rule that I try to adhere to is that the Faces Context does not go beyond the presentation layer itself as shown in Figure 5.3. This can help in keeping the necessary abstraction between layers.

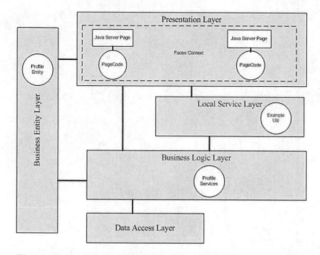

Figure 5.3   Layered architecture with JSF

The example used in this chapter shows a number of different components at different layers, taking full advantage of the guidance provided by the architecture team. Because we are building a user profile, the business logic layer contains existing profile services that in a real application would also probably provide access to data access services. The entity layer contains the profile entity that is available across all layers. In addition some utility services are provided via a local service layer that lies outside of the Faces Context to provide functionality across web applications within the container.

> **Beware of the Wizard**
>
> With JSF tooling much of the back-end connectivity can often be performed with built-in wizards. Whether you are connecting to a database or web service, you can often drag and drop connectors onto a page that will examine the schema and build simple CRUD functionality automatically. Although this feature looks good for simple demos, this generated code often does not conform to your architectural standard and sometimes it is not truly production ready. Use these wizards to learn from, but think about where you will deploy these assets within your production environment, if at all!

As you learn how the application works and how JSF manages its lifecycle the concepts will become clearer. Taking a look at the actual project folder (see Figure 5.4) for the application, you can see how all the pieces should fit together. In reality some of these components should be JAR files that are included in the project from other service layer projects.

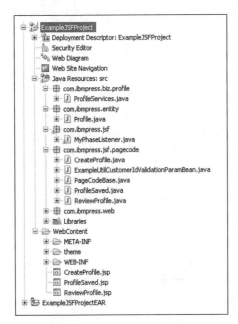

Figure 5.4   Project layout

The packages have been broken down as follows:

- **com.ibmpress.biz.profile:** This package contains the business layer components that should be available to the application. Normally I would expect this set of features to be present in a set of external libraries, which are included in this project. For simplicity's sake this package is just a simple class with one or two example methods.
- **com.ibmpress.entity:** Entities are classes that emulate model objects within the application. These classes also would not normally be designed within this layer, but exist as components of the data access layer.
- **com.ibmpress.jsf.pagecode:** Page code classes are the UI backing classes that contain much of the UI functionality required by the JSPs. This relationship is usually one-to-one, with one page code bean for each JSP. Care should be taken to ensure that these beans do not get engorged with application or data access code so be sure to provide specific guidelines to help avoid this occurrence.
- **com.ibmpress.web:** Additional utility services or local services might be located here. These can be classes that are created directly for this web application or imported classes from a local service layer.

Create Profile Page

With the phase listener in place and some logging interspersed throughout the application there is some logging that will be provided upon application startup:

```
PhaseListener I MyPhaseListener beforePhase RESTORE_VIEW 1
PhaseListener I MyPhaseListener afterPhase RESTORE_VIEW 1
PhaseListener I MyPhaseListener beforePhase RENDER_RESPONSE 6
SRVE0242I: [ExampleJSFProjectEAR] [/ExampleJSFProject]
 [/CreateProfile.jsp]: Initialization successful.
Profile I com.ibmpress.entity.Profile getCustomerID <Null Message>
Profile I com.ibmpress.entity.Profile getLastName <Null Message>
Profile I com.ibmpress.entity.Profile getFirstName <Null Message>
Profile I com.ibmpress.entity.Profile getBirthDate <Null Message>
PhaseListener I MyPhaseListener afterPhase RENDER_RESPONSE 6
```

Notice that phases 1 and 6 are called in this initial rendering of the `CreateProfile.jsp`. The jsp is initialized successfully because this is the first time this jsp is called, and the entity bean does not provide any information with which to preload data onto the page as illustrated in Figure 5.5.

It may be the case that the entity (the profile bean) would be called using a data access service with the model being pre-populated with data related to the current user of the application. In other words, it would automatically come up with its own data. To simplify things, in this example we just bring up an empty bean, which will allow us to start adding some data.

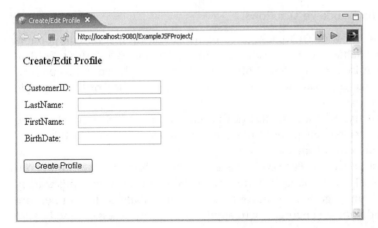

Figure 5.5   Create profile

Built into the page are actually a number of events, such as a value change listener assigned to the `customerID` component. This listener is triggered when the `customerID` value is changed. The listener is composed of two parts. The first part is a small method within the page code bean for this page. The second part is assigning the listener to a component. This listener is assigned by adding the `valueChangeListener` to the component within the JSP page itself.

```
<td align="left">CustomerID:</td>
<td style="width:5px"> </td>
<td>
<h:inputText id="textCustomerID"
value="#{profile.customerID}"
styleClass="inputText" required="true"
valueChangeListener="#{pc_PageCreateProfile.customerIdChanged}">

</h:inputText><h:message for="textCustomerID"></h:message>
</td>
```

This method is one of those that walks the fine line between presentation and business logic and is designed to allow for a clean separation between layers. Because value change events rely on the Faces Context you need to use this method to abstract the Faces Context information from underlying services. The `customerIdChanged()` method is provided within `CreateProfile.java`, which is the page bean for this JSP. You also could have identified a separate bean or service that might, for example, be part of the business layer to do some validation if an important value changes.

```
public void customerIdChanged(ValueChangeEvent event) {

        //extract the field value to send to the external method
        String newValue = event.getNewValue().toString();

        logger.logp(Level.INFO, getClass().getName(),
        "ValueChangeListener.customerIdChanged", "New Value: " +
        newValue);
```

```
        //we could do more stuff here like reset values
        //but for now use the business layer to validate the id.
        String customerID =
        getExampleUtil().customerIdValidation(newValue);

        //now set the new ID so the model can be updated.
        getTextCustomerID().setValue(customerID);

}
```

The `customerIdChanged()` method performs three main functions:

- Extracts the value in the `customerId` field
- Passes that value to the `customerIdValidation()` method for some action
- Resets the returned value into the field for use in subsequent phases

The `customerIdValidation()` method is a member of the `Example Utils` class that could also represent a part of the local service layer.

```
public String customerIdValidation(String id) {

        id = id+"_0000";

        //ok we could really do something important here...

        logger.logp(Level.INFO, getClass().getName(),
        "customerIdValidation", "id: " +id);

        return id;
}
```

The `customerIdValidation()` method doesn't really do much, although it could if required. At this point all the method does is to append the value _000 to the id that is passed into the method and returns the resulting composite value. Figure 5.6 illustrates the value before it is modified.

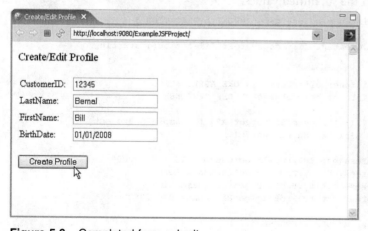

Figure 5.6   Completed form submit

After you complete the form and submit it the phase listener will allow you to examine where these activities will take place.

```
PhaseListener I MyPhaseListener beforePhase RESTORE_VIEW 1
PhaseListener I MyPhaseListener afterPhase RESTORE_VIEW 1
PhaseListener I MyPhaseListener beforePhase APPLY_REQUEST_VALUES 2
PhaseListener I MyPhaseListener afterPhase APPLY_REQUEST_VALUES 2
PhaseListener I MyPhaseListener beforePhase PROCESS_VALIDATIONS 3
Profile       I Profile getCustomerID <Null Message>
Profile       I Profile getLastName <Null Message>
Profile       I Profile getFirstName <Null Message>
Profile       I Profile getBirthDate <Null Message>

CreateProfile I CreateProfile ValueChangeListener.customerIdChanged New
Value: 12345

ExampleUtil   I com.ibmpress.web.ExampleUtil customerIdValidation id:
12345_0000

CreateProfile I CreateProfile geTextCustomerID begin

PhaseListener I MyPhaseListener afterPhase PROCESS_VALIDATIONS 3
```

Phase 3 is where the value change listener is activated and the `customerId` is reset from 12345 to 12345_000.

```
PhaseListener I MyPhaseListener beforePhase UPDATE_MODEL_VALUES 4

Profile       I com.ibmpress.entity.Profile setCustomerID 12345_0000
Profile       I com.ibmpress.entity.Profile setLastName Bernal
Profile       I com.ibmpress.entity.Profile setFirstName Bill
Profile       I com.ibmpress.entity.Profile setBirthDate 01012008

PhaseListener I MyPhaseListener afterPhase UPDATE_MODEL_VALUES 4
```

Phase 4 is where the model is updated with the new values. Note that this is after all conversion and validations on the submitted values.

```
PhaseListener I MyPhaseListener beforePhase INVOKE_APPLICATION 5

CreateProfile I pagecode.CreateProfile doCreateProfileAction() starting
Action...

PhaseListener I MyPhaseListener afterPhase INVOKE_APPLICATION 5
PhaseListener I MyPhaseListener beforePhase RENDER_RESPONSE 6

ServletWrappe I   SRVE0242I: [ExampleJSFProjectEAR] [/ExampleJSFProject]
[/ReviewProfile.jsp]: Initialization successful.

Profile       I com.ibmpress.entity.Profile getCustomerID 12345_0000
Profile       I com.ibmpress.entity.Profile getLastName Bernal
Profile       I com.ibmpress.entity.Profile getFirstName Bill
Profile       I com.ibmpress.entity.Profile getBirthDate 01012008

PhaseListener I afterPhase RENDER_RESPONSE 6
```

Review Profile Page

The review profile page does not allow you to edit the values; it is simply designed to let you review the data (see Figure 5.7) before saving the data values that were submitted in the create profile form. Note the customer ID field with the modified value in Figure 5.7.

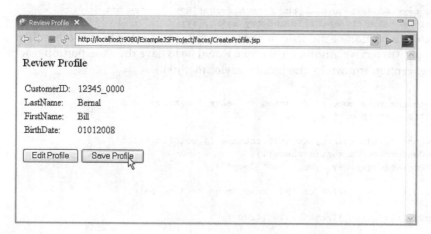

Figure 5.7   Review profile

The Save Profile button has an action assigned that performs the save data functionality. This action is assigned as an attribute to the button in the `ReviewProfile.jsp`.

```
<hx:commandExButton type="submit" value="Save Profile"
    id="saveProfileButton"
    styleClass="commandExButton"
    action="#{pc_PageReviewProfile.doSaveProfileAction}">
</hx:commandExButton>
```

Once again the action is composed of two parts. The first is a method in the page code bean for the JSP page, but this is simply a wrapper for the actual service that will validate and persist the data within the entity bean. The second part is the `doSaveProfileAction()` method in `ReviewProfile.java`, which examines the result from this external service to determine which actions to take. A simple `if-else` statement allows the navigation to proceed to the next page or provides an error message to the user with a redisplay of this page.

```
public String doSaveProfileAction() {

        logger.logp(Level.INFO, getClass().getName(),
        "doCreateProfileAction()", "starting Action...");

        String result = getProfileServices().persistData(getProfile());

if (result.equals("profilesaved")) {

        logger.logp(Level.INFO, getClass().getName(),
        "doSaveProfileAction()", result);
```

```
} else {
        logger.logp(Level.INFO, getClass().getName(),
        "doSaveProfileAction()", result);

        FacesContext facesContext = FacesContext.getCurrentInstance();

        facesContext.addMessage(null,new FacesMessage("Hey, you're not
        Joey! Please edit this profile and try again."));
```

Note that in the else portion of the statement can react to any returned value other than what we were hoping to receive. Another technique would be to have the else portion react to a message or exception thrown by the profile service method.

```
        //I would use this code if I wanted to leave a message to a
        //specific element on the page.

        //facesContext.addMessage(getTextFirstName1().getClientId(
        //facesContext.getCurrentInstance()),
        //new FacesMessage("Hey, you're not Joey!"));

        //disable the save button so they have to go back to edit.

        getSaveProfileButton().setDisabled(true);

}
return result;
}
```

If the save fails then a message is sent to the user and the page is redisplayed. The Save Profile button is also disabled so that the user cannot try to continue forward again. The only option left for the user is to return to the Create/Edit Profile page and change the values for first name.

So what exactly went wrong? Well the persistData() method, which is in the ProfileServices.java services class, is part of the profile services that are provided to your application. Potentially ProfileServices is in the business layer and is designed to provide a set of services to all applications in the presentation layer.

```
public String persistData(com.ibmpress.entity.Profile profile) {

        //if the first name is set to "Joey" then we'll pretend that
        //everything happens correctly.  If the first name is set to
        //anything else then there is a problem.

        logger.logp(Level.INFO, getClass().getName(), "persistData",
        "FirstName: " +profile.getFirstName());

        String result = "profilenotsaved";
        if (profile.getFirstName().equals("Joey")) {

                logger.logp(Level.INFO, getClass().getName(), "persistData",
                "I should save the profile here...");
```

```
                    result = "profilesaved";

            }
    return result;
    }
```

From an architecture perspective this interaction will work with several layers. You can see in Figure 5.8 how the interaction occurs.

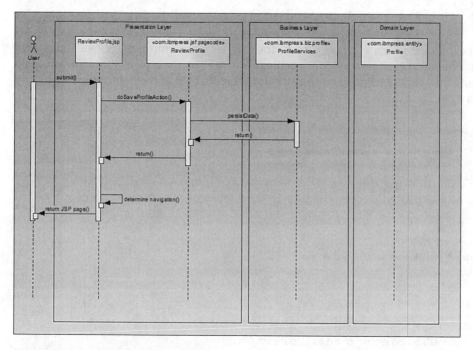

Figure 5.8   Interaction between layers

I hope this diagram helps make clear where the interaction between layers actually occurs. This key point in the architecture needs to be well defined before development actually takes place on the application.

The phase listener also illustrates what is going on within the submit process for this page. Phases 1 through 4 are not very interesting, but phase 5 shows the action in process. Remember that the persistData() method simply looks for a first name with the value of "Joey" and fails if it is not the value that was entered.

```
PhaseListener I MyPhaseListener beforePhase INVOKE_APPLICATION 5
ReviewProfile I pagecode.ReviewProfile doCreateProfileAction() starting
Action...
ReviewProfile I pagecode.ReviewProfile getProfileServices begin
ReviewProfile I pagecode.ReviewProfile getProfile begin
Profile       I Profile getFirstName Bill
```

```
prez           I ProfileServices persistData FirstName: Bill
Profile        I Profile getFirstName Bill
ReviewProfile  I ReviewProfile doSaveProfileAction() profilenotsaved
PhaseListener  I MyPhaseListener afterPhase INVOKE_APPLICATION 5

PhaseListener  I MyPhaseListener beforePhase RENDER_RESPONSE 6
Profile        I .Profile getCustomerID 12345_0000
Profile        I Profile getLastName Bernal
Profile        I Profile getFirstName Bill
Profile        I Profile getBirthDate 01012008
PhaseListener  I MyPhaseListener afterPhase RENDER_RESPONSE 6
```

The review profile screen is redisplayed to the user with an error message (see Figure 5.9).
Note that this message is not tied to a specific component on the screen, although you could
have done this. The Save Profile button has also been disabled so the user cannot try to save
the data again.

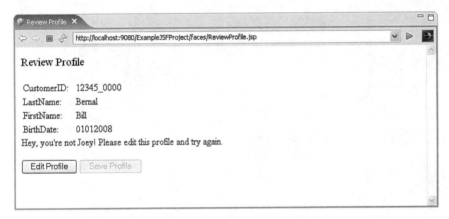

Figure 5.9   Validation error; return to Create Profile

At this point nothing is left to do except go back to the Create Profile page and change the
value of the field (see Figure 5.10). Changing the first name value on the Create Profile page
should not trigger any major changes. If you do change the customer ID then the value
change listener will trigger again and append the _000 data to the ID.

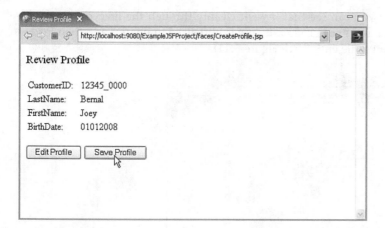

Figure 5.10   Save Profile with correct name

Now that you have the values correct you can go ahead and try to save the profile.

```
PhaseListener I MyPhaseListener beforePhase RESTORE_VIEW 1
PhaseListener I MyPhaseListener afterPhase RESTORE_VIEW 1
PhaseListener I MyPhaseListener beforePhase APPLY_REQUEST_VALUES 2
PhaseListener I MyPhaseListener afterPhase APPLY_REQUEST_VALUES 2
PhaseListener I MyPhaseListener beforePhase PROCESS_VALIDATIONS 3
PhaseListener I MyPhaseListener afterPhase PROCESS_VALIDATIONS 3
PhaseListener I MyPhaseListener beforePhase UPDATE_MODEL_VALUES 4
PhaseListener I MyPhaseListener afterPhase UPDATE_MODEL_VALUES 4

PhaseListener I MyPhaseListener beforePhase INVOKE_APPLICATION 5
ReviewProfile I pagecode.ReviewProfile doCreateProfileAction() starting
Action...
ReviewProfile I pagecode.ReviewProfile getProfileServices begin
ReviewProfile I pagecode.ReviewProfile getProfile begin
Profile      I Profile getFirstName Joey
prez         I ProfileServices persistData FirstName: Joey
Profile      I Profile getFirstName Joey
prez         I ProfileServices persistData I should save the profile
here...
ReviewProfile I ReviewProfile doSaveProfileAction() profilesaved
PhaseListener I MyPhaseListener afterPhase INVOKE_APPLICATION 5

PhaseListener I MyPhaseListener beforePhase RENDER_RESPONSE 6
ServletWrappe I   SRVE0242I: [ExampleJSFProjectEAR] [/ExampleJSFProject]
[/ProfileSaved.jsp]: Initialization successful.
Profile      I Profile getCustomerID 12345_0000
Profile      I Profile getLastName Bernal
Profile      I Profile getFirstName Joey
Profile       I Profile getBirthDate 01012008
PhaseListener I MyPhaseListener afterPhase RENDER_RESPONSE 6
```

Watching the log output you can see that it went cleanly through the lifecycle phases. In this cycle you can see that the `ProfileSaved.JSP` is initialized in phase 6 and then loaded with the values from the Profile entity (see Figure 5.11).

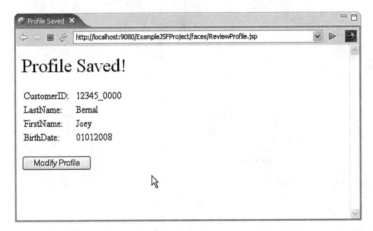

Figure 5.11   Profile saved

It's a lot to digest, I know, but if you walk through the example, or better yet, run your own examples, you will get the hang of how everything works together. Very important is the abstraction of layers within the overall architecture and how JSF fits within your prescribed architecture.

Masking and Conversion Errors

There are a lot of features that I did not get to cover in this chapter. Field validation is one of the many interesting features of JSF that help make it the framework of choice for developers today. Applying a mask to a field enables developers to very easily guide the end user into entering the right set of data. Figure 5.12 illustrates how I have applied a mask to the birth date field of the type ##/##/####. This mask can ensure that the end user enters a set of numbers in the required sequence.

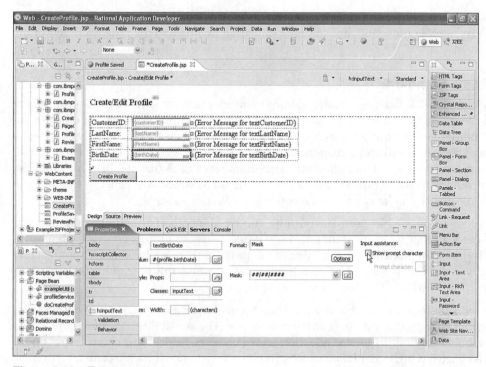

Figure 5.12 Edit component properties

Using a mask is by far not the only option. You might set the mask and still not have the application prompt the user for the numeric values. This can result in a conversion error (see Figure 5.13) if the user does not enter numbers in the right sequence, so be cautious on how you implement these types of features.

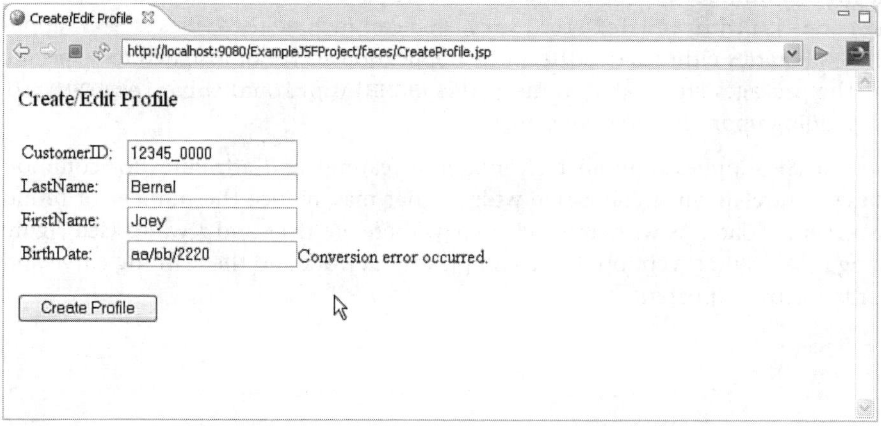

Figure 5.13 Conversion error

You can see how JSF can be used in this context to make some aspects of web development very easy, leaving the mundane aspects of validating user data to the inner workings of the framework.

JSF as a Standard

As a standard, JSF has been slowly gaining new adopters and advocates. The prevailing framework over the last few years has been Struts; however, Struts was never an official standard, but rather something the industry adopted as a whole. JSF has been fully adopted by Sun and hence versions and support options are available by several vendors, including IBM. As I mentioned before, standards are the minimum set of rules that can be made available. Many vendors strive to provide additional functionality, which will enhance the development experience and, of course, make building applications simpler.

The adoption on JSF has been fairly strong and by some reports the initial adoption was stronger than that for Struts during its early years. There are no proven studies, but adoption is often determined by the number of job postings there are looking for specific types of skills in the workplace. Indeed.com is one location where this type of historical analysis can be performed.

Both industry adoption and being a recognized standard are a couple reasons why adopting JSF within your organization may be the right choice. The availability of resources and developers should continue to grow as adoption grows; however, the learning curve, as mentioned in this chapter, is high so in-house developers will need additional training and time to come up to speed on this or any new technology. In addition to Struts, other open source presentation frameworks, such as SpringMVC, may be of interest to you for your project.

IBM's JWL

IBM's version of JSF is the JavaServer Faces Widget Library. This library integrates widgets or components from a number of sources and makes them available for your use. Supplied as two JAR files, `odc-jsf.jar` and `jsf-ibm.jar,` you can include these files in your application as shared libraries either across the entire application server or assigned to a specific application. The packages are located in the `${WAS_HOME}\optionaLibraries\IBM\jwl` directory, depending upon the latest version.

IBM's version of JSF supplies a number of enhanced features and attributes for common widgets. These features include client-side widgets that may reduce the number of round trips to the server for data. As with any technology, there are risks and rewards (see Figure 5.14) for using it. JSF is no exception. It is a complex framework and the learning curve and potential for missteps is apparent.

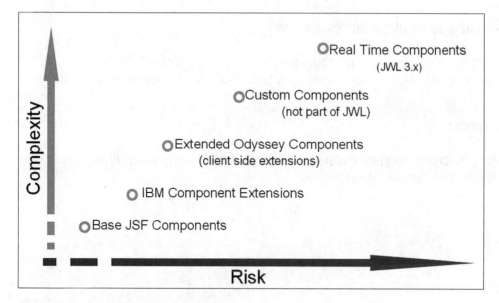

Figure 5.14 Using JSF in your projects

This chapter presented a tentative direction and outline of what is available within the JWL framework. This availability may change by the time this book is released. This overview should give you a good idea of how the presentation layer should fit into your overall application. Other options exist for implementation of the presentation, but ensuring layer separation should be at the top of your list.

Conclusion

This chapter has covered a lot. The presentation layer is the most visible layer within your application, so it is something that you should pay close attention to when designing the application. The choices are numerous and the debate of which approach is the best can get heated. I choose to cover JSF in this chapter because it is an industry standard. I think this is an important point to consider when evaluating the use of any framework within your application.

Keep in mind that like any framework, a good understanding of its use and potential areas of misuse is important. The choice of using a standards-based approach can help when trying to secure resources that are knowledgeable in the framework and how best to adapt it to your application.

Links to developerWorks Articles

A5.1 JSF for Non-Belivers, Richard Hightower:
http://www.ibm.com/developerworks/views/java/libraryview.jsp?search_by=nonbelievers:

References

Fowler, M. (2003). "Distribution Strategies." In *Patterns of Enterprise Application Architecture* (p. 89). Boston: Pearson Education, Inc.

Chapter 6

Investing in a Portal

A good follow-up to the discussion about the presentation layer is the concept of using a portal framework. Portals are based on a pluggable component architecture and are all about delivering diverse information that is relevant to the end user. The presentation of this information is accomplished via an aggregation framework that assembles the appropriate markup fragments within the context of a consistent user experience. In Chapter 5, "Presentation Frameworks," I discussed briefly some of the features that a presentation framework might bring to your project, enabling you to standardize on an approach and enabling your developers to focus on the features that are important to the users of your application. Portals go way beyond that aspect by providing a framework that enables you to merge many applications in a standardized way. Developers have to look beyond any single application and understand how portals can transform the way we build and present services and functionality to end users.

Probably the most difficult question to answer is, "when do I need to use a portal?" The answer can really go both ways. You can always take advantage of portal functionality within your application, and you can probably always go the custom route and build your own aggregate interface for your application. The fact is that simple standalone applications with minimal navigation needs would probably not benefit from being housed in a portal. Any application requirements beyond that and you can probably start to look at taking advantage of a portal framework, and anytime you need to bring multiple applications or disparate services into a common presentation layer, then a portal is probably the better choice.

A6.1

That being the case, does that single application really need to stand out there on its own, or should it be merged with other applications within a common shared infrastructure; that is, a portal infrastructure? This chapter gives you some of the information needed to make that decision within your own organization or project.

Incorporating a Portal into Your Architecture

One of the biggest paradigm shifts that will take place within your design is the idea that an application now becomes a small piece of functionality on the screen. Often this transition is harder to make than one might first imagine, with the end result being the original application trapped inside a portal framework, thus taking little advantage of the portal capabilities and features. Not taking advantage of the portal environment results in a direct loss of business value and the ROI that could have been realized. When not used correctly, the portal becomes additional software in the infrastructure that is not needed, yet requires ongoing maintenance and support.

Portals provide the ability to combine people, processes, and content within a common shared interface. In the example of a company intranet or employee portal, it can be a powerful concept. Combining or aggregating information and Web sites from across the company into a single solution for your employees can provide a cost-benefit ratio that is truly impressive. Imagine combining Web sites from HR, IT, Finance, Operations, and other areas of your organization and providing employees with a single site to access all of this information. Now imagine being able to plug in additional features and information at will as new requirements arise within the organization. The reduced infrastructure costs alone from the consolidation effort are probably worth taking a look at adopting a portal framework. Figure 6.1 shows an example of IBM's own Intranet portal with many common features.

Figure 6.1   IBM's W3 - On Demand employee portal

The concept of a portal has been around for several years and is continuing to grow in popularity within the enterprise. There has been an evolution that portals continue to follow within the enterprise. Some portions of this evolution are as follows:

1. The basic portal provides basic functionality, content aggregation, and key information.

2. The portal provides role-based access to content and applications.

3. It provides personalization of content that is targeted to roles as well as user attributes.

4. Collaboration capability is introduced, including expert location, team spaces, and file sharing.

5. Business process integration with human tasks is surfaced through the portal.

6. Business services are surfaced within the portal as the presentation layer within your Service Oriented Architecture (SOA) framework.

Portals provide the framework that facilitates the evolution of this capability in such a generic way as to allow you to build in the required functionality. You might consider some of the features of the framework as the plumbing upon which you can attach your own fixtures. I have focused a bit on the idea of an employee portal; however, no limitation exists for how you might apply portal technology to meet your needs. Let's look at some of the ways that a portal may be useful to your application.

Virtual Portal Technology

There are times when you need a different subset of functionality delivered to different groups of users. With a portal framework, a couple ways exist to partition or provision the desired functionality. One technique is to leverage the access control subsystem provided by the portal to deliver the targeted functionality to the right user at the right time. However, you need to consider the situation where the targeted functionality needs to be delivered to a given user population that may first access the portal as anonymous users. In this case, leveraging the access control capabilities of the portal do not suffice. An alternative approach you can use is based on the concept of virtual portals. Virtual portals use the same infrastructure and, in fact, the same portal server instance to deliver a separate view to different groups. This separation is really only logical within the portal but it provides a very clean separation on many levels.

The look and feel can be branded different for every group. For example, suppose you wanted to deliver insurance information branded for different companies or sets of customers. Each group could have a different look and a slightly different URL, but the functionality or portlets are the same for everyone using the portal. Recent advances also allow for users to be separated by virtual portal so that access is not allowed to another virtual portal view, and even administration tasks can be delegated to administrators at the virtual portal level.

Virtual portals can maximize your hardware and software investment by enabling you to provide additional services to your customers and make use of unused capacity. These additional services can be one of the core ideas around using a portal framework, enabling you to provide different views, or even completely separate logic entities to groups of customers based on need. Of course, this capability has to be weighed against the fact that you actually do have additional capacity available. Your governance model has to be very strong to withstand different parts of the business all competing for your resources.

Business-to-Employee (B2E) Portals

You saw a bit about business-to-employee portals earlier in the example of IBM's W3 portal. Company intranets have been the number one entry point for portal technology, and I admit that most of the portal projects I have worked on were internal employee portals. While sometimes ROI on an employee portal can be hard to measure, there are cases where having a consolidated portal is a worthwhile investment. I often refer to employee portals as the 4-Tab view, where the top categories are Home, Work, Life, and Career, or usually something to that effect.

The results on IBM's employee portal are truly impressive. W3 is the go-to site for employee self-service worldwide. With an average 1.7 million page viewers per day at the time of this writing, it is one of the most robust examples of using a portal framework. Even more impressive is the cost savings of moving many of the day-to-day interactions to a self-service model hosted on the portal. I personally can attest that in the last seven years or so, I have never talked to HR or used anything other than intranet self-service for many of my personnel matters, except for my initial hiring process, which was before many of the self-service components were in place.

Business Process or Forms-Based Portal

A portal as a front end to business processes can be invaluable. The value comes not so much from being able to provide an interface for human tasks, but in the fact that they can be integrated with other activities to build composite applications. The composite application can be composed of portlets and pages that enhance the end users' experience and thereby make them more productive with regard to completing the task. Dynamic page creation can be invoked along with the workflow to allow end users to be assigned to or choose a task, work on that activity, and then have the workspace cleaned up as tasks are completed.

The ability to invoke and route forms along with business processes provides a level of ability that can mimic anything we do outside the computer today. The use of a form allows data to be entered, approved, signed, stored, and restored as needed for business use. All of these wonderful abilities do come at some cost. The framework is provided for you, but filling in the details is often not a trivial task. Often people are asked to change the way they work to achieve the benefit of an automated world. This means that as architects, our job is to understand how these technologies work best in our environment and then adapt our approach; however, trying to change either side too much often results in problems. By that I mean that trying to bend the technology to work the way we do is often painful and never very successful, but trying to completely change business processes is equally challenging, because that means changing people and the way they work. A compromise and buy-in from all parties is usually required.

Portals Versus the Web App

I made this point a little earlier in this chapter, but you need to consider several areas when trying to decide when to use a portal framework. Often it may be an organizational decision that all new applications will use the portal; this is especially true if a single shared infrastructure has been implemented to house these applications. Again, if your requirements are strictly for a standalone disparate application that serves a distinct purpose then a portal may not be the right approach. It is an interesting discussion, and the vision has to be made very clear and followed closely. Without that vision you will find very little advantage with using a portal, and in some ways it may hinder your ability to function. This vision should include many of the key features that a portal provides

Role-based Navigation and Content Delivery

Combining content and applications from multiple sources within a single page view can be one of the key benefits of using portal technology. Portals have the ability to provide the right access to the pages and portlets that you decide on, based on roles defined within the portal. These roles are usually mapped to LDAP groups or attributes so that users see the information that they are supposed see and are limited from seeing information that pertains to other roles. For example, a manager's page could be defined that provides information on employee data, or last week's sales, or the ability to order more paper cups. This page can be blocked from anyone who is not a manager within the organization. The beauty of portal navigation is that it is defined by an administrative interface and not dependent upon some code components created by the developer. Navigation functionality is probably one of the most important concepts in implementing a portal project.

Security and Single Sign-on

Portals take security pretty seriously, and WebSphere Portal is no exception. Much of the authentication subsystem of WebSphere Portal leverages the WebSphere Application Server security features. Keep in mind that the authentication subsystem primarily protects the entry points into a portal, while the authorization subsystem of a portal protects the specific portal resources. Therefore, the portal is protected from authenticated requests by the WebSphere Application Server.

The WebSphere Application Server authentication subsystem supports custom form-based authentication, integration of third-party authentication proxy servers, and certificate-based authentication. Once the WebSphere Application Server determines the end user's identity, a distinguished name is handed off to the portal, which can then make the necessary access control decisions.

Content Personalization

A portal can determine which pages and portlets to display to the user, but the portal does not usually have any insight into what is displayed within the portlet window itself. This requires the developer to understand what should be displayed and whether the content is user dependent. To make the decision to display targeted content, you can often look at the roles or groups to which a user belongs. However, displaying targeted content could be quite complex and based on a combination of attributes, metadata, and business rules. This type of complex calculation requires additional system capacity when you consider that complex queries may be expensive in terms of computational capacity.

Personalization engines such as the one built into WebSphere Portal can provide that additional capability. This type of engine enables you to identify metadata on resources such as content and build rules to display that content based on user attributes. These can be simple types of rules such as, "if manager then display sales data," or they may be increasingly complex such as determining whether a user is a silver, gold, or platinum member based on some account balance or usage of a service.

Portlet Aggregation and Composite Applications

One of your long-term visions is to gain the ability to combine portlets or applications in ways that you haven't even thought of today. Portals provide the ability not only to combine portlets on a page or set of pages, but also to wire them together through a set of APIs that allows them to communicate and pass data to one another. Many good examples of this type of composition come to mind, including call centers where a call center representative may click on the user's name in one portlet, and several other portlets then populate with data to display previous orders or call history.

The real power of this approach is in how easily you can add new portlets into the mix and then wire them up. Doing this in a standard web application would usually require a substantial rewrite to the application. Within a portal you can deploy the new portlet and wire it to the other portlets within the page or on other pages with no changes to the existing application—assuming you have built the necessary hooks into your functionality to allow this exchange to happen.

Interestingly enough, all of these features are fairly similar in that security and targeting data is the end goal. The combination of these features allows you to ensure that you have a secure system that is providing the right access to the right information. Some of these features are out-of-the-box capability that you can use right away, while others such as personalization and composite applications require some design work to be used correctly.

Applications as Portlets

So where does the portlet fit into your overall architecture? You can really approach it in a fashion similar to other presentation layer applications. You can consider each portlet or set of portlets as a standalone application that happens to live in a shared environment, possibly even sharing the same page or view. Figure 6.2 shows a simple example of a layered diagram where multiple portlets can live within the Portlet Container.

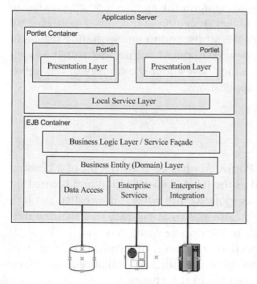

Figure 6.2   Portal layers

Note that there is a local service layer provided, which you can use to manage access to any and all resources that are required by the portlets. This layer could actually live within each portlet if sharing is not necessary across applications. Figure 6.3 illustrates how specific classes are defined within each layer to provide a well-defined architecture.

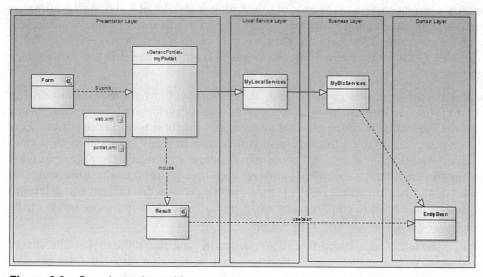

Figure 6.3   Sample portlet architecture

The presentation layer is made up of the actual portlet class and the required deployment descriptors, as well as any JSPs that are needed for HTML output. Additional components are actually defined within separate layers depending upon the architectural approach you take within your organization. This approach makes designing and building portlets easy regardless of the framework you choose; that is, JSF, Struts, and so on. Separating logic and data enables the portlet itself to become the view component within the overall Model-View-Controller (MVC) structure. Some organizations have adopted a strategy of very lightweight portlets that contain the view of some applications.

The Java Portlet API

Within the WebSphere Portal world, the Java Portlet API has been both a bit of a blessing and a curse. The initial version 1.0 was created as the JSR 168 specification and focused on standalone portlet applications. Later it was incorporated into what is now called the Java Portlet API. Version 2 of the Portlet specification, also known as JSR 286, was finalized during the writing of this book and will be available in WebSphere Portal version 6.1. The focus of JSR 286 is to enable coordination between portlets and address the construction of composite applications based on portlet components, as well as other API enhancements. None of the additions will change the code that is presented in this chapter

The blessing is that a pretty strong open standard upon which to build portlets now exists. Vendors should be very excited about this because it affords the opportunity to try to build portlets that will run on multiple portal servers. This standard can provide an easy way, with just a little extra effort, to leverage portlet development and integrate systems easily with any and all portal servers that have portlet containers that adhere to the Java Portlet API.

The curse is that the API can be considered pretty sparse in functionality. At least version 2.0, which is being voted on at the time of this writing, adds a lot of additional features that will make the API much more functional. Of course, vendors themselves will often add proprietory features and APIs that can enhance existing functionality. WebSphere Portal provides this functionality in the form of custom APIs and services that you can leverage within your code.

My advice to customers is to go ahead and take advantage of any additional functionality or services if they make sense for your application. Often development teams want to stay close to the spec with the argument that vendors and products within their organization will change over time. I think this argument is ridiculous in many cases and in most cases the business would not or should not allow major changes in vendor technology without a compelling reason. The specifications can never keep up with vendor-added functionality, which is one of the main reasons why IT organizations perform due diligence in determining which product suite to choose. Choosing a product and then not using much of the available functionality seems somehow wrong.

Before I get too far off base, let me talk about portlets in general and the Portlet API. One of the key tenets of the Portlet specification was that portlets are different from servlets.

Originally a portlet was really just a subset of a servlet with some additional API features. But really portlets are different from servlets in that they have a lifecycle that splits rendering into two distinct phases. The responsibility of the first phase, referred to the action phase, is to handle actions from the portlet. It is the recommended phase for updating the application state and interacting with the business model. The second phase, referred to as the render phase, is focused on transforming the business data into the target markup. A description of the events in the portlet lifecycle follows:

- **Init:** As with a servlet, the portlet gets initialized in this phase.
- **Process action:** In this phase an action is triggered or some processing takes place. Messages get passed, preferences get set, and so on.
- **Render:** In this phase the markup is generated for the portlet based on the current mode and window state. The render phase can be called independently or will be called after a process action phase.
- **Destroy:** Again, as with servlets, the portlet is removed from service.

Contrast this lifecycle with a servlet's lifecycle events: Init, Service, and Destroy. Note that the Service event becomes two events in a portlet's lifecycle, each having its own use cases (see Figure 6.4).

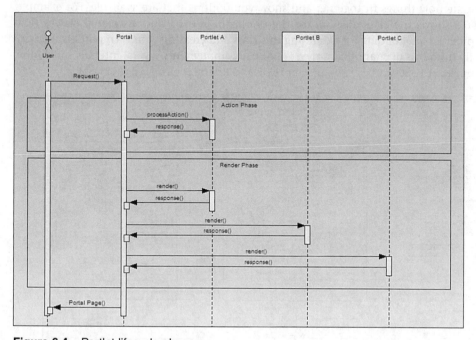

Figure 6.4   Portlet lifecycle phases

The render phase is used most often and is called for every portlet that generates some output. During the aggregation of a portal page, each portlet on that page must render some content to be displayed, assuming, of course, that the portlet is not minimized or is in some other state that precludes rendering some output. The render phase for each portlet is called in no particular sequence, although empirically it seems to go from top to bottom within the page. Unfortunately, you cannot rely on the order of execution, so ensuring that one portlet is called before another can be difficult.

The action phase is the result of a direct interaction by the user with the portlet. It is usually triggered by some type of form input or processing request. Process action phases are called when required, which in some cases can trigger the process action of another portlet—for example, when portlet messaging is used and messages need to be passed between portlets. Actually, portlet messaging is not part of the JSR 168 specification. It will be part of version 2.0 and is an added API that is currently available within WebSphere Portal. This messaging process occurs during the process action phase of the portlet lifecycle. After the process action phase, then the render phase can be called, this time for every portlet that resides on the displayed page.

Java Portlet API 2.0

The best way to learn about a new technology or framework is to download the API samples and look at them. Javadoc is sometimes interesting but often you need a good class diagram to illustrate how things fit together and show you options that are available. For example, Figure 6.5 shows the class diagram for the `GenericPortlet` and associated classes. This visual provides a lot of data for extending this class and creating your own portlets. You can see easily from this diagram that `GenericPortlet` implements several interfaces including `Portlet`, `PortletConfig`, `EventPortlet`, and `ResourceServingPortlet`.

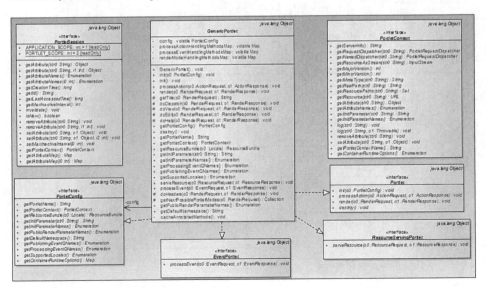

Figure 6.5   Generic portlet class diagram

Taking a look at the code that comprises the class `GenericPortlet` you can see that these interfaces are implemented and return maps to hold processing data. More information about the code samples and how to download them is available in Appendix B, "Running the Examples."

```
public abstract class GenericPortlet implements Portlet, PortletConfig,
EventPortlet, ResourceServingPortlet {

private transient PortletConfig config;

private transient Map<String, Method> processActionHandlingMethodsMap =
new HashMap<String, Method>();

private transient Map<String, Method> processEventHandlingMethodsMap =
new HashMap<String, Method>();

private transient Map<String, Method> renderModeHandlingMethodsMap = new
HashMap<String, Method>();
```

Some other features that are important to portlets are the mode and view of a portlet. Portlets generally have several modes:

- **View mode:** Usually the default mode for normal function
- **Edit mode:** Allows the setting of user-specific settings such as preferences
- **Help mode:** Displays help information about the portlet or application
- **Custom modes:** Usually vendor specific, such as Configure mode in WebSphere Portal, which is an administrative view for shared settings

Besides modes, portlets also have state. Those states include Normal, Maximized, or Minimized view. As portlets often share space on the same page, they need to understand how to work nicely together. For example, all the portlets on the same page may be in the Normal state, which means they all need to share the same window space. However, a portlet may be maximized, in which case it is expanded and will take over the entire page.

This chapter just scratches the surface in helping you understand the Portlet API and how to approach your portlet architecture. An entire class diagram is shown in Figure 6.6, which can help you understand what is available from the specification for leveraging within your application.

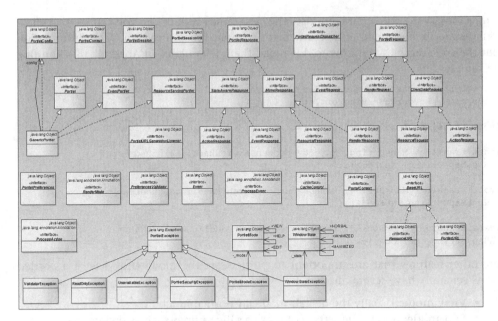

Figure 6.6   Portlet API 2.0 class diagram

In general I suggest reading the specification itself as well as some of the books available. I am a co-author of both the first and second editions of the book, *Programming Portlets*, by IBM Press (Lynn, 2007). This guide walks beginners through all aspects of developing their own portlet applications.

Portlet Preferences

The Portlet API has way too many features to discuss in this chapter, but there are some concepts that can be helpful to understand. I mentioned earlier that one of the core tenants of the portlet spec was to differentiate it from the servlet spec. Portlets really are different animals, and they live in a shared space, so your application architecture should put a bigger emphasis on helping portlets work together and share resources as much as possible.

The state of a portlet is really defined by a combination of factors. Some of the factors include

- Session state, similar to a servlet session
- The current portlet mode and view state; that is, Edit mode, or maximized view
- Preferences set by the administrator or user

Preferences are a feature specific to portlets and are used to represent points of variability. They are a means by which an end user or administrator can specify how a portlet looks or behaves. For example, a stock portlet may allow the setting of user preferences that define which particular stock's values will be shown. The specification itself is downloadable from the Java Community Process Web site (jcp.org) and can walk you through all the requirements of the API. Often when I give presentations on this topic, I build the slides directly from the latest specification document to illustrate constraints, requirements, and examples.

A Simple Portlet Example

I think an example will best illustrate how you might build your own portlet. The example is based on one of the sample portlets from Rational Application Developer built using the portlet project wizard. I have noted before that I am not a huge fan of wizards, because they sometimes make assumptions that don't scale well in production systems. But for getting started, they can nicely shortcut many of the mundane steps that are easy to mess up. In this case the sample portlet is a simple bookmarks portlet, as shown in Figure 6.7.

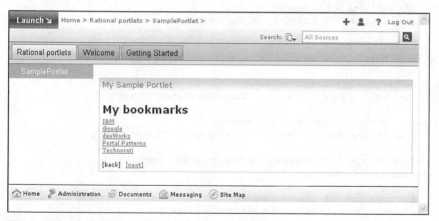

Figure 6.7 Sample portlet

The bookmarks portlet allows users to edit their bookmarks, which are stored as preferences within the portlet framework. Each user has the ability to set his or her bookmarks, which are then displayed in the view mode of the portlet.

Looking at the portlet class, the overall structure is fairly simple. The class `SamplePortlet` extends the class `GenericPortlet`, discussed earlier. This is really what makes the class a portlet and provides a base set of methods that you can build upon. The next part is a set of constants or static strings that are used to ensure continuity across different methods within the class and any of the JSPs used by the portlet. While not always strictly required, the use of statics does follow good programming practices and can provide some continuity across the code modules. A better method might be to externalize the strings even further to a properties file, but that might be considered overkill for many situations.

```
public class SamplePortlet extends GenericPortlet {

// JSP folder name
public static final String JSP_FOLDER     = "/_SamplePortlet/jsp/";

// JSP file name to be rendered on the view mode
public static final String VIEW_JSP       = "SamplePortletView";

// JSP file name to be rendered on the edit mode
public static final String EDIT_JSP       = "SamplePortletEdit";

// Bean name for the portlet session
public static final String SESSION_BEAN   = "SamplePortletSessionBean";

// Action name for adding a preference
public static final String PREF_ADD       = "SamplePortletPrefAdd";

// Action name for removing a preference
public static final String PREF_REMOVE    = "SamplePortletPrefRemove";

// Parameter name for the preference name
public static final String PREF_NAME      = "SamplePortletPrefName";

// Parameter name for the preference value
public static final String PREF_VALUE     = "SamplePortletPrefValue";

// Parameter name for the validation error message
public static final String ERROR_MESSAGE = "SamplePortletErrorMessage";

public void doView(RenderRequest request, RenderResponse response)
throws PortletException, IOException {

    // Set the MIME type for the render response
    response.setContentType(request.getResponseContentType());

    // Check if portlet session exists
    SamplePortletSessionBean sessionBean = getSessionBean(request);
    if( sessionBean==null ) {

                response.getWriter().println("<b>NO PORTLET SESSION
                YET</b>");
        return;
    }
```

Finally, the doView() method is called when the portlet is first displayed and whenever the portlet is refreshed on the page; that is, whenever the page is refreshed or a processAction() method is called. The doView() method is very straightforward. In this case, the doView() method delegates the actual management of the rendering effort to the JSP. By inspecting the method, you can see that the PortletRequestDispatcher is used to include the JSP in the request. Something to note is that JSP forwards are not allowed within the render phase.

```
// Invoke the JSP to render
   PortletRequestDispatcher rd =
   getPortletContext().getRequestDispatcher(getJspFilePath(request, VIEW_JSP));

   rd.include(request,response);

}
```

As a recommended practice, the View mode of a portlet is for viewing information whereas the Edit mode is for entering information that may change the state of the portlet. Switching between various modes may be vendor specific depending upon how the vendor has implemented this within their portal. In the case of this WebSphere Portal, two approaches are used. The first is using the portlet context menu (see Figure 6.8) to allow the user to switch to Edit mode. In the case of WebSphere Portal this menu option is called Personalize. If you think about it, this name makes a lot of sense. The purpose of Edit mode is to allow the user to define his or her specific preferences or personalization options. From an end user perspective, different modes like Edit and Configure might get confusing, but Personalize makes some sense in that the user can now tailor the portlet to his or her personal preferences. The second approach is to switch modes programmatically, which will be covered later in this chapter.

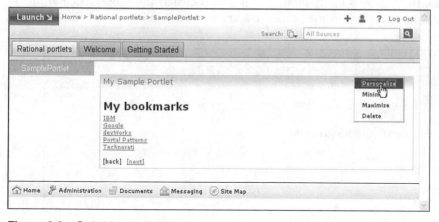

Figure 6.8   Switching to Edit mode

Switching to Edit mode now triggers the doEdit() method rather than the doView() during the render phase of the portlet. Suprisingly, the doEdit() method does little more than the doView() method in this portlet. However, one thing that is important is that the doEdit() method calls a different JSP to display the markup. This is key to distinguishing the different modes within a single portlet. Although it may be the case that the doView() or doEdit() methods call more than one JSP during a given portlet's interaction with an end user, the starting place is usually different because of the function that each mode plays in the operations of a portlet.

```
public void doEdit(RenderRequest request, RenderResponse response) throws
PortletException, IOException {

        // Set the MIME type for the render
        responseresponse.setContentType(request.getResponseContentType());

        // Check if portlet session exists
        SamplePortletSessionBean sessionBean = getSessionBean(request);
        if( sessionBean==null ) {

                response.getWriter().println("<b>NO PORTLET SESSION YET</b>");

                return;
        }

        // Invoke the JSP to render
        PortletRequestDispatcher rd =
        getPortletContext().getRequestDispatcher(getJspFilePath(request,
        EDIT_JSP));

        rd.include(request,response);
}
```

View mode for this portlet is pretty boring; all it does is display the bookmarks. But in Edit mode you actually interact with the portlet to add and remove bookmarks from the list.

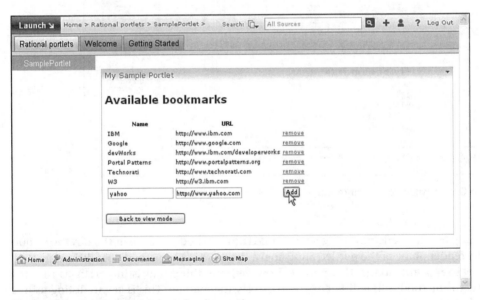

Figure 6.9   Adding a bookmark (preference)

Let's take a look at how Edit mode works by starting with the JSP and seeing how these functions work. The initial heading in the JSP is fairly standard. The imports are important because they allow you to leverage any beans that are passed within the session or on the request. Also some portlet JSP tag libraries are defined and initialized within the JSP. This makes portlet objects available within the JSP. The rest of this section is simple display heading information for the list of preferences that may be displayed.

```
<%@page session="false" contentType="text/html" pageEncoding="ISO-8859-
1" import="java.util.*,javax.portlet.*,com.ibmpress.portlet.sampleportlet.*
"%>
<%@taglib uri="http://java.sun.com/portlet" prefix="portlet" %>
<portlet:defineObjects/>

<H3 style="margin-bottom: 3px">Available bookmarks</H3>

<FORM ACTION="<portlet:actionURL/>" METHOD="POST">
<TABLE CELLPADDING=0 CELLSPACING=4>
<TBODY>
        <TR>
                <TH><B>Name</B></TH>
                <TH><B>URL</B></TH>
                <TH></TH>
        </TR>
```

The next section of the JSP actually displays the preferences that are available within this portlet. Preferences are generally user specific, although ways exist for making preferences read only or for creating more general preferences for all users. The code creates a collection of preferences that are stored as name/value pairs. This collection can now be iterated over and displayed as a list of bookmarks and associated names. Notice that the preferences are after an attached prefix, "url." This allows the separation bookmark preferences from other preferences that may be set within the portlet. In actuality, the portlet container itself may prefix your preferences so that it knows which portlet they belong to.

The final thing to note in this section is the addition of the Remove link to each preference. This is actually a specific URL that is generated to trigger an action within the portlet. The URL contains a parameter named PREF_REMOVE, and the value of this parameter is the actual name of the preference or bookmark. You will see how this action gets handled; for now, understand that this is an actionURL as opposed to a renderURL.

```
<%
PortletPreferences prefs = renderRequest.getPreferences();

for( Enumeration prefNames=prefs.getNames();
        prefNames.hasMoreElements(); ) {

        String name = prefNames.nextElement().toString();
        if( !name.startsWith("url.") ) continue;
        %>

        <TR>
        <TD><%=name.substring(4)%></TD>
        <TD><%=prefs.getValue(name,"<undefined>")%></TD>
        <TD><A HREF ='<portlet:actionURL><portlet:param
```

```
name="<%=com.ibmpress.portlet.sampleportlet.SamplePortlet.PREF_REMOVE%>"
value="<%=name%>"/></portlet:actionURL>'>remove</A></TD>
        </TR>

<%  }   %>
```

The final section of the Edit JSP is a simple form display that allows you to add a preference or bookmark to the current list. The form has two parameters: the name of the bookmark and the actual URL that the bookmark points to. This addition gets triggered by the form submit button called Add.

```
<TR>
<TD><INPUT
NAME="<%=com.ibmpress.portlet.sampleportlet.SamplePortlet.PREF_NAME%>"
TYPE="text"></TD>

<TD><INPUT
NAME="<%=com.ibmpress.portlet.sampleportlet.SamplePortlet.PREF_VALUE%>"
TYPE="text"></TD>

<TD><INPUT
NAME="<%=com.ibmpress.portlet.sampleportlet.SamplePortlet.PREF_ADD%>" TYPE="submit"
value="Add"></TD>
</TR>
</TBODY>
</TABLE>
</FORM>
```

The exciting part actually happens when a submission from this page occurs. It triggers an action request to the portlet. The processAction() method gets called during this request and can now operate on the request as required. The goal of the method is to determine the nature of the request and then perform the requested action: That is, to add a bookmark or to remove one from the list. This is handled by examining the parameter that is associated with the request URL to perform the requested action. Remember that the generated actionURL has a parameter with a name and a value associated with it. The name is actually one of the constants that is declared at the beginning of the portlet class file: PREF_REMOVE or PREF_ADD.-

One thing to note is that the processAction() method can actually get fairly large, because action requests from all modes of the portlet will trigger this one function. It is interesting that each mode will get its own render method, but the action method is shared across all modes. If the request is to remove a preference then the code will call the reset method to remove the preference from the list. The value of the request parameter is used to match the actual preference name.

```
public void processAction(ActionRequest request, ActionResponse response)
throws PortletException, java.io.IOException {

if( request.getParameter(PREF_REMOVE) != null ) {

        // Reset or remove a portlet preference
        PortletPreferences prefs = request.getPreferences();
        prefs.reset(request.getParameter(PREF_REMOVE));
        prefs.store();
```

```
            // Reset bookmark start position
            SamplePortletSessionBean sessionBean = getSessionBean(request);
            if( sessionBean != null )
                    sessionBean.setStartPosition(0);
```

Adding a preference is a little more complicated. The preference or bookmark name will get the value of "url." as a prefix to identify it as an actual bookmark. This prefix is necessary to distinguish the preference from other settings you may have in your portlet. If the parameter is "PREF_ADD", then the processAction() method calls the setValue() method of the PortletPreferences object. This sets the object in the preferences but does not commit the value. The value will not be committed until the store() method is called. Note that the store() method must also be called with the reset() method in order to commit the removal of the preference. Several exceptions are handled that one could expect from the preferences interaction. Finally, the start position of the list of bookmarks is reset to 0. This resetting to 0 is just so we can count during the display of the bookmarks. This count is reset and then is used in the display of the bookmarks to ensure we can show five bookmarks at a time and so that users can navigate between pages of bookmarks.

```
} else if( request.getParameter(PREF_ADD) != null ) {

            // Set a portlet preference
            PortletPreferences prefs = request.getPreferences();
            String prefName = request.getParameter(PREF_NAME);
            if( "".equals(prefName) ) prefName = "(no name)";
            prefName = "url." + prefName;

            try {
                    prefs.setValue(prefName,request.getParameter(PREF_VALUE));
                    prefs.store();
            }
            catch( ReadOnlyException roe ) {
                    response.setRenderParameter(ERROR_MESSAGE,"Read-only portlet
                    preference '"+prefName+"' cannot be changed.");
            }
            catch( ValidatorException ve ) {
                    // I gotta do something here!
                    @todo
            }

            // Reset bookmark start position
            SamplePortletSessionBean sessionBean = getSessionBean(request);
            if( sessionBean != null )
                    sessionBean.setStartPosition(0);

}

}
```

Switching Modes Programmatically

When the user is finished updating the bookmarks, he or she needs to switch back to the View mode of the portlet (see Figure 6.10). They can do so in the same manner that was used previously with the portlet menu; however, you can also provide a shortcut to your users to increase usability of the portlet. In this case it can be accomplished through the use of a button on the page. This programmatic approach is another option available for providing the right functionality to users.

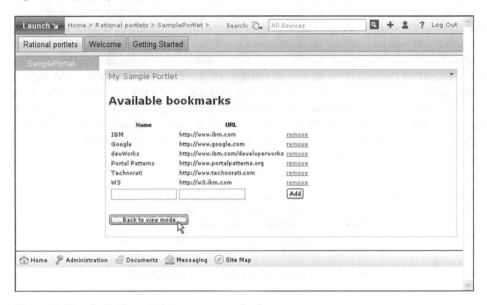

Figure 6.10   Switching modes programmatically

The code for creating this button is quite simple. You can use the URL generation capability of the Portlet API to create a `renderURL` that points back to the portlet. Within that URL the portlet mode is set back to the View mode. Clicking that button merely triggers the link. It could also be displayed as an HTML link as opposed to an actual button.

```
<FORM ACTION='<portlet:renderURL portletMode="view"/>' METHOD="POST">
        <INPUT NAME="back" TYPE="submit" VALUE="Back to view mode">
</FORM>
```

I kind of approached this portlet backwards by talking mostly about Edit mode first instead of View mode. But in this case it was important to show how preferences get created before they are displayed within the portlet view. The bookmarks view is pretty simple. It just iterates through all the bookmarks and displays them as links to the user. This potentially has limited value to the user because a browser can achieve the same functionality. However, it could have great value to an administrator. Suppose an administrator wanted to provide a set of links or bookmarks to your users—how could he do so? It could be a separately defined project, or this project where an administration or the business forces the set of bookmarks that a user has access to.

One feature that has been incorporated into this display is limiting the display of bookmarks to only five. This ensures that the user does not have potentially dozens of bookmarks to view at once and that the portlet does not take up too much of the page real estate. If we were to display all bookmarks in the portlet at once, the page could scroll quite a bit, and leave another portlet stranded at the bottom of a very long page. Provided with those five links is a set of back and next buttons (see Figure 6.11) that allow the user to scroll through the set of links. Setting the list to be displayed each time the portlet is rendered is a matter of determining the starting position in the list. Once the starting position is determined, the next five entries from that point in the list are displayed. This approach illustrates how data can be passed to the JSP from the portlet controller class using a data bean.

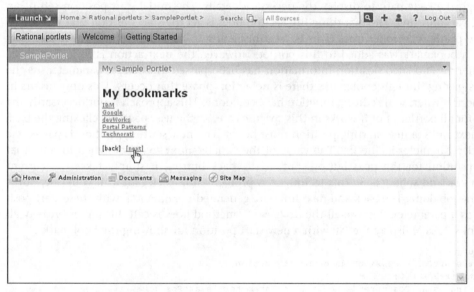

Figure 6.11 Paging thru bookmarks

Walking through the code for the view JSP you can see that the JSP actually gets the sessionbean from the portlet session. Looking back at the doView() and doEdit() methods you have seen where the sessionbean is set. In the processAction() you also saw that the value in the bean for the startPosition was set to 0. After getting the bean from the portlet session, the JSP then retrieves the set of preferences from the request for display. If this set is empty, then some generic text is displayed to the user.

```
<%
        com.ibmpress.portlet.sampleportlet.SamplePortletSessionBean
sessionBean =
(com.ibmpress.portlet.sampleportlet.SamplePortletSessionBean)renderRequest.getPortlet
Session().getAttribute(com.ibmpress.portlet.sampleportlet.SamplePortlet.SESSION_BEAN)
;
```

```
%>

<H3 style="margin-bottom: 3px">My bookmarks</H3>

<%
    PortletPreferences prefs = renderRequest.getPreferences();
    Enumeration prefNames = prefs.getNames();
    if (!prefNames.hasMoreElements()) {
        // no bookmarks
%>
        No bookmarks available.
        Please use edit mode to add bookmarks.
        <BR>
<%
```

If the set of preferences actually contains some bookmark information, then the portlet goes through the code path to display the necessary details. The initial start position setup can be a little confusing. The first thing this section does is get the start position that was set up by the portlet controller class. This is probably going to be a zero initially as it was reset when a bookmark was added to this portlet. However, the next action is to look and see whether any updated position information has been passed as a render parameter. As the user is paging through bookmarks there is no action phase that occurs. This only occurs in this portlet when some editing function has been done. This approach is not necessarily the same for all portlets, but it works in this specific case. As the user pages by clicking the back and next links, a new starting position must be set. The new starting position is passed via a render parameter in the JSP. The value of the variable `nextPos` is designed to hold that next position for the next button, but in the back button, it simply takes the current `startPos` and subtracts 5. This technigue is probably not as elegant as it could be, but it gets the job done. The back and next links are generated `renderURLs` with these start positions as a parameter. Because all the `doView()` method does is call this JSP, essentially all the links do is redisplay the JSP with a new start position for showing the bookmarks.

```
} else {
    int startPos = sessionBean.getStartPosition();
    int nextPos = 0;
    String _startPos = renderRequest.getParameter("startPos");
    if( _startPos != null ) {

        try {
            startPos = Integer.parseInt(_startPos);

        } catch (NumberFormatException nfe) {}
            sessionBean.setStartPosition(startPos);
        }

        while( prefNames.hasMoreElements() && nextPos < startPos+5 ) {
            String name = prefNames.nextElement().toString();
            if( !name.startsWith("url.") ) continue;
            if( nextPos >= startPos ) {
%>
```

```
        <A HREF='<%=prefs.getValue(name,"<undefined>")%>'>
        <%=name.substring(4)%></A><BR>

        <%
        }
        nextPos++;
        }
        %>
        <BR>

        <%
        if( startPos > 0 ) {
        %>
            <A HREF='<portlet:renderURL>
            <portlet:param name="startPos"
value="<%=String.valueOf(Math.max(0,startPos-5))%>"/>
            </portlet:renderURL>'>[back]</A> 
        <%
        } else {
        %>
            [back] 
        <%
        }

        if( prefNames.hasMoreElements() ) {
        %>
         <A HREF='<portlet:renderURL><portlet:param name="startPos"
value="<%=String.valueOf(nextPos)%>"/></portlet:renderURL>'>[next]</A>
        <%
        } else {
        %>
             [next]
        <%
        }
}
%>
```

Finally, take a look at the layout of the portlet within the project itself (see Figure 6.12). A portlet project looks very similar to any other web application with some additional items. The portlet.xml deployment descriptor is required by the portlet container to help identify specific portlet features that may be required. For example, the portlet.xml identifies which modes this portlet will use. This helps the portal to know which modes it should display within the portlet menu that is used to switch from view to edit mode.

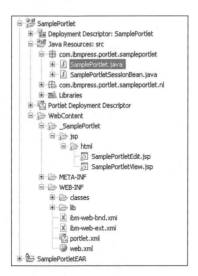

Figure 6.12   Portlet layout

There is a bit of a learning curve to understanding the differences between portlets and other web applications, but understanding servlet and JSP programming will help you learn how to develop portlets.

Conclusion

Overall you can see that portlets can fit nicely within your overall architecture. They can be used to provide unique interfaces for services or systems within your organization. They can be combined to create what is called a composite application that allow your users to perform new and exciting things within a single user interface or application.

There is much that is not covered here, as suggested by some of my other books in the portal space such as our Programming Portlets book referenced at the end of this chapter, but the main point was to show how you can integrate a portal into your overall architect. In reality the architecture should not change dramatically with the inclusion of a portal. One of the main factors that lead me to write this book was the idea of helping portal teams understand how to build well-defined applications, with or without portals, within the WebSphere family of products.

An important point to remember is that incorporating a portal server imposes a new infrastructure and additional rigor within your organization. The value of a portal is undeniable. It allows your organization to bring together people, content, and applications as never before. One issue that often comes up is the idea of keeping the portal and portlets lightweight and moving all the heavy processing to the business and other layers. The idea is that doing so will allow the portal to scale better and hold more portlets and applications. Overall, I think this can be a good approach, but there are several things to consider:

- A single portal environment has an upper bounds; at some point you will probably need to put up another infrastructure to hold additional portlets. This could be solely due to memory limitations within the application server. Some applications may be better off living on their own.
- More portlets and applications within a shared environment mean you must have tighter control over the development and deployment of these artifacts. The information in Chapter 2 now becomes a lot more important within your organization. One bad portlet can spoil the bunch if control is not maintained.
- Moving the heavy lifting to other layers now requires that those layers be built and scaled to handle the appropriate load. Service-level agreements should be made with those services to ensure that they know what to expect as load from the presentation/portal layer.
- Distribution implies lower performance. While this is not the worst thing that could happen, make sure you understand the impact of taking this approach and take every opportunity to make sure performance is not an issue.

This list is not designed to scare you away from using a portal; if anything my recommendation would be the opposite in most cases. It is simply designed to inject a bit of experience into your decision making.

 ## Links to developerWorks Artic

A6.1 developerWorks WebSphere Portal Zone: http://www.ibm.com/developerworks/websphere/zones/portal/

A6.2 Portlet Development Workbook, Tim Hanis: http://www.ibm.com/developerworks/websphere/library/techarticles/0608_hanis/0608_hanis.html

References

Lynn, Bernal, Blinstrubas, Memon, Marston, Hanis, Ramamoorthy, and Hepper. (May 2007). *Programming Portlets, From JSR 168 to IBM WebSphere Portal Extensions*. IBM Press.

Chapter 7

SOA and Web Services

A7.1

S OA or service-oriented architecture has been one of the growing trends in the information technology realm over the last few years. Support for this approach has been on the rise, partly due to industry and vendor marketing hype, but also because IT organizations are looking for concrete solutions to manage their growing infrastructure and to be able to respond to the changing business demand. According to Kostas, (Kostas et al., 2007) service orientation has been touted as one of the most important technologies for designing, implementing, and deploying large-scale service provision software systems.

But what is SOA really, and why is it having such an influence on how we are architecting systems today? This chapter offers some discussion around that question and provides some basics around implementing web services within your architecture.

Pinning Down SOA

Arriving at a concrete definition of SOA can be somewhat difficult. The Open Group provides a robust and consumable definition of SOA (Group, 2006) as follows.

> Service-oriented architecture (SOA) is an architectural style that supports service orientation. Service orientation is a way of thinking in terms of services and service-based development and the outcomes of services. A service
>
> - Is a logical representation of a repeatable business activity that has a specified outcome (for example, checking customer credit, providing weather data, or consolidating drilling reports)
>
> - Is self-contained

- May be composed of other services

- Is a "black box" to consumers of the service

An architectural style is the combination of distinctive features in which architecture is performed or expressed.

The SOA architectural style has the following distinctive features:

- It is based on the design of the services—which mirror real-world business activities—comprising the enterprise (or inter-enterprise) business processes.

- Service representation utilizes business descriptions to provide context (that is, business process, goal, rule, policy, service interface, and service component) and implements services using service orchestration.

- It places unique requirements on the infrastructure—it is recommended that implementations use open standards to realize interoperability and location transparency.

- Implementations are environment-specific—they are constrained or enabled by context and must be described within that context.

- It requires strong governance of service representation and implementation.

- It requires a "litmus test," which determines a "good" service.

This definition is a bit long but it helps to define the concepts around a service. Going forward with some of the points provided, a service is a self-contained consumable resource. Often when we talk about SOA and services we think about web services. One important point that has been made abundantly clear over the last few years is the idea of separating the concept of a SOA from the actual technology used in the implementation; that is, web services. While a web service and SOA seemingly go hand-in-hand, one does not always imply the other. One can embark upon an SOA strategy using technologies other than web services, and conversely, implementing web services within your organization does not mean that you are embracing a service-oriented strategy.

As Brenda Michelson states (Mamdouh et al., 2007), "Service-oriented architecture is much broader than the technology underpinnings that often describe it. Service-oriented architecture provides a means to express business activities as modular, configurable and composable software services." This idea is important because it allows organizations to design a robust enterprise architecture that incorporates a number of implementation technologies, although standardization can also be an important factor. Web services definitely have a place within most infrastructures, providing a platform for interoperability between heterogeneous applications, but limitations also exist, depending upon the functional requirements of the applications being designed.

How to Implement SOA

Implementation patterns for SOA cross a wide range of technologies again based on existing systems and end requirements. Enterprise Service Bus is one such pattern that allows for the integration of new and existing systems using JMS, RMI, or of course, web services, but also provides for heterogeneous integration with translation, mediation, and other capabilities that are required in complex environments. Providing on-the-fly interoperability plays a big role in SOA and web services alone cannot fill that gap.

Service Modeling

Most SOA experts will tell you that building a service model is one of the first steps that is necessary. The need for a cohesive information model behind your collection of services is important because it allows services to be built intelligently within the organization. Simply wrapping data sources as services can result in a cumbersome approach that is just as ugly as the current point-to-point integration approach.

In addition to a specific set of models, a roadmap for implementing SOA within your organization is required. IBM provides roadmaps and best practices around specific industries and approaches and is available to any organization. Currently roadmaps are available for banking, healthcare, insurance, telecommunication, retail, and industrial organizations. These roadmaps enable your organization to undertake an SOA approach at a pace that your team can afford, allowing you to get the most benefit from SOA within your enterprise.

Modeling your business and understanding the benefits and impact from each service deployed within the organization can help provide a cost-benefit analysis of services and when and where they should be deployed.

Services as Business Functions

As a segue from service modeling, one important question that often gets raised is "what types of services should I build?" As Luciano and Feng state (Luciano and Feng, 2007) in their paper on service data objects, "These services [SOA] will offer business functionality as a unit or as a whole. These services will access data from different data source types and potentially need to aggregate data from different data source types with different data formats. In this type of environment, handling of different forms of data poses a big challenge for application developers, and the challenge increases in size when you consider the broad diversity of programming models in use."

With this in mind extending the technology beyond just the use of web services has been a major goal of many vendors. Message Queue and Enterprise Service Bus technology are examples of growing trends in SOA, as well as the use of additional technologies to help take advantage of SOA implementations within the enterprise. Business process management and process services are additional technology advancements that are becoming increasingly useful as organizations continue to embrace SOA.

Other Types of Services

The concept of application and infrastructure type services is also continuing to grow within many IT shops. These utility types of services are perhaps even more important in some ways than business services, because they get used by all or many different applications. The idea of managing or retrieving a user profile comes to mind as a reusable IT services that can be made available across multiple applications within the enterprise. Often a user profile can be considered a standard business function or an extension of Customer Data. However, user profile information can come from different sources, so it may be a unique service that gets aggregated into the composite Customer Data service, or it may be used independently as some type of authentication or authorization service.

Managing Service Data Elements

Two seemingly minor advancements that will have a big impact on managing service data elements are the use of Service Data Objects (SDO) and the concept of a Service Component Architecture (SCA). Working together these technologies will further allow the abstraction of unique sources and provide for increased interoperability in areas other than web services. With the release of SDO specification version 1 in early 2007 by the OSOA (OSOA, 2007), application server vendors are starting to provide technical previews and build this functionality into their products. Think of SDOs as data or value objects on steroids, providing a robust API that allows you to combine, share, and update from multiple heterogeneous data sources.

You can think of SCA as a service layer abstraction that allows you to build services using a number of technologies and within any tier of your infrastructure, and then expose those services using a variety of communication protocols.

A Commitment from the Business

Governance and management of services play a big role in SOA. Without a strong commitment from IT management, and from the business owners, the benefit of SOA cannot be realized effectively. Development, evolution, and maintenance of SOA-based systems demands rethinking traditional roles for performing these activities (Mira, Grace, and Dennis, 2007). Some of the key factors that play into this effort include ensuring that everyone who is involved understands the investment required to embrace an SOA strategy. Additionally there are many technical issues, like scaling services as demand increases, locating existing services, and service maintenance, as new requirements are put into place. Exiting roles change when in the course of an SOA transition, traditional silo'ed applications no longer exist. A silo'ed application is one that exists by itself and cannot interoperate with other applications. New applications are being composed out of many new and existing services, and all service owners are involved and are responsible for the success of these new applications. Conversely, when an application fails, some amount of advanced detective work is necessary to understand whether the cause lies within the application itself, or is because of some underlying service that does not have the necessary service-level agreements in place to keep up with performance requirements (Liam, Paulo, and Len, 2007).

New approaches for managing these problems are being proposed such as a stakeholder-driven service lifecycle model (Qing and Patricia, 2007), where stakeholder roles such as service provider and service consumer gain new responsibilities and commitments to the organization.

The business is also finding new responsibility for defining services that will drive the organization. Business Process Management, or BPM, is gaining new ground in determining which processes can help to drive the business and help maintain a competitive edge by using Business Process Modeling to analyze business processes (Bala, Kaori, Makoto, Akio, and Jay, 2006) and drive process transformation across the business.

One fact that everyone—vendors, academics, and IT shops—can agree on is that SOA is not easy. The benefits appear to be high. Increasing service granularity and improving reuse can allow the business to respond more quickly to changing business demand (Joseph, 2006). But the cost of achieving the benefits of SOA is not trivial when trying to build a flexible and scalable set of services across a large organization. Many organizations have adopted a strategy of applying SOA in stages across many projects and years in an attempt to manage investment and realize appropriate value. A green field or clean slate approach to designing a new application is simply not feasible for any organization that has been around for any length of time and that has existing legacy applications.

Things to Consider about Web Services

Web services, or most types of services, offer several great advantages, two of which are interoperability and distribution. Interoperability allows systems and applications to work together in ways that they never were able to before. Organizational IT departments are filled with a mish-mash of legacy systems that were never designed to work with other systems. In some cases, legacy could mean a system that is only a few years old and still cannot be used outside of its own world. But, if we can expose those systems through some standard service protocols then we can begin to see how applications can work together, or parts of a legacy system can be consumed and used by the business in new ways. The power can be intoxicating. Distribution of web services can be more of a concern when considering performance, which is discussed in detail in Chapter 8, "Caching and Performance."

But what are the disadvantages of this type of approach? Are there really any? Well, not in the sense that there really is a disadvantage, but there are risks that can occur if you jump headlong without checking the waters for hidden boulders. Let's take a look at a few potential boulders.

Performance

Performance is a big issue, and one that worries me the most. There are two main components to this concern:

- **Distribution:** Distribution of services raises several questions. Latency is one aspect, but also how services will be used. How course grained are the services to be defined? Will you have to make several calls to retrieve the data that you need, how responsive are the services designed, and over what speed will the network calls be provided? There are many questions to be answered in the design phase of the service project.

- **Dependency:** We now have applications that are dependent upon other applications. When a problem occurs, the end user–facing application is the one that will get blamed. I have learned this firsthand working in the portal space with IBM WebSphere Portal.

Just these two factors alone can work against you. Combine them with the fact that composite services are dependent upon other services within the enterprise or legacy back-end systems, and you can see that problems can occur that are very difficult to recover from without redesigning the application.

Standardization

Standards are slowly converging into some generally recognized approaches, but they are still slow in coming and there are still gaps to be filled. Even with sets of industry standards available, you still have battles to fight within your own organization. Microsoft, IBM, Sun, and other vendors all have their own agenda in getting you to adopt their standard approach. You might think that web services are all about integration so it shouldn't matter, but publishing a service with one standard or technology and trying to consume or use that service with a different standard can sometimes cause problems. Usually you can overcome these issues, but the goal is to streamline the development approach, not make it harder.

Web Service Interoperability (WS-I) is an important idea that has been established across the industry. The WS-I organization at http://www.ws-i.org/ is designed to confirm and publish the best practices for web service interoperability across platforms, operating systems, and languages.

Manageability

Managing and governance over a service or set of services is probably the biggest issue of all. Once the simplest service is put in place within the enterprise the trouble may start. Other applications begin to consume and depend upon that service. Any change can now break these dependencies, wreaking havoc across the enterprise.

Maybe the result wouldn't be that drastic, but those dependencies will exist. And the owners of each part of the application may be different. Some of the questions that need to be asked around this aspect include

- What services are available within the enterprise?
- Who is using which services and what are their SLA requirements?
- What versions exist for different services, and what is the maintenance schedule?

Obviously, this discussion barely scratches the surface of the this topic, but you can see that as services and their dependencies grow, then the effort and investement needed to manage those services needs to keep up with this growth. Standards are currently lacking in this area, but IBM is providing some leadership with best practices and products to help fill the gap. WebSphere Registry and Repository is a complete system for managing and versioning services within an organization.

Web Services Feature Pack for WAS

As of this writing, IBM has implemented the Java API for XML Web Services (JAX-WS) programming model in the form of a Web Services Feature Pack for WebSphere 6.1. The feature pack takes an open standards approach toward building web services and includes the following standards:

- Web Services Reliable Messaging (WS-RM)
- Web Services Addressing (WS-Addressing)
- Java API for XML Web Services (JAX-WS 2.0)
- Java Architecture for XML Binding (JAXB 2.0)
- SOAP Message Transmission Optimization Mechanism (MTOM)
- SOAP 1.2
- SOAP with Attachments API for Java (SAAJ 1.3)

This model allows developers to create web services using JAX-WS annotations. Additional tooling, shown in Figure 7.1, helps with implementation and is also available within the latest Rational Application Developer (RAD) versions.

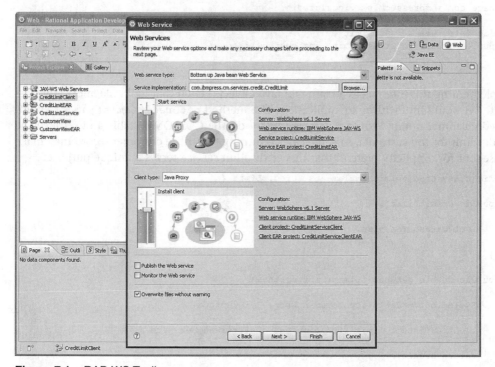

Figure 7.1   RAD WS Tooling

The feature pack also supports the Java Architecture for XML Binding 2.0 (JAXB) specification. This binding replaces the WS-RPC binding scheme.

Annotations are a major attraction of this feature pack and allow you to build web services as easily as you built EJBs in Chapter 3, "Persistence Matters."

Credit Limit Service

Walking through a simple example will illustrate how easy implementing a simple web service can be using the Web Service Feature Pack. Keep in mind that this example is kept simple and does not take into account any security or exception handling that would definitely be necessary in any enterprise service. The example is a simple web service that provides the credit limit for any given customer. This task could be realistic in the sense that credit limits would be stored or calculated separately from other customer data. Because this information is sensitive, access may be limited to specific sets of users within the organization.

Start by defining a simple interface that outlines the service function. This interface defines one method, getCreditLimit(), which is in line with the goal of keeping things as simple as possible for examples. All of the sample code discussed within this book is listed in Appendix B, "Running the Examples," along with information on where to download the samples.

```
package com.ibmpress.cm.services.credit;

public interface ICreditLimit {
   public double getCreditLimit( int custnum);


}
```

Implementing this interface is a Plain Old Java Object (POJO) that looks like most any class that you would find within an application. The method getCreditLimit() uses the provided customer number to do a database query on the CUSTOMER table and retrieve the credit limit for the customer. In some cases returning the entire customer record may make sense, but for simplicity pretend that this credit limit service serves a unique purpose.

```
public class CreditLimit implements ICreditLimit {

   public CreditLimit() {

      ...get datasource here.

   }

   public double getCreditLimit( int custnum) {

      System.out.println("customer number: " + custnum);

      ...look up credit limit with provided customer number here

      return result;     }
}
```

So far you have seen nothing new, but now you can create a web service using JAX-WS and some custom annotations. By creating a wrapper class with the annotations the application server will create a dynamic WSDL and the bindings needed to call the class when the web service is accessed. Figure 7.2 shows the class diagram of the credit limit service.

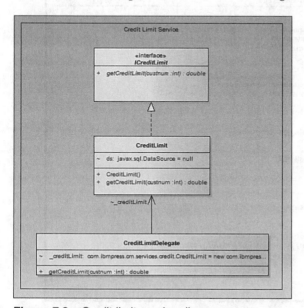

Figure 7.2   Credit limit service diagram

The wrapper class, called `CreditLimitDelegate()`, creates an instance of the actual class and provides a wrapper to the methods within that class.

```
package com.ibmpress.cm.services.credit;

@javax.jws.WebService
(targetNamespace="http://credit.services.cm.ibmpress.com/",
serviceName="CreditLimitService", portName="CreditLimitPort")
public class CreditLimitDelegate{

    com.ibmpress.cm.services.credit.CreditLimit _creditLimit = new
com.ibmpress.cm.services.credit.CreditLimit();

    public double getCreditLimit(int custnum) {
    return _creditLimit.getCreditLimit(custnum);
}
```

The first annotation you will notice is the `@WebService` annotation. It identifies this class as a web service. Because the WSDL is created dynamically from this class, this annotation is all that is needed. Once the code is deployed, you can browse to view the WDSL that has been defined via the annoations. Browsing to http://localhost:9081/CreditLimitService/CreditLimitService/creditlimitservice.wsdl shows the results in Figure 7.3.

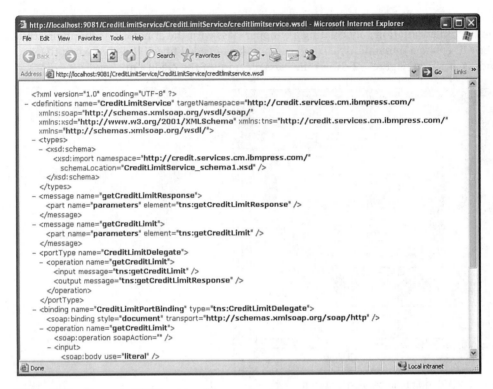

Figure 7.3 Dynamic WSDL generation

This example is, of course, the simplest implementation of a web service using JAX-WS, where the service was created via a bottom-up scenario. This means that the Java object was created first, and then the web service was created from that definition. In many cases your service will need to adhere to a specific type of WSDL. In these cases a top-down approach will probably be desired by defining the WSDL first and then creating the Java object stubs to fill with the required business logic.

Testing the Service

Rational Application Developer (RAD) tools for the Web Service Feature Pack allows the generation of a test client that you can use to test the created web service. This full-featured client, shown in Figure 7.4, is eerily reminiscent of the Web Services Universal Test Client that also comes with RAD.

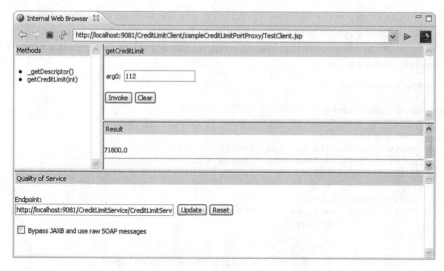

Figure 7.4   Web service test application

Nevertheless this application generates all the client code that will be necessary to create your own application. Ignoring all the JSPs that make up most of the user interface, two parts are the core of the application. The `CreditLimitPortProxy` class can be used to call the web service from your own application. Figure 7.5 shows the web service client code that is generated by the wizard.

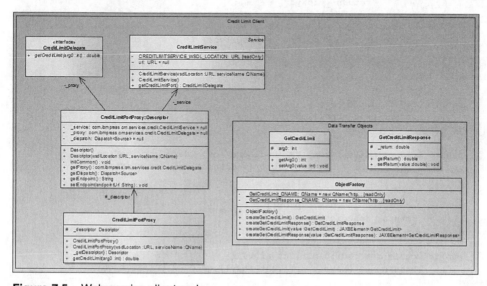

Figure 7.5   Web service client code

The `CreditLimitPortProxy` is the entry way into accessing the web service. This class has an inner class called a `Descriptor` that allows the dispatch information to be encapsulated into a member of the proxy class. This nice use of an inner class helps organize much of the mess that web services seem to raise.

```java
public class CreditLimitPortProxy{

protected Descriptor _descriptor;

    public class Descriptor {
            private CreditLimitService _service = null;
            private CreditLimitDelegate _proxy = null;
            private Dispatch<Source> _dispatch = null;

            public Descriptor() {
                    _service = new CreditLimitService();
                    initCommon();
            }

            public Descriptor(URL wsdlLocation, QName serviceName) {
                    _service = new CreditLimitService(wsdlLocation,
                    serviceName);
                    initCommon();
            }

            private void initCommon() {
                    _proxy = _service.getCreditLimitPort();
            }

            public CreditLimitDelegate getProxy() {
                    return _proxy;
            }

            public Dispatch<Source> getDispatch() {
                    …
            }
    }

    public CreditLimitPortProxy() {
            _descriptor = new Descriptor();
    }

    public CreditLimitPortProxy(URL wsdlLocation, QName serviceName) {
            _descriptor = new Descriptor(wsdlLocation, serviceName);
    }

    public Descriptor _getDescriptor() {
            return _descriptor;
    }

    public double getCreditLimit(int arg0) {
            return _getDescriptor().getProxy().getCreditLimit(arg0);
    }

}
```

At the bottom of the proxy class is the method that you are after, which wraps the web service method call into a simple local function. Additionally the data transfer objects, GetCreditLimit and GetCreditLimitResponse, are generated to be used by JAXB. As you may remember JAXB defined a Java-to-XML translation protocol, which is used in this sample instead of a standard SOAP message protocol.

The CreditLimitDelegate interface defines the @WebService and @WebMethod information in place of a WSDL file in the local client. These annotations allow the JAX-WS libraries to generate a dynamic WSDL to access the remote service.

```
package com.ibmpress.cm.services.credit;

import javax.jws.WebMethod;
import javax.jws.WebParam;
import javax.jws.WebResult;
import javax.jws.WebService;
import javax.xml.ws.RequestWrapper;
import javax.xml.ws.ResponseWrapper;

@WebService(name = "CreditLimitDelegate", targetNamespace =
"http://credit.services.cm.ibmpress.com/")
public interface CreditLimitDelegate {


@WebMethod
@WebResult(targetNamespace = "")
@RequestWrapper(localName = "getCreditLimit", targetNamespace =
"http://credit.services.cm.ibmpress.com/", className =
"com.ibmpress.cm.services.credit.GetCreditLimit")
@ResponseWrapper(localName = "getCreditLimitResponse", targetNamespace =
"http://credit.services.cm.ibmpress.com/", className =
"com.ibmpress.cm.services.credit.GetCreditLimitResponse")
public double getCreditLimit(
        @WebParam(name = "arg0", targetNamespace = "")int arg0);

}
```

Building a New Client Application

You can now use the generated web service client code in any application or local service layer to access this web service. A new web application, shown in Figure 7.6, can be developed that allows a user to interact more comfortably with the credit limit service.

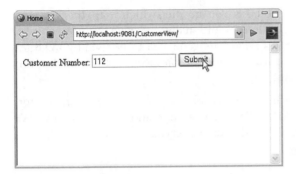

Figure 7.6 Service client

By posting the entered customer number to a servlet, the generated proxy can be instantiated to serve as an interface for this application.

```
protected void doGet(HttpServletRequest request, HttpServletResponse response)
throws ServletException, IOException {

    PrintWriter out = response.getWriter();

    Short  customerid = Short.valueOf(request.getParameter("customerid"));

    out.println("Customer ID: " + customerid);

    out.println("<br><br>getting proxy.<br><br>");
    CreditLimitPortProxy myProxy = new CreditLimitPortProxy();

    out.println("Credit Limit: " + myProxy.getCreditLimit(customerid));

}
```

This servlet uses the proxy to access the service with very little code written on our part
except to instantiate the proxy and use the available methods. Figure 7.7 illustrates the outcome of the client application.

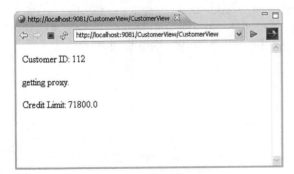

Figure 7.7 Access the web service

You can easily imagine the next steps of moving this proxy to a utility library or local service layer that can proxy the service, and perhaps adding additional information to the query. For example, instead of retrieving just the credit limit, you could have the local customer lookup retrieve additional customer information and return a data object containing all the information about that customer.

Figure 7.8 shows just this case, where the proxy has been moved to a business layer that processes a number of lookups and then provides an aggregated view of the customer information.

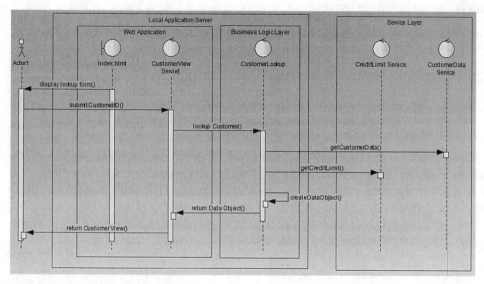

Figure 7.8   Service integration

Simple REST-Based Services

Recently there has been a trend in another direction when building web services. Representational State Transfer or REST has seen a surge in popularity for building quick and simple services, especially for work with the presentation layer. Put another way, you can think of REST as a protocol for transferring the representation of some resources current state, either what it currently is, or by modifying the state to what you need it to be by updating or perhaps deleting the resource.

REST builds off of those aspects of the World Wide Web that have made it so popular—using a simple HTTP protocol and generic interfaces to access available resources. These interfaces follow the current HTTP approach using GET, POST, PUT, and DELETE. Using the HTTP protocol, responses are streamed directly in XML rather than using SOAP to wrap the request/response cycle.

REST-based services, in conjunction with Ajax or Asynchronous Java with XML, have become very popular because you can update the display of a page without having to do a full page refresh on the server. Just specific sections of the page can be updated either in real time or when the user requests an update.

Building a REST service using the servlet interface can be a simple exercise. Note that you are not using any web service tooling here; it is just a simple output of basic XML. The example servlet works like any other servlet but the output will not be HTML.

```
public class CurrentCreditLimit extends javax.servlet.http.HttpServlet
implements javax.servlet.Servlet {

static final long serialVersionUID = 1L;
javax.sql.DataSource ds = null;

public CurrentCreditLimit() {

    super();
    ...setup data source

}
```

The doGet() method has been implemented to return the current representation state of a customer's credit limit. The servlet output is a simple XML stream for use by any client. Also present is a helper method that does the credit limit lookup. The implementation of this aspect is not important for this example.

```
protected void doGet(HttpServletRequest request, HttpServletResponse
response) throws ServletException, IOException {

    PrintWriter out = response.getWriter();
    response.setContentType("text/plain");

    int custnum = Short.valueOf(request.getParameter("customerid"));
    System.out.println("customer number: " + custnum);

    out.println("<customer>");
    out.println("<customerid>" + custnum + "</customerid>");
    out.println("<creditlimit>" + getCreditLimit(custnum) +
"</creditlimit>");
    out.println("</customer>");

}


private String getCreditLimit(int custid){

    ...Lookup credit limit for customer

}
```

Finally, some additional servlet methods are included that map directly to the generic interfaces that the REST architecture suggests you should follow such as the put method. These methods have not been implemented in this example.

```
protected void doPost(HttpServletRequest request, HttpServletResponse
response) throws ServletException, IOException {

        ...modify resource

}

protected void doPut(HttpServletRequest request, HttpServletResponse response) throws
ServletException, IOException {

        super.doPut(request, response);
        ...create resource

}



protected void doDelete(HttpServletRequest request, HttpServletResponse response)
throws ServletException, IOException {

        super.doDelete(request, response);
        ...delete resource

}
```

As mentioned, there is no defined WSDL for these types of services. This can be both good and bad. Without some type of service definition it is hard for the client to know how to use the service and what the response will look like.

Client Interaction with REST

Much of the focus in the industry today is to use REST within the presentation layer, but this does not necessarily have to be the case. REST services can be placed anywhere within the enterprise for consumption by other clients. One could easily use some java.net code to create a URL and interact with a REST service, but these services do lend themselves well to presentation layer functionality because of the commonality with web-based protocols. Ajax has played nicely into that collaboration with the use of asynchronous data calls to services. The simple client shown in Figure 7.9 illustrates how you might consume a REST service within your web page.

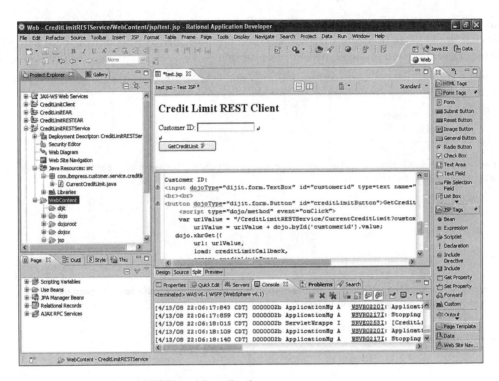

Figure 7.9   Building a REST-based application

Much of the page is routine Ajax. The function `creditLimitCallback()`can be used to parse and use the XML that is returned from the service. This function will be passed the data from a good response to the service.

```
<%@ page language="java" contentType="text/html; charset=ISO-8859-1"
pageEncoding="ISO-8859-1"%>
<!DOCTYPE html PUBLIC "-//W3C//DTD HTML 4.01 Transitional//EN"
"http://www.w3.org/TR/html4/loose.dtd">

<html>
<head>
<meta http-equiv="Content-Type" content="text/html; charset=ISO-8859-1">
<title>Test JSP</title>

<style type="text/css">
   @import "dojoroot/dijit/themes/soria/soria.css"
   @import "dojoroot/dojo/resources/dojo.css"
</style>

<script type="text/javascript" src="dojoroot/dojo/dojo.js"
djConfig="parseOnLoad: true"></script>
```

```
<script type="text/javascript">

  dojo.require("dijit.form.TextBox");
  dojo.require("dijit.form.Button");

  function creditLimitCallback(data,ioArgs) {
     alert(data);
  }
  function creditLimitError(data, ioArgs) {
     alert('Error when retrieving data from the server!');
  }

</script>

</head>
```

The body of the page has two form elements: a textbox and a button. In the button is an embedded script that creates a URL to the service, adding the customer ID that should be entered into the text box. This script then performs an xhrGet command to send the request to the servlet and pass the returned data to the creditLimitCallback() function that was shown earlier.

```
<body>
<h2>Credit Limit REST Client</h2>

Customer ID:
<input dojoType="dijit.form.TextBox" id="customerid" type=text name="customerid"/>
<br><br>


<button dojoType="dijit.form.Button" id="creditLimitButton">GetCreditLimit
    <script type="dojo/method" event="onClick">
    var urlValue = "/CreditLimitRESTService/CurrentCreditLimit?customerid=";
        urlValue = urlValue + dojo.byId('customerid').value;
    dojo.xhrGet({
        url: urlValue,
        load: creditLimitCallback,
        error: creditLimitError
    });
    </script>
</button>

</body>
</html>
```

Figure 7.10 shows the page in action. The user should type in a customer ID in the text box and click the button; the script will make a GET request to the service with the customer ID parameter. The resultant XML is then shown in an alert box.

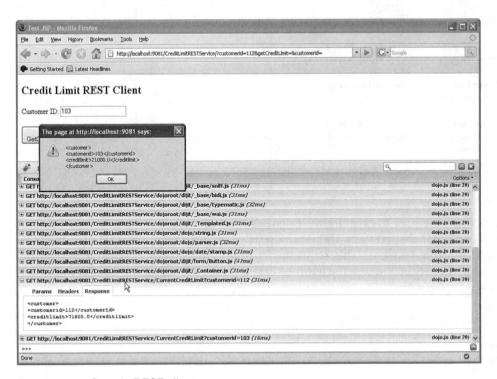

Figure 7.10   Sample REST client

This simple example hopefully enables you to see how you can incorporate REST services into your application. As with most things, REST and Ajax are tools to help you deliver the best value to your customer and end user. Used in this way, the approach actually goes against the SOA principle of reuse. Consider that not every feature within your application has to be Ajax enabled, as that may be considered a poor use of business dollars. But do not let that dissuade you from understanding the principles and approach where REST may add good value to your application.

Conclusion

You may have noticed that there was no manual WSDL building within this chapter. That is actually not common in SOA and web service work. The Web Service Definition Language is the contract that your services need to abide by, and hence are pretty important. But they are also ugly and complicated to build, so anytime you can use tooling to do the dirty work you should try to take that route. Not everyone in an organization is going to be an expert at using a WSDL document so you should make it as easy as possible to create and consume web services across the enterprise. With the new WSDL 2.0 specification these tasks are getting easier, but as requirements increase, things also tend to get more complicated.

Links to developerWorks Articles

A7.1 developerWorks SOA and Web Services Zone, http://www.ibm.com/developer-works/webservices

A7.2 Developing Web services for WebSphere using JAX-WS Annotations, Jeff Barrett, Dustin Amrhein, Bruce Tiffany, http://www.ibm.com/developerworks/websphere/library/techarticles/0711_tiffany/0711_tiffany.html

References

Bala, R., Kaori, F., Makoto, K., Akio, K., and Jay, B. (2006). *Business process transformation patterns & the business process transformation wizard.* Paper presented at the Proceedings of the 38th Conference on Winter simulation. Retrieved October 2, 2007, from http://delivery.acm.org.dml.regis.edu/10.1145/1220000/1218232/p636-ramachandran.pdf?key1=1218232&key2=5810404911&coll=ACM&dl=ACM&CFID=41408235&CFTO-KEN=96264195

Group, Open Group (2006, June 8, 2006). Service Oriented Architecture (SOA). Retrieved October 10, 2007, from http://www.opengroup.org/projects/soa/doc.tpl?gdid=10632.

Joseph, B. (2006). Service-oriented architecture (SOA): a new paradigm to implement dynamic e-business solutions. *Ubiquity, 7*(30), 1-1.

Kostas, K., Grace, A. L., Dennis, B. S., Marin, L., Hausi, M., Stefan, S., et al. (2007). *The Landscape of Service-Oriented Systems: A Research Perspective.* Paper presented at the Proceedings of the International Workshop on Systems Development in SOA Environments. Retrieved October 2, 2007, from http://portal.acm.org.dml.regis.edu/citation.cfm?id=1270298&coll=ACM&dl=ACM&CFID=41408235&CFTOKEN=96264195#

Liam, O. B., Paulo, M., and Len, B. (2007). *Quality Attributes for Service-Oriented Architectures.* Paper presented at the Proceedings of the International Workshop on Systems Development in SOA Environments. Retrieved October 2, 2007, from http://portal.acm. org.dml.regis.edu/citation.cfm?id=1270300&coll=ACM&dl=ACM&CFID=41408235&CFTO-KEN=96264195#.

Luciano, R., and Feng, R. (2007). *Handling heterogeneous data sources in a SOA environment with service data objects (SDO).* Paper presented at the Proceedings of the 2007 ACM SIGMOD international conference on Management of data. Retrieved October 2, 2007, from http://doi.acm.org/10.1145/1247480.1247582.

Mamdouh, H. I., Kerrie, H., Nicolai, M. J., Brenda, M., Dave, T., and John, D. (2007). *The future of SOA: what worked, what didn't, and where is it going from here?* Paper presented at the Companion to the 22nd ACM SIGPLAN conference on Object-Oriented Programming Systems and Applications Companion. Retrieved October 2, 2007, from http://portal.acm.org.dml.regis.edu/citation.cfm?id=1297975&coll=ACM&dl=ACM&CFID=41408235&CFTO-KEN=96264195#

Mira, K.-M., Grace, A. L., and Dennis, B. S. (2007). *A Framework for Roles for Development, Evolution and Maintenance of SOA-Based Systems*. Paper presented at the Proceedings of the International Workshop on Systems Development in SOA Environments. Retrieved October 2, 2007, from http://delivery.acm.org.dml.regis.edu/10.1145/1280000/1270304/29600007. pdf?key1=1270304&key2=2695304911&coll=ACM&dl=ACM&CFID=41408235&CFTOKEN =96264195

OSOA (2007). Service Component Architecture Specification – Assembly Model V1.00, Open Service Oriented Architecture (OSOA). Available from http://www.osoa.org/display/Main/ Service+Component+Architecture+Specifications.

Qing, G., and Patricia, L. (2007). *A stakeholder-driven service life cycle model for SOA*. Paper presented at the 2nd International Workshop on Service Oriented Software Engineering: in conjunction with the 6th ESEC/FSE joint meeting. Retrieved October 2, 2007, from http://portal.acm.org.dml.regis.edu/citation.cfm?id=1294930&coll=ACM&dl=ACM&CFID= 41408235&CFTOKEN=96264195#.

Chapter 8

Caching and Performance

Performance problems are probably one of the biggest issues that applications on the Web face today. Actually, the problems that can occur are not confined solely to the Web, but that is where the focus lies for this book. This chapter outlines some of the steps you can take to incorporate good performance characteristics into your application early in the development lifecycle. Provided in this chapter are discussion points, options, and some examples on how to leverage the caching infrastructure provided by the WebSphere Application Server product line. Specifically this chapter presents two basic examples:

- Using the distributed map to save any custom Java objects
- Using servlet/JSP fragment caching to cache the HTML output of a servlet directly

Designing for Performance

The performance of your application can be looked at in several ways. The first part of any development cycle is to try to optimize your code so that it performs as well as possible. There are a lot of performance factors to take in to consideration, including some of the following:

- The use of string buffers versus string concatenation
- Creating objects that are never used within the code
- Lack of common logging or exception handling
- Overloading back-end resources
- Use of third-party libraries
- Minimizing memory usage, such as session information

The list can get pretty long and more information on these topics is available on the Web. Some of these topics are discussed in detail within this book, and many of these types of issues should come up within your code review process.

In deep code analysis, you can review code path length to ensure that you are optimizing the execution of your code. This helps ensure you are not performing unnecessary actions or using poorly performing features of the language. Often you might not be worried about a few unnecessary steps, but over time they can build up to take up a large chunk of your system resources. However, these types of issues are commonly not defined as part of the architecture of the system.

Other areas of concern are resources, third-party applications, and application frameworks that surround your own application. These might be items like databases, services, the operating system in use, or the application server itself in use. Tuning of these applications and environments is important to ensure that you are not handicapping the application before you even really get started. Chapter 2, "Setting a Standard," which focuses on standards within the development cycle, offers suggestions for getting well-formed and hopefully performing code from your development team.

Architecture Concerns

Often you hear the statement that performance should be considered early in the design/development cycle. But actually architecting for performance can be challenging. Consider how distributed your architecture actually will be during the design cycle. Where will different components and layers sit within the infrastructure? How can you minimize requests to back-end systems such as databases or business logic components? Developers continue to learn new techniques, and ongoing enforcement of their adherences to best practices is necessary to ensure the same issue does not crop up more than once within a project or across the organization.

More than likely you will have user registries involved in the authentication and authorization of users within the application—how are those registries presented and accessed? LDAP protocol or perhaps a web service is used in many cases, but using a remote service during login can be quite expensive unless service-level agreements are in place with the providing service. Navigation and access control or authorization are also processes that sometimes require an external service.

Much broader issues need to be understood by the application architect when defining the application layers. Initial performance is a concern; that is, response time by a single user, but scalability is of perhaps a larger concern, because you do not want response time to go up as the user load increases.

Thinking about how your application or service will react under load is one of your main concerns. Should your application really make a database call for every request by every user? Can the database handle perhaps thousands of requests per minute, and how complex will the queries actually be? Remember that the database and other back-end services has to be able to scale with the application, so if your app suddenly becomes very popular will it overwhelm other systems that are not designed for this increased load?

Performance Terminology

When discussing performance it is always important that everyone uses and understands the same terms. Performance testing is a topic of great importance and unfortunately not something discussed in this chapter. But even without this detail we can agree on the proper terms. One of my favorite books on this topic is *Performance Analysis for Java Web Sites* (Joines, 2003). This book is a few years old but still very relevant to understanding the basic concepts of performance testing today.

You should have a general understanding of a few terms. I have taken these terms from my 2007 article in developerWorks (Bernal, 2007) for use here:

- **Load:** This is the amount of pressure against a Web site. This always makes me think of a water hose, either turned down to a trickle or turned all the way up to full blast. With Web sites, we talk about load in terms of concurrent users, which does not necessarily mean that every user is requesting a page at the exact same moment, which is a common misconception. It is better to think about load over time; for example, a number of users accessing the site within a specific time frame, perhaps over five minutes or per hour.
- **Response time:** This is the time it takes for the portal or site to respond to the request. This is really end-to-end time from the browser's perspective, and does not normally include time spent by the browser generating or displaying the page. Consider that in many applications response time generally will change (it will probably increase) as the load against the site increases, potentially increasing to the point where it is unacceptable to users. Response time is one measurement that gets a lot of attention, and tuning your portal to provide a consistent response time range with the expected volume of user load is your ultimate goal. Response time goals are chosen to follow industry standards; for example, a goal for the site might be to respond to 95% of page requests to respond within five seconds.
- **Throughput:** This is the rate at which a portal can respond to requests. Generally, you can think of this as either the hit rate or page rate of the system, with the page rate measurement being more consistent. Throughput, coupled with response time and a model of your users' activity, can help you determine how many users your system can handle (load) within a given timeframe. Throughput is often measured in relation to load, determining where the boundaries of the system might be as user load continues to grow.

These three main terms, working together, will help you understand how your portal might perform when you get to that phase in your development cycle.

Caching Considerations

Caching is the process of moving some resource that is needed closer to the location where you need it. Not a very scientific definition, I admit, but a cache doesn't always have to be about computer data. For example, you may keep a small cache of drinks in a mini-fridge within your home office, which saves you trips to the kitchen all the time. This is exactly the same type of performance-enhancing effect you want to achieve with your applications.

The goals of caching are simple. Achieve better performance, scalability, and availability of your applications by reducing the overall amount of data that is transferred or reducing round trips between your application and any data sources or other applications that provide data or information. Additionally, with interim (local) caching you can potentially reduce the amount of processing actually done within your application. This is similar to code path length reduction where you want to be as efficient as possible, but being able to do so is very heavily dependent upon the implementation. Coupled with this desire for efficiency is the need to ensure that security constraints are enforced.

Caching Design Options

A8.1

The best caching is useless if users have access to data that should not be permitted. In fact, this brings up an interesting point. If you have very high security or personalization requirements, then you may have to take the performance hit and simply ensure that your hardware and infrastructure is large enough to handle the expected load. When thinking about caching you have many design options to consider including

- **Staleness of cached data:** This includes the likelihood that the underlying data will change, leaving a cache that is useless because it is not up to date. What happens when the cache is updated on a single server? Will the changes need to be replicated on other servers, or is there an approach that will allow the caches to be flushed and rebuilt when data changes? The performance impact of replicating data can be a large one.
- **Cache loading policies:** Here we want to talk about **proactive** versus **reactive** loading. Can data be pre-cached at startup so that it can be readily available, or should you fetch it upon first use? Memory and timeout considerations help drive this discussion along with how expensive it really is to retrieve the data initially.
- **Size of the cache:** Caches should probably never be unbounded. There is just too much opportunity for a problem to occur without your knowing the maximum size or amount of memory that your cache can consume. What makes sense for your cache: 100 entries or 1,000? You can make this design decision early, and hopefully it will help you better understand the details of your application.
- **Cache key generation:** The cache key is used to store and retrieve the data within a cache. This key is unique for each cache entry. Cache keys are usually based on the user or the data itself. For example, a zip code or customer ID may be the cache key that is used. In complex scenarios the cache key may be a combination of factors such as [user role + geographical location + department code]. This type of approach allows a complex caching capability that can be shared across groups of users. You need to determine whether the value of this complex caching outweighs the cost of running the SQL query.
- **Expiration policies:** Data changes over time, so caching can cause problems if the data in the cache is not updated appropriately. This issue goes hand in hand with the staleness of the data as discussed previously. Time-based expiration is the most often-used type of policy where the cache simply clears an entry after a given amount of time. Notification-based expiration is also an option, where some type

of trigger allows you to clear the cache on demand. This approach may be good for data that does not change as often. For example, content-based repositories may only change a few times a week. Allowing for the ability to clear the cache on demand only when the content needs to be refreshed can be the right approach.

- **Types of caches:** Generically, you have two types of caches to think about: **memory resident caches** and **disk resident caches**. Memory resident is the most popular and generally provides the best performance. Again a consideration for any memory resident cache is the size of the cache and the size of each cache entry. Care should be taken with a disk resident cache policy. Writing to disk is generally expensive and may outweigh the benefit that you expect the cache to provide. If you need cached data to live beyond a server crash or restart then a disk resident approach can be a good option.

This list is not exhaustive but it should provide a good idea of the types of considerations you need to think about when designing your cache.

Sizing a Cache

Mentioned earlier is the idea that caches generally have a maximum size. That means there is a maximum number of entries that a cache can hold. So how do you determine this size? There is no set equation although I'm sure you could come up with some that are related to your environment. The problem is that the cache size should be driven partly by the amount of available memory within your system. Caches take up memory, so any tradeoff needs to be determined between the value of the cache and the amount of memory that it consumes.

Determining the size of each cache entry will make it easier to figure out the overall size of the cache. Weigh this figure against the total number of entries to be stored in the cache and whichever expiration policy needs to be put into place, to calculate some general memory consumption assumptions. The first problem is how to determine the size of the cache entry and whether the size will vary between each entry. Ways exist for analyzing the system heap to make this determination, but you can also build some `sizeof()` type of methods into your code, which can be turned on perhaps via a logging statement to gather the memory size of objects when necessary. Java 5 offers the possibility of providing instrumentations via agents to gather size data in a test mode scenario. When there is the possibility that the cache entry size is actually different between different cache entries, then you should calculate the average size to help determine the overall cache memory size. Additionally, the cache itself may provide some overhead, which you might need to consider. If you can determine the average size of each cache entry you might consider that number close enough unless you want to go digging through JVM heap dumps to calculate the total size with the most accuracy.

Additional caching tools are available, and the industry as a whole is catching up on the need for better tooling in this area. Of particular interest is the availability of viewing object cache instances within WebSphere Application Server. A preview product with this capability is available at http://www.ibm.com/developerworks/websphere/downloads/cache_monitor. html. Also for very large caches the Websphere Extended Deployment (XD) has advanced caching features for large-scale environments http://www-306.ibm.com/software/ webservers/appserv/extend/?S_TACT=105AGX10&S_CMP=LP.

When Not to Cache

Sometimes a cache is not the best approach. But you should consider these times as carefully as when thinking about when to cache. Putting a cache in place after the fact can be very difficult, especially when it is an object- or data-level cache. Caches at the front end of your application that cache HTTP data are easier to implement later in the development cycle, but these types of caches have limitations when content is very personalized across users or groups or users.

Think about not caching when building the cache key is very expensive, or when the data will expire within a very short time period, say, under a minute. In some cases even a five minute cache can help under an extreme user load and may not be noticed by your business sponsors or the end user. Expensive cache keys are those that take a lot of processing or getting data from the back end to create; for example, if you have to retrieve the current user's customer ID, office location, position, title, and/or current role within the organization. This is an example of how you might personalize the data that is being displayed. While having these kinds of requirements is perfectly acceptable for the business, accounting for the performance impact that this type of calculation will need on a large scale is also important.

In some cases the business sponsor will make it clear that it does not want some data cached. For example, in the retail industry the application may display information about product recalls. This type of information has to be immediately sent to the field for local stores to begin removing products from the shelves. Perhaps in this case a more complex framework can be built to provide the required performance without sacrificing the urgency needed.

In any case, when a decision is made not to cache, then any performance hit must be discussed and accounted for. Back-end systems need to be tested or scaled to handle the increased load. The main point is that you have to pay for performance, in one way or another.

User Session Caching

Generally, the session is not considered a cache, but it can be a convenient location to store user data. Early in the life of Java programming using session state was a common practice. Programmers who are familiar with .Net programming are also comfortable with using session and application state to store information for their users. Putting information in a user session that needs to be saved between user requests is a no-brainer; everyone who has been building web applications for any length of time has done this, probably without even thinking too much about it.

There is a tendency for things to get out of hand when easy solutions like this one are around. Pretty soon everything gets stored in the session within the application. This can lead to a couple of key problems, one of which is session bloat, where more memory is used per user than should be. This reduces the amount of available memory that would allow your application to handle additional users. Remember that a user session is stored in memory until it expires. This is usually some set time after the last request has been made. Because you don't know if a user is reading some information on the current page, filling out a form, or has actually closed the browser window, you need to keep session information in memory until a set time period when you can assume the user will not be coming back.

The general recommendation is to keep the session timeout as short as possible. Again, there are perfectly legitimate reasons for maintaining a long session timeout. There are cases where a user will open a browser window in the morning and leave it open all day; however, the infrastructure must account for the cost of leaving objects in memory for long periods.

When things get out of hand there always tends to be a whiplash effect where new rules are put in place. In this case the new base rule that emerged was *do not* use the session for data storage. In many cases and with proper guidance, not using the session at all is probably better than overflowing it with too much data. But with proper guidance the rule can be tempered to something that provides a useful function without becoming the black hole of overloaded data. You can use advanced strategies such as storing session data to disk, or using lightweight session data to restore active data when needed; however, you should use these strategies on a case-by-case basis.

Caching in WebSphere Application Server

WebSphere Application Server and many WebSphere products provide a lot of caching capability to leverage within your application. One of the ways that WAS provides this ability is through a service called the **dynamic cache**. Dynamic caching or **dynacache** as it is often called, contains a number of interfaces and services that allow you to cache data in different ways. Figure 8.1 illustrates in a very simple way some of the capability that is provided in the Dynamic Cache service.

A8.2

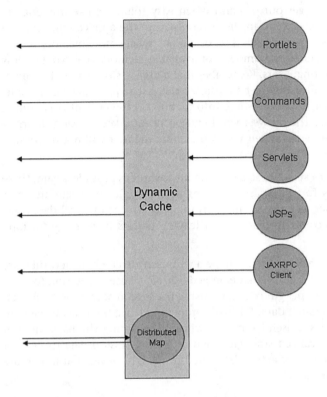

Figure 8.1   WebSphere dynamic caching

Dynacache provides the capability to cache the output of different objects within your application. For example, servlets and Java Server Pages often output HTML to the browser. Dynacache provides servlet/JSP fragment caching, which allows you to actually save the HTML fragments or the entire page, helping to reduce expensive calls to the same servlet over and over again. At the same time, dynacache also provides mechanisms for caching data objects that can be stored and retrieved locally instead of having to go back to the data source for the same information more than one time. Cacheable Command objects are another approach for data caching, where the CacheCommand interface can be implemented to provide a similar data caching ability. You can see in the diagram that other interfaces are available such as the capability to cache portlets or web service client results.

How does this capability fit together with your application? Figure 8.2 illustrates how you might use some of the capability within your web applications. Some data is cached natively or as objects, while other services cache the output of your application. The capabilities are usually mixed and matched to give you the best possible results depending upon the application requirements and your user base.

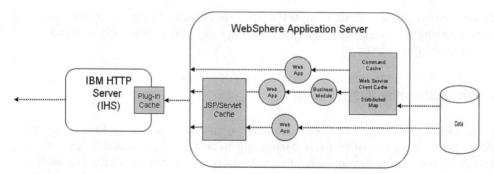

Figure 8.2   Where to cache

The ability to cache at several layers provides the best flexibility for an application. Figure 8.2 above does not illustrate every possible caching location. Additional opportunities exist for caching further out within the infrastructure. The general rule as stated at the beginning of this chapter is that the closer you can get to the end user with your caching the better off you will be in terms of performance. In Figure 8.2 several applications are sandwiched between different caching capabilities, something you might call back-end versus front-end caching. You can see that different applications take advantages of different capabilities, while some applications may not be able to use any of the features or services provided because of application requirements.

IBM HTTP Server and the Caching Plug-in

Static items are something that can cause a lot of churn within the application server. A server working hard to respond to requests for static items is that much less able to work on page requests to the system. Static items are just that: items that do not change very often, if at all. Images, style sheets (CSS), and script files such as Java script or JS files usually do not change on a day-to-day basis. These files specifically should be cached as close to the user as possible. Luckily, the browser does a lot of this work by caching static files between requests, but you still have to expect the initial hit from every new user as they request a page in your application.

In the early days of web programming developers generally tried to move static files to a different location, like perhaps out to the HTTP server itself where they would get served without ever bothering the application server for the request. This approach is fine, but it does put an additional burden on the developer to ensure that all URLs within the page access this external source. To help ease that burden and for those development teams who do not follow this approach, the WAS Web Server Plug-in using the ESI cache has been designed with some caching capability so that some types of files are cached automatically upon the initial request, and then subsequent requests are pulled from the cache and do not get routed back to the application server.

Although configuring and optimizing this cache will not usually save your Web site from performance problems, in some cases it can provide a substantial reduction in overall activity to the application server.

Using the Distributed Map

The distributed map (dMap) has become a very popular approach to caching data within WAS. It operates very similar to a HashMap might in Java, with the added benefit of being cluster aware if necessary. If you are familiar with using a Java collection such as a HashMap then you know how easy they are to use: You simply instantiate the object and start adding values. Using the dMap takes a little more foresight. You have to create an instance on the application server and then using JNDI you can get a handle to the correct Dmap instance that you need to use. Don't worry; you'll see how to do all this in the later example.

The one downside, if you are looking for one, is that there is no real security policy on the distributed map cache. That means that anyone can access the cache if he or she knows the name and look at data. This is generally not a problem within a controlled environment, but it may influence your decision.

Creating a New Distributed Map

Creating separate distributed map instances for different caching areas is a good idea. This approach allows you to separate where different data is cached and provides some opportunity for tuning caches independently based on the size of the cache and the data for each entry.

Object caching is something done internally to your code as opposed to the servlet/JSP caching that is provided to cache the HTML fragments that are output by your code. In this example you use the distributed map, which is an instance of an object cache, to cache internal data that you need to compute some value.

You can create a new object cache instance within the Integrated Solutions Console (admin console). Before creating a new instance you need to determine the scope of the instance. To do so:

1. In the scope drop-down box choose Cell scope for the instance.

2. To create a new instance navigate to **Resources, Cache instances, Object cache instances,** and click on the **New** button, as shown in Figure 8.3.

   To create a new orders instance enter the following values:
   Name: orders
   JNDI name: services/cache/orders
   Description: Dmap cache for orders servlet

3. You can leave the rest of the settings as shown in Figure 8.4 as the default. Enabling disk offload of the cache would not be recommended unless you were very sure of what you were doing. Click **OK** to continue. The object cache instance is created.

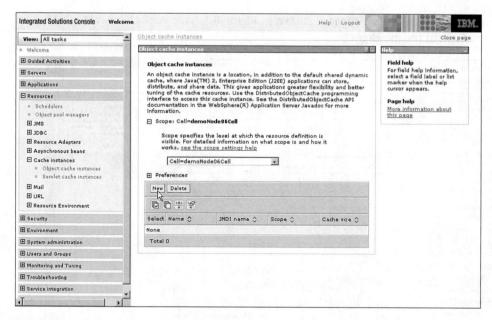

Figure 8.3   Create a new object cache instance

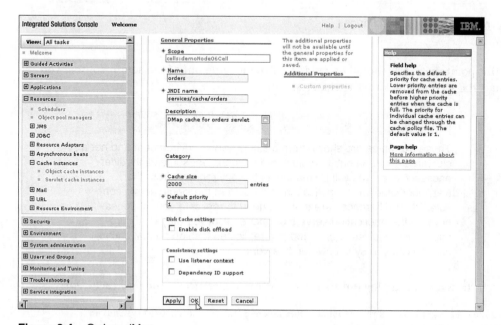

Figure 8.4   Orders dMap

4. On the screen that appears, shown in Figure 8.5, save your changes by clicking on
Save in the messages box.

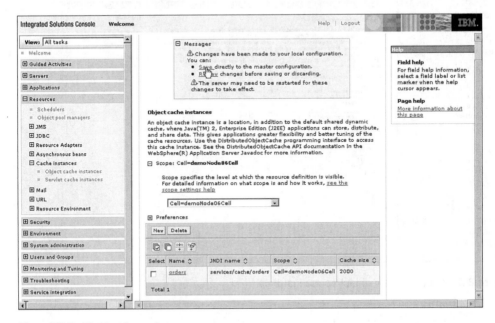

Figure 8.5 Saving your changes

At this point the server should be restarted. After logging out of the admin console you can
restart the server to pick up the changes.

> **NOTE**
>
> These examples are shown from a single server environment and not a
> clustered environment. In a clustered environment some slight differ-
> ences exist, as you will be managing the environment from the
> Network Deployment application and not from the single admin con-
> sole. Other differences are that you need to replicate your changes
> down to the application servers or nodes. Also, you may configure
> caches themselves to be setup in a replicated fashion so that cache
> changes stay in sync between hservers.

Watch the System.out log during the restart for a reference to the new cache entry.

```
[3/24/08 12:44:43:015 EDT] 0000000a ResourceMgrIm I   WSVR0049I: Binding
orders as services/cache/orders
```

Once the cache entry has been created successfully and you can see the entry being initialized in the logs, it is ready for use by your application.

Testing the Distributed Map

To test out the map I revised our old friend the ClassicModelsWeb application that was used in Chapter 2 with the EJB 3 example. To use this I have changed the interface slightly to allow you to actually input which order number you want to use. This allows you to request a specific order number and cache it as necessary. The algorithm to use is as follows:

1. The user submits a request to view a specific order.

2. The servlet checks the cache to see whether the order has been requested before.

3. If the order is in the cache, simply display the order information.

4. If the order is not in the cache, then request the order information from the database and cache the order for the next time it is requested.

Figure 8.6 shows the new `index.html` page that is used within the application. This page provides an input box for submitting the order number. Note: We have output to the bottom of the screen some of the order IDs for easier testing.

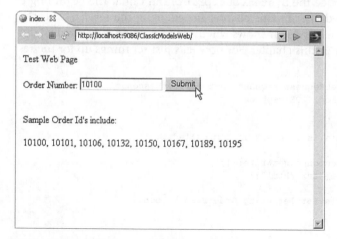

Figure 8.6   Submit an order request

The code for this page is pretty simple. A form is displayed that allows the entry of an order ID, and then a submit button allows for posting that ID to the OrdersTestServlet. The full example code is described in Appendix B, "Running the Examples," along with the location where you can download all of the examples.

```
<body>
<p>Test Web Page</p>

<form action="/ClassicModelsWeb/OrdersTestServlet" method="post">
Order Number: <input type="text" name="orderid" size="20">
<input type="submit" name="submit" value="Submit">
</form>
```

```
<p><br></p>
<p>Sample Order Id's include:</p>
<p>10100, 10101, 10106, 10132, 10150, 10167, 10189, 10195 </p>
</body>
```

Once the form is submitted the OrdersTestServlet takes over. Because you are posting the form data use a simple call in the doPost() to pass the information to the doGet() method in the servlet.

```
protected void doPost(HttpServletRequest request, HttpServletResponse
response) throws ServletException, IOException {


        doGet(request, response);


}
```

The doGet() is where the real magic happens so let's examine this servlet in detail. It shows a mixture of System.out calls and PrintWriter options. The PrintWriter outputs data to the browser in the form of an HTML page. This allows you not to use a JSP and simplify the testing of this approach. Notice the System.out.printline call at the beginning of the method. This is actually used later in this chapter for enabling the servlet/JSP cache, which will cache the output of this servlet. It shows whether this method is even called during a request. More on that later in this chapter. For now let's just set things up for the rest of the method.

```
protected void doGet(HttpServletRequest request, HttpServletResponse
response) throws ServletException, IOException {


        System.out.println("This is to check if I'm called...");

        PrintWriter writer = response.getWriter();
        response.setContentType("text/html");

        writer.println("OrderTestServlet using OrderFacade(Local)
        <br><br>");
```

The next step is to get the order ID from the request. This is the ID that is entered in the form and submitted to the servlet. You can use that ID as the cache key to store and retrieve information from the Dmap. You can use the dmap.get() method with the ID as the input parameter to attempt to retrieve an Order object from the map.

```
        //get the submitted order ID from the request
        Short orderid = Short.parseShort(request.getParameter("orderid"));

        //get the requested order from the distributed map
         writer.println("Checking dmap cache for order object " + orderid +
        "...<br>");

        Orders myOrder = (Orders)dMap.get(orderid);
```

Next, check whether you actually got something out of the Dmap. If you did that means this order has been requested before and has already been retrieved from the database. If you got a null, then you have to go back to the database and retrieve the information for this order. If the result is null then you do have to go retrieve the information. In this case you call the `findOrdersByOrdernumber()` method with the same order ID that was originally requested by the user. The next step is to now cache the result so next time, you don't have to go back to the database to look it up.

```
//check if we got an order out of the map
if (myOrder == null) {

    //Order does not exist in dMap, go ahead and get it from the DB
    writer.println("Not in dmap cache, retriving order data from
    DB...<br>");

    myOrder = ordersFacade.findOrdersByOrdernumber(orderid);

    //Now place it in the map for next time.
    writer.println("Storing retrieved order in dmap
    cache...<br>");
    dMap.put(orderid, myOrder);
```

If the `Orders` object is not null, that means you successfully retrieved the object from the Dmap. The code actually does not need this `else` section of the statement for any practical reasons, but you can make a note to the user explaining where you got the data.

```
} else {
        writer.println("Order retrieved from dmap cache
        successfully.</br>");
}
```

At this point in the code the `Order` object is available and should be stored in the cache for the next time this order is requested.

```
writer.println("<br><br>");
        writer.println("Ordernumber: " + myOrder.getOrdernumber() +
        "<br>");
        writer.println("Customernumber: " +
        myOrder.getCustomernumber() + "<br>");
        writer.println("Orderdate: " + myOrder.getOrderdate() +
        "<br>");
        writer.println("<br>order details<br>");

        List<Orderdetails> orderDetails =
        myOrder.getOrderdetailsCollection();

        Iterator<Orderdetails> it = orderDetails.iterator();

        Orderdetails od;
        while (it.hasNext()) {

        od = (Orderdetails) it.next();
        writer.print("orderlinenumber: " +  od.getOrderlinenumber()
        + " ");
        writer.println("item: " + od.getProductcode() + "<br>");

        }
```

The last part of the method is designed to display some more information on using the dMap cache. This section does a lookup of all the entries that are stored in the cache and then iterates through them to display the cache keys. Specifically, the `dMap.keySet()` method retrieves a set of keys for the entire cache.

```
writer.println("<br><br>Cache Keys:<br>");
Set set = dMap.keySet();
Iterator it1 = set.iterator();
while (it1.hasNext()) {
        String value = it1.next().toString();
        writer.println("Key: " + value + "<br>");
}


}
```

The result of all this is shown in Figure 8.7. The request is submitted and the data is not found in the cache. This results in a lookup and then the data is displayed. This specific order ID has been retrieved from the database and is now to be stored in the cache for any future lookups.

Figure 8.7   Looking up in the cache

The final piece of code to look at in this example is where the distributed map is actually defined within the servlet. JNDI calls can be expensive, especially when they are used over and over unnecessarily. Because of this I have opted to define the map only once and then store the handle as an instance variable in the servlet. Generally the use of instance variables are frowned upon because a servlet is a multiuser type of object. But in this case a shared instance is okay because I am sharing the cache across all users. Other cases may call for abstracting the cache instance in a service or utility class.

I have broken my own rules here for better clarity and used System.out calls to handle the initialization of the servlet. Because it is only used once it lets me know whether the dMap has been set up correctly or not. The dMap is declared as an instance variable or globally within the class, and the initialization performs a context lookup on the JNDI name that we defined when creating the dMap in the admin console.

```
private DistributedMap dMap;

public OrdersTestServlet() {
      super();

      try {
            System.out.println("in constructor - getting dMap handle");
                 InitialContext ic = new InitialContext();
            dMap =(DistributedMap)ic.lookup("services/cache/orders");
                 System.out.println("Cachesetup constructor...
                 Finished");
      } catch (Exception e) {
                 System.out.println("Cachesetup.constructor - Exception");
      e.printStackTrace();
      }
}
```

On any subsequent requests for a particular order we should see the result shown in Figure 8.8. This shows that the order was successfully retrieved from the cache and is being used to display the data.

Figure 8.8 Order found in the cache

In this example all the caching occurred within the servlet class, or the presentation layer of this application. This may be fine for some applications, but more than likely you would provide this type of caching within a different layer within the architecture. The business logic layer or local service layer are good candidates for this type of caching.

HTML Fragment Caching

The servlet/JSP fragment caching component of dynacache can also be a powerful tool. In some cases this feature has been implemented to produce a multifold improvement in performance in an application. Fragment caching actually caches the HTML that a servlet or JSP component provides. This means that the next request for that servlet will result in a display from the cache and not the servlet. This protects the servlet from even being called on these subsequent requests. Be aware, however, that the closer to the end user that a cache exists, the less flexible the cache contents become. Caching at this high of a level is best for more generic or public data that is shared across all users, or at least large groups of users, or perhaps for content that is very expensive to generate and that you want to only create once for a given user and then keep it around for the length of that user session.

One good example is a public home or landing page. This generally is the page that everyone hits when they first access a Web site or application. Because there is no authentication the content is usually pretty generic and doesn't change often (maybe daily or weekly). This is a perfect candidate for a servlet cache. The first user to access the page triggers the cache. Any subsequent requests are displayed from the cache, which usually brings response time down to zero for these requests.

The default caching service has to be enabled to run at startup. You can accomplish this through the WebSphere Integrated Solutions Console by drilling down to the server that you are using and enabling the service at startup. Figure 8.9 shows the check box for turning on the dynamic caching service for a particular server.

Once dynacache is enabled it is ready to use with your application, and you need to tell it what applications to actually cache. This configuration is provided through the `cachespec.xml` file that is deployed with your application. The `cachespec.xml` configuration file is pretty powerful, which means that it can be confusing to new users. The `cachespec.xml` has several components that are discussed in detail in the WebSphere InfoCenter at http://publib.boulder.ibm.com/infocenter/wasinfo/v6r1/topic/com.ibm.websphere.nd. multi-platform.doc/info/ae/ae/rdyn_cachespec.html?resultof=%22%63%61%63%68%65%73%70% 65%63%2e%78%6d%6c%22%20.

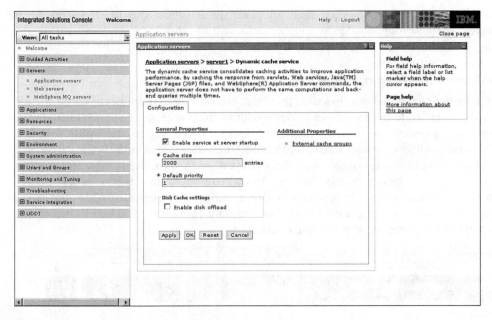

Figure 8.9 Turning on fragment caching

Specifically for this implementation, the `cachespec.xml` describes the fact that we are caching the output of the servlet called `com.ibmpress.cm.web.OrdersTestServlet.class`. This triggers the fact that we need to cache the output when this servlet is called. Additionally, we define a `cache-id` that provides the cache key for this particular servlet. The cache key in this case is the ordered parameter that is passed into the servlet from the initial request form. This allows us to cache the output of the servlet once for every unique order that is displayed.

Finally, we define a cache timeout of 180 seconds. This timeout is actually pretty short—only three minutes, but it is enough to perform a test without having to wait too long for the cache entries to time out.

```xml
<?xml version="1.0" ?>
<!DOCTYPE cache SYSTEM "cachespec.dtd">
<cache>
  <cache-entry>
      <class>servlet</class>
      <name>com.ibmpress.cm.web.OrdersTestServlet.class</name>
      <cache-id>
        <component id="orderid" type="parameter">
            <required>true</required>
        </component>
         <timeout>180</timeout>
      </cache-id>
  </cache-entry>
</cache>
```

That's it! Putting the cachespec.xml in place should allow this to start working as expected. For a web application the cachespec.xml file should be deployed within the WEB-INF directory of the war file.

Monitoring the Fragment Cache

For the earlier distributed map example there was no real way to monitor the cache entries. We added some code to the bottom of our servlet so that we could see which entries were cached during testing. But usually there is no out-of-the-box way to accomplish this. You would need to build a separate servlet that showed the state of all of your system caches. For the fragment cache this is not the case. There is an out-of-the-box way to view and monitor the state of this cache at any point in time. WebSphere Application Server comes bundled with an application called the CacheMonitor.ear, shown in Figure 8.10. This application needs to be deployed to the same server that you want to monitor and will show you the status of what is going on with the fragment cache.

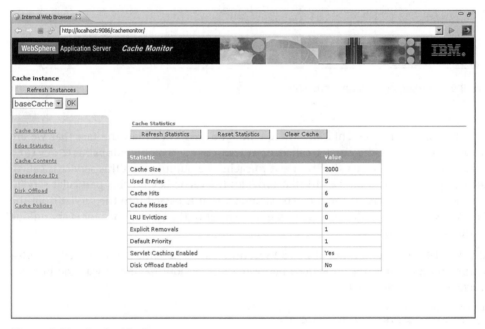

Figure 8.10   Cache Monitor

The Cache Monitor can provide basic statistics about the fragment cache. Watching the base statistics can be enlightening. Of particular interest is the number of cache hits versus misses. If you are getting too many missed then you may adjust the size of your cache or look at the cache key that you are using for each entry. Figure 8.11 shows the cache entries themselves that have been stored in the servlet cache.

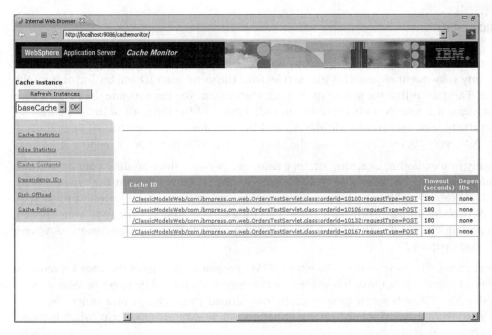

Figure 8.11 Cache entries

Drilling down into the actual cache contents will show you the actual entries that are being cached. Notice that each entry has a different order ID associated with it.

ESI Plug-in Caching

Not shown here is the enablement of the ESI (Edge Side Includes) cache within the HTTP Server plug-in. This plug-in allows for the caching of static entries that are usually displayed on a web page. Statics consist of images, Javascript files, or stylesheets that are generally used by all users, but are not something that the application server itself would need to provide every time. The plug-in is enabled by default when deployed so you receive the benefit of this approach without even trying, but the settings are configurable within the `plugin-cfg.xml` file that is deployed to the web server.

```
<?xml version-"1.0"?>
<Config>
        <Property Name="esiEnable" Value="true"/>
        <Property Name="esiMaxCacheSize" Value="1024"/>
        <Property Name="esiInvalidationMonitor" Value="false"/>
```

There is an ESI monitor that is similar to the cache monitor that you deployed in this chapter that can show you what is being cached in the plug-in. The WebSphere Info Center can guide you on setting this up and tuning the plug-in.

Conclusion

So what is actually happening here? This is important because once an entry is in the cache, then any subsequent requests for that servlet with the same order ID will be drawn from the cache. This means that the servlet itself is not even called. You can imagine the performance improvement if your servlets are not even called much of the time. All of this is dependent upon the type of data you are displaying and the functional requirements of your application. Not every application will gain the same benefits with this type of caching.

Actually implementing a caching strategy requires not only understanding your application requirements, but also knowing what tools are available to you within the environment. You have seen two different approaches to caching using some of the features provided by the WebSphere infrastructure. Object-level caching can be done internally to your application and provides you with a handy holding space for data that you don't want to retrieve with every request.

Servlet caching is a way to store the entire HTML page or fragments of the page for reuse by groups of users. This approach is extremely fast, especially for public pages or Web sites. In addition the ESI web server plug-in cache can offload static images and other files from being served from WebSphere. This combination can be extremely powerful when incorporated into your application.

Links to developerWorks Articles

A8.1 Revisiting Performance Fundamentals: http://www.ibm.com/developerworks/websphere/techjournal/0708_col_bernal/0708_col_bernal.html

A8.2 Static and Dynamic Caching in WebSphere Application Server, Bill Hines, http://www.ibm.com/developerworks/websphere/techjournal/0405_hines/0405_hines.html

References

Bernal (2007). "Revisiting Performance Fundamentals." *DeveloperWorks Technical Journal*, Comment Lines Series. http://www.ibm.com/developerworks/websphere/techjournal/0708_col_bernal/0708_col_bernal.html

Joines, Willenborg, Hygh (2003). *Performance Analysis for Java Web*: Addison-Wesley Professional Computing Series.

Chapter 9

Keeping Things Secure

Security is a topic that usually gets more attention than the topic of performance, but of course, the stakes are higher. Slow performance means unhappy customers or end users; poor security can have much more dire consequences. This chapter looks at security in several different ways, both from a WebSphere perspective using built-in security functionality, and from the viewpoint of application architecture and how you can build security into your applications where required.

Security from a code perspective should be a first line of defense. Applications need to be written securely, reviewed, and tested, to ensure that you are not allowing large security holes into your application and potentially into your enterprise. Common security attacks are around cross-side scripting and SQL injection. This chapter looks at SQL injection and provides some insight into how you can avoid that kind of attack.

In addition to securing your code, you can also use WebSphere Application Server, which provides several different mechanisms to help secure your application. Many project teams use their own security scheme not knowing or understanding how WAS security actually works. This chapter will look at enabling WAS security and applying it to your application.

Why Security Is Important

I am sure I don't really have to answer the question of why security is important. In today's IT world not understanding the risks and attacks that take place against us on a daily basis is almost impossible. Just look at our desktop machines pummeled by mal-ware constantly, in the same way Web sites are being assessed and attacked at a constant rate by intruders looking for weaknesses, or ways to get inside the system to steal data, or to plant their own information that can be used to attack other sites.

Beyond this type of attack, security also includes events of nonprofessional hackers who can sometimes cause problems. Think about a scenario where one employee simply by changing an ID within a home page could see another employee's personnel information. A simple example is shown in Figure 9.1 where a change in the query string will result in displaying a different employee's contact information.

Figure 9.1   Example query string manipulation

The same effect can be caused by changing hidden values within a form, or even cookie data that is being stored by the application on the local browser. The application shown in Figure 9.1 is actually designed as an open people search application, so manipulating the query string does not do any real damage. But the example being discussed is relevant as other applications may not have the same open requirements.

The threats on the front end are many, and the challenge of ensuring security is becoming greater all the time as new attacks are being developed and perfected constantly. The truth is that keeping up on the latest security threats is very hard for the average programmer, so you need to look to experts or perhaps tooling to keep the threat information current and relevant to the organization and specific applications.

The Role of the Security Architect

Many organizations would do well to create the role of a security architect within the organization. This specialized type of role would need to have broad skills within the realm of enterprise security and also some responsibility for ensuring that applications within the organization are secure. Figure 9.2 illustrates this role within the overall role of architects in the organization.

A9.1

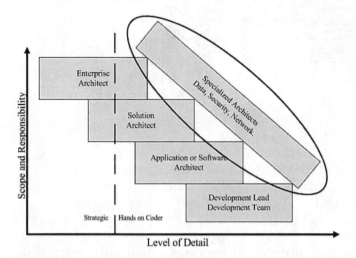

Figure 9.2   Security architect role

The security architect would be in a good position to guide development teams on the predefined roles that are available within the organization and how those can be mapped to required functionality. Additionally, the security architect should be able to provide some formal review or testing on potential security flaws within the design or completed application. The development team cannot always keep up with the latest attacks but a security expert tasked with keeping the organization safe from these attacks can help guide the team in the right direction. The security architect can assist the entire organization by creating checklists and internal documents that outline the security standards for the development team. For example, common security standards may include ensuring that all user input is validated to help protect against SQL injection attacks.

Security protection within an application can be tricky. Many times instance variables within a servlet can cause some security issues. Security and session cookies that are not in sync can cause problems with shared computers; for example in a system on the shop floor where employees need to check and then sign up for health care benefits.

SQL Injection Example

A9.2

One common attack is that of using SQL injection to retrieve more information from the
database than was originally intended. The central idea is to inject SQL into the application
that is then run; the results are then displayed to the end user. Consider the screen in Figure
9.3. This form is designed to display some results based on the customer number that is submitted within the form.

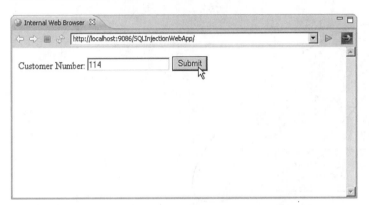

Figure 9.3   Customer lookup submit

The form itself is only a few lines that submits the entered data with a POST to the
CustomerDetail servlet. All of the sample code is described in Appendix B, "Running the
Examples," along with the location for downloading the examples.

```
<form action="/SQLInjectionWebApp/CustomerDetail" method="post">
Customer Number: <input type="text" name="customerid" size="20">
<input type="submit" name="submit" value="Submit">
</form>
```

Once the customer number is submitted the servlet does an SQL query on the database and
displays a few results from the customer table. For brevity this result set, shown in Figure
9.4, is very simple and only provides a few key pieces of information.

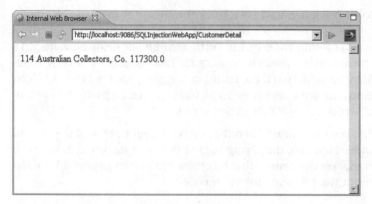

Figure 9.4 Customer lookup results

The CustomerDetail servlet gets the `customerid` from the request and then submits it within an SQL call to the database.

```
String customerid = request.getParameter("customerid");

try {

   conn = ds.getConnection();
   stmt = conn.createStatement();

   query  = "SELECT CUSTOMERNUMBER, CUSTOMERNAME, CREDITLIMIT FROM
DB2ADMIN.CUSTOMERS WHERE CUSTOMERNUMBER = " + customerid;

   rs  = stmt.executeQuery(query);
```

The result set is written out directly to the browser by iterating through the result set and displaying each column in the set. Granted, this would not be the way production-ready code would be delivered, but you might be surprised the amount of code that requires this degree of flexibility.

```
   ResultSetMetaData rsmd = rs.getMetaData();
   int cols = rsmd.getColumnCount();

   while (rs.next()) {
      for (int i = 1; i <= cols; i++) {
      writer.print(rs.getString(i)+"     ");
      writer.println();
      }
   }
```

So what is the big deal? Well the big deal is in the way that the form input is directly injected into the SQL stream like so:

```
query  = "SELECT CUSTOMERNUMBER, CUSTOMERNAME, CREDITLIMIT FROM
DB2ADMIN.CUSTOMERS WHERE CUSTOMERNUMBER = " + customerid;
```

This provides a security hole big enough to drive a truck through in many cases. All that a hacker has to do is perform a simple test to see whether this application is vulnerable to an SQL injection attack. He or she would enter in the customer number field the value, 114 AND 1=1. Because 1 does equal 1, this equates to AND TRUE. This result is a valid SQL statement that can be evaluated by the database. If the results of the query are the same as before, that is, the application returns the same results as if 114 were entered by itself, then potentially the application is vulnerable to an SQL injection attack.

When a potential victim has been identified, then the real work begins. By looking at error messages and trying to understand the underlying data structure, a hacker can do much damage. After a while, the attacker determines that he or she can extract payment information from the application with the following injection code,

```
114 UNION SELECT CUSTOMERNUMBER, CHECKNUMBER, AMOUNT FROM
DB2ADMIN.PAYMENTS WHERE CUSTOMERNUMBER = 114,
```

resulting in the output shown in Figure 9.5.

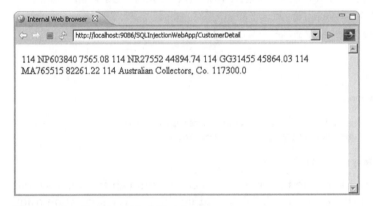

Figure 9.5   Results with SQL injection

One can see how dangerous this type of attack could become.

Protecting against SQL Injection Attacks

Validation of input values is the key to protecting against SQL injection attacks. Other ways exist to protect against these types of attacks, such as ensuring that information found in error messages does not provide the attacker with clues to your data and application structure. In this example, a simple line change would have provided some better protection. Validating that the data input is indeed a numeric value will strip out all the additional SQL that could be added in.

```
Short  customerid = Short.valueOf(request.getParameter("customerid"));
//String customerid = request.getParameter("customerid");
```

> **NOTE**
>
> I am using a short value in the preceding code because it matches
> what is set up in the database. The customer number in the DB was
> defined as a small integer.

Making this change will cause the servlet to throw an error when a non-numeric value is
appended to the field value.

```
[4/7/08 15:26:21:375 EDT] 00000030 WebApp        E   [Servlet Error]-
[CustomerDetail]: java.lang.NumberFormatException: For input string: "114 AND 1=1"
   at java.lang.NumberFormatException.forInputString(NumberFormatException.java:63)
   at java.lang.Integer.parseInt(Integer.java:490)
   at java.lang.Short.parseShort(Short.java:135)
   at java.lang.Short.valueOf(Short.java:168)
   at java.lang.Short.valueOf(Short.java:193)
```

This is just one example of how an attack can occur. Someone in the organization has to be
very diligent in keeping up with different types of attacks and how to protect against them
as vulnerabilities occur. Using a persistence framework can also help, as validation often
occurs as a part of that framework. To get more detail on persistence frameworks see
Chapter 3, "Persistence Matters."

WebSphere Security Basics

We skipped ahead a little at the beginning of this chapter in order to show an example of
some of the security issues that can occur within applications. Computer Science 101 outlines a number of security functions that you should consider within application design. In
this chapter we will look at two of them and how they fit within WebSphere Application
Server. The two areas of consideration are

A9.3

- Authentication is the act of identifying users and ensuring that they are who they
  say they are. Is this really John Smith?
- Authorization is the act of determining which permissions or access rights the user
  has on the system or application. Does John Smith have permission to view this
  data?

You need to consider many other areas when designing your application, such as transaction integrity, auditing, confidentiality, and nonrepudiation. These topics will need to be
handled in a separate book. But there is more than enough to cover with authentication and
authorization.

Authenticating Application Users

I actually still get surprised when I see applications that do not use WebSphere (WAS) security. Unauthenticated or public applications aside, many applications have used a home-
grown security approach. This makes me uncomfortable for several reasons:

- How secure is the application? Are there security holes in the approach that are unknown because no code or security review was done?
- Did the team end up reinventing the wheel or in this case the security architecture? This is simply a waste of business value, unless a conscious decision was made not to use the provided framework.
- How extensible is the custom security model? WebSphere security is designed to be pluggable with new capabilities as needed. For example, if a new single sign-on framework such as Tivoli Access Manager, or CA's SiteMinder was put into place, it could be incorporated into WAS security fairly easily.

Setting up application security within WebSphere is fairly simple, but does require some explanation. Figure 9.6 shows a variation of the WebSphere Security Management screen.

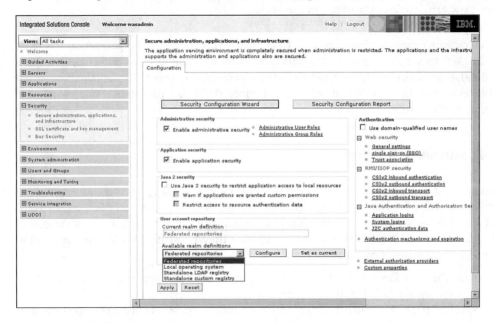

Figure 9.6   WebSphere security setup

You can define different types of security within WAS, such as administrative security, application security, and Java 2 security, but setting up security requires a user registry to hold the user and group information needed by WebSphere to provide the security needed for authentication or authorization. Several different repositories are available:

- Federated repository
- Local operating system
- Standalone Lightweight Directory Access Protocol (LDAP) registry
- Standalone custom registry

Administrative security is enabled by default with a file-based federated repository configured as the main user repository. A simple way to check whether security is enabled is to use the snoop servlet. This servlet is part of the samples that are often deployed with a WebSphere profile. Security is one of those features that requires a restart of the application server. After the restart, navigate to the snoop servlet if it is installed and see whether you are prompted with a Basic Authentication prompt, as shown in Figure 9.7.

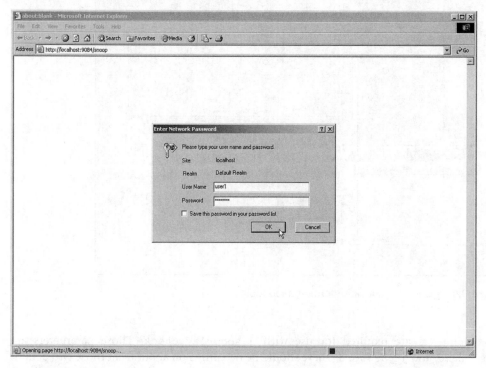

Figure 9.7 Using basic authentication to access a Web resource

Using j_security_check

The web container provides a mechanism for protecting resources within your web application. Part of the servlet specification identifies the use of the `j_security_check` to provide a login process for your application. The use of `j_security_check` is available once application security is enabled within WebSphere.

You can identify the login form that is to be used by the security check within the `web.xml` of your application.

```
<login-config>
    <auth-method>FORM</auth-method>
    <form-login-config>
        <form-login-page>/login.jsp</form-login-page>
```

```
        <form-error-page>/loginError.jsp</form-error-page>
    </form-login-config>
</login-config>
```

When a resource is protected, any call to that resource results in a redirect to the identified login page for authentication. The process is illustrated in Figure 9.8.

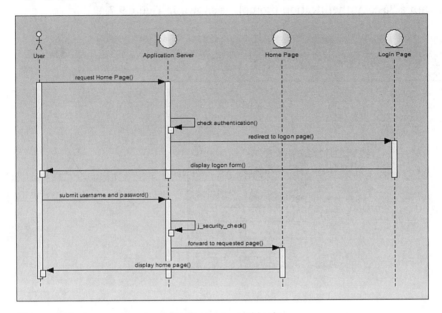

Figure 9.8   j_security_check for forms-based login

Two parameters are required for use with j_security_check. Those parameters are j_username, and j_password. There should be no confusion about what those two parameters are used for. Here is an example of what your login.jsp should look like:

```
<form method="POST" action="j_security_check">

User ID:
<input type="text" name="j_username" id="name" maxlength="40">
Password:
<input type="password" name="j_password" id="pswd" maxlength="40">

<input type="submit" name="Submit" value="Log In">

</form>
```

As you can see in Figure 9.7, you should not actually link directly to the login.jsp. Rather let WAS do the redirecting as you try to go directly to some secured resource. The j_security_check login process will remember the URL that you originally tried to access, and will redirect you back to that URL after you have successfully logged in.

Securing Resources

One distinction that we have not made is that of roles versus groups within an application. The following definitions describe what they mean and how they work together:

- **Roles** are generally defined by the application and can be organizational or functional roles such as HR manager or sales rep, or they can be application-specific roles, such as administrator.
- **Groups** are generally defined within the user repository and may or may not map to application type of roles. Often an attempt is made to define groups that emulate roles within the organization, but more often than not, it is simply groups of users that need access to some application or function.

Although sometimes mapping groups to roles can be difficult, generally this separation provides the ability to create complex authorization mappings that fit the business need. Figure 9.9 shows an approach that is designed to allow for separation of concerns within the application development space, but that also provides the needed flexibility to work with most organizational security schemes.

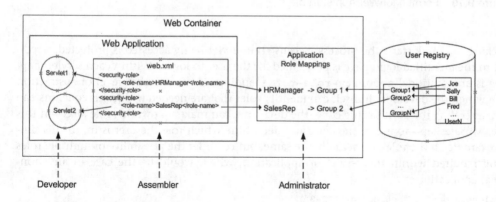

Figure 9.9   Role to group mapping

Role mappings can be done in many different ways, and many security practices often define the approach based on the organizational security model. Often roles are mapped to many groups within applications. For example, an editor role might be mapped to groups that contain managers, administrators, as well as actual editors.

You can see how this all fits together by looking at the `web.xml` from the sample FormLogon application. The application itself is pretty simple. It has two major functions: one for HR managers to view employee data, and one for sales reps to view customer data. Obviously the two areas should be separated so that a sales rep, for example, cannot look at other employee data. When started, the application displays a main menu (see Figure 9.10) for the user to choose which function he or she needs to view.

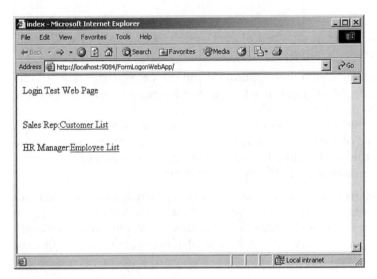

Figure 9.10   FormLogonWebApp start page

Clicking on a link starts the process. Because the servlet being accessed is protected, a redirect to the identified login page is performed for the user to log in. Within each servlet mapping is an additional `security-role-ref` mapping. This is another level of abstraction with which the developer himself can identify roles that are needed within his code. Instead of hard coding roles within the code, the developer can make up own his role alias—in this case, MySalesRep—to use in the code and determine which role the user is in. In this simple example all the roles are actually the same, but consider the possibility of multiple roles being required within the servlet or application, which would be the case in any non-trivial application

```
<?xml version="1.0" encoding="UTF-8"?>
<web-app id="WebApp_ID" version="2.4" xmlns="http://java.sun.com/xml/ns/j2ee"
xmlns:xsi="http://www.w3.org/2001/XMLSchema-instance"
xsi:schemaLocation="http://java.sun.com/xml/ns/j2ee
http://java.sun.com/xml/ns/j2ee/web-app_2_4.xsd">

<display-name>FormLogonWebApp</display-name>

<servlet>
   <display-name>CustomerList</display-name>
   <servlet-name>CustomerList</servlet-name>
   <servlet-class>com.ibmpress.web.customer.CustomerList</servlet-class>
   <security-role-ref>
      <role-name>MySalesRep</role-name>
      <role-link>SalesRep</role-link>
   </security-role-ref>
</servlet>
```

The EmployeeList servlet is described in the same manner with the `security-role-ref` being defined so that the developer can code to a specific name without worrying about what the real role name might end up being. The servlet mapping and the `welcome-file-list` items just tell the web container how to access each servlet and what the default welcome page will be.

```
<servlet>
        <display-name>EmployeeList</display-name>
        <servlet-name>EmployeeList</servlet-name>
        <servlet-class>com.ibmpress.web.employee.EmployeeList</servlet-class>
        <security-role-ref>
                <role-name>MyHRManager</role-name>
                <role-link>HRManager</role-link>
        </security-role-ref>
</servlet>
<servlet-mapping>
        <servlet-name>CustomerList</servlet-name>
        <url-pattern>/CustomerList</url-pattern>
</servlet-mapping>
<servlet-mapping>
        <servlet-name>EmployeeList</servlet-name>
        <url-pattern>/EmployeeList</url-pattern>
</servlet-mapping>
<welcome-file-list>
        <welcome-file>index.html</welcome-file>
</welcome-file-list>
```

The `security-role` identifies the actual roles that need to be mapped within the web container. These are the same roles that are linked within the servlet `security-role-ref` section.

```
<security-role>
        <role-name>HRManager</role-name>
</security-role>
<security-role>
        <role-name>SalesRep</role-name>
</security-role>
```

The web container will provide the capability to map user groups or sets of users to these roles within the administration console. Figure 9.11 shows an example of this mapping in the WebSphere Administration Console.

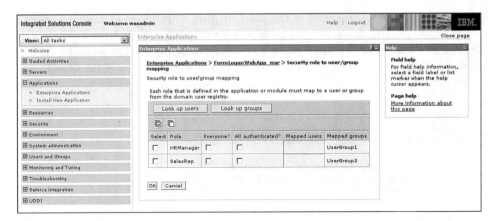

Figure 9.11   Security role to user group mapping

Of interest to note is that you can set several default settings, such as **Everyone** or **All Authenticated**, for each role.

I have added an error JSP for completeness to the application. This is different from the `LogonError.jsp`, which is at the bottom of the xml file. The `LogonError.jsp` triggers if a problem occurs logging into the application, such as if there is an incorrect username or password. The `error-page` triggers after a successful login when the user is not authorized to view the page.

```
<error-page>
        <error-code>403</error-code>
        <location>/403Error.jsp</location>
</error-page>
```

This error is a common occurrence in many applications and I add it here to ensure that you can follow the security path through the application. With the default error page too much uncertainty exists as to whether the problem was supposed to occur or whether a bug exists in the application. With a custom error, as shown in Figure 9.12, you know exactly which error occurred within the application.

Everything in the `web.xml` up to now has been necessary, but has really been items that work behind the scenes. Actually securing resources within the application is performed within the `security-constraint` section of the file. This section contains two parts: the `web-resource-collection`, which identifies what resources need to be secured, and the `auth-constraint` section, which identifies which role has access to those resources.

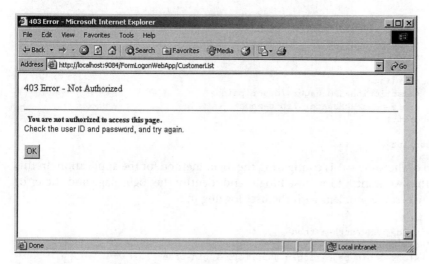

Figure 9.12 403 Error-Not Authorized

In this section I have created a constraint for each servlet in the application and set a different role for each one. This allows us to fully test the capability without too much effort. In the `web-resource-collection` are several parameters, which allow you to set different constraints on different aspects of the application. In this example I have only constrained the GET and POST methods of each servlet, but other options are available. For most applications finer grained control would probably be necessary.

```
<security-constraint>

        <display-name>CustomerList</display-name>

        <web-resource-collection>
                <web-resource-name>CustomerList</web-resource-name>
                <url-pattern>/CustomerList</url-pattern>
                <http-method>GET</http-method>
                <http-method>POST</http-method>
        </web-resource-collection>

        <auth-constraint>
                <description>SalesRep</description>
                <role-name>SalesRep</role-name>
        </auth-constraint>

</security-constraint>

<security-constraint>

        <display-name>EmployeeList</display-name>

        <web-resource-collection>
                <web-resource-name>EmployeeList</web-resource-name>
```

```
        <url-pattern>/EmployeeList</url-pattern>
        <http-method>GET</http-method>
        <http-method>POST</http-method>
</web-resource-collection>

<auth-constraint>
        <description>HRManager</description>
        <role-name>HRManager</role-name>
</auth-constraint>

</security-constraint>
```

The final section of the web.xml is configuring the login method for the application. In this case we define that we want a form-based login and identify the login page and the error page in case there is some problem with the user logging in.

```
<login-config>
        <auth-method>FORM</auth-method>
        <form-login-config>
                <form-login-page>/login.jsp</form-login-page>
                <form-error-page>/loginError.jsp</form-error-page>
        </form-login-config>
</login-config>
```

On the surface this looks a little complex, but once you see how all the pieces fit together it makes some sense.

Running the Example

So what happens when you try to access a protected resource? As you might imagine the web container will see that you are trying to access a secure URL and redirect you to the login page, shown in Figure 9.13. This login page has been identified in the web.xml of the application.

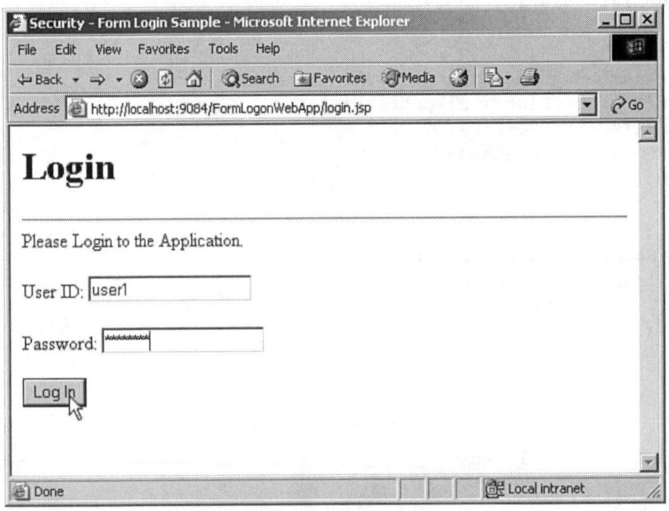

Figure 9.13   Redirect to login.jsp

On the login page you enter the username and password. If you are authorized to view the URL then you will get forwarded on to the CustomerList servlet shown in Figure 9.14. If you are not in the right role then you will see a result similar to Figure 9.12 (shown earlier).

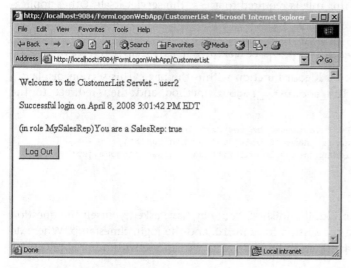

Figure 9.14 Successful login

The CustomerList servlet shows a few pieces of information that may be relevant to many applications. The first item is to get the username of the user who is logging in. In this case we get the name as an attribute within the session.

```
protected void doGet(HttpServletRequest request, HttpServletResponse response) throws
ServletException, IOException {

PrintWriter out = response.getWriter();

String userName = (String)request.getSession().getAttribute("USER_ID");

if (userName != null) {
        out.println("Welcome to the CustomerList Servlet - " + userName);
} else {
        out.println("Welcome to CustomerList Servlet");
}
```

Second, a timestamp can often be used to log or determine when a user actually logged in. Again as an attribute on the session we can display this information.

```
String timeStamp = (String) request.getSession().getAttribute("LOGINTIME");
if (timeStamp != null) {
        out.println("Successful login on " + timeStamp);
} else {
        out.println("Successful login");
}
```

Finally, the isUserInRole() method can be used to determine whether a user has permissions to specific features within the application. In this case a Boolean holds the role value of a specific user and then displays whether that value is true or false. For this servlet the value has to be true because this role is required to access the servlet itself. Other applications may have a number of roles, any one of which could be true or false.

```
boolean salesrep = request.isUserInRole("MySalesRep");
out.println("(in role MySalesRep)You are a SalesRep: " + salesrep);
```

For completeness I have added a logout function within the page. This section displays a form that can trigger the ibm_security_logout method and then redirect to the logout.jsp page.

```
out.println("<form method='POST' action='ibm_security_logout'>");
out.println("<input type='submit' name='Submit' value='Log Out'>");
out.println("<input type='hidden' name='logoutExitPage' value='/logout.jsp'>");
out.println("</form>");

}
```

Interestingly enough we are not quite finished. You may have asked yourself the question about the values we got from the session for userid, and the login timestamp. Where do these values come from and are there additional values we can use within our application?

Adding a Filter to the Login Process

The specification allows for a filter to be injected into the login process so that you can do some pre- and post-processing of the logon event. By itself j_security_check does not provide a lot of information. The spec is pretty silent on implementation so it is left to the implementation to determine what features are available. The filter allows us to wrap the login process and give the application the additional information that it requires.

Adding the filter to the application is done by inserting a filter tag into the web.xml. This provides a filter class and the filter-mapping so that container knows what URL needs to be filtered. For the login process we need to put the filter on the j_security_check process.

```
<filter>
<description>Login Filter to provide additional Login Info</description>
<display-name>LoginFilter</display-name>
<filter-name>LoginFilter</filter-name>
<filter-class>com.ibmpress.web.login.LoginFilter</filter-class>
</filter>
<filter-mapping>
<filter-name>LoginFilter</filter-name>
<url-pattern>/j_security_check</url-pattern>
</filter-mapping>
```

A servlet filter consists of several parts based on its lifecycle. The three components to the lifecycle are init(), doFilter(), and destroy(). The init() and destroy() methods are pretty generic, but the doFilter() method provides the ability to manage data both before and after the login is performed. Within the doFilter() the first part of the method casts the ServletRequest and ServletResponse to an HTTPServletRequest and HTTPServletResponse for use within the code.

```
public void doFilter(
  ServletRequest req,
  ServletResponse resp,
  FilterChain chain)
  throws ServletException, IOException {

  HttpServletRequest hreq = (HttpServletRequest)req;
  HttpServletResponse hres= (HttpServletResponse)resp;
```

In the pre-login section we can extract the username and password from the request and place them on the session for future use.

```
// pre login action
// get username
String username = hreq.getParameter("j_username");
hreq.getSession().setAttribute("USER_ID", username);
```

After the pre-login section we pass control back to the web container to perform the login. This is the common way of working with servlet filters and allows filters to be chained together to perform many actions.

```
chain.doFilter(req, resp);
```

The post-login process creates a timestamp for the login and again places this value on the session. We now have the username and the time he logged in available on the session for this web application.

```
// post login action
// log the time stamp for login
String timeStamp = null;
Locale locale = req.getLocale();
DateFormat df= DateFormat.getDateTimeInstance(DateFormat.LONG,
DateFormat.FULL, locale);
  timeStamp = df.format(new Date());
  hreq.getSession().setAttribute("LOGINTIME", timeStamp);
}
```

Attaching a filter opens up the possibilities for pre- and post-login processing (say that three times fast) and provides the application with a flexible and secure approach to managing access to its resources.

Architecting for Security

This chapter has covered a couple of cool security topics, but the higher goal is to help you figure out how to combine security into your architecture, especially in regards to a layered and likely distributed architecture described throughout this book. Maintaining a security context across a distributed environment can be a challenge. Many options are available to help with this challenge such as

- WebSphere LTPA Single Sign-on
- Principle/Credential Mapping with JAAS

- Secure Association Service (SAS) used for backward compatibility for EJB authentication
- Common Secure Interoperabilty Version 2 (CSIv2): Object Management Group standard for EJB authentication
- Java 2 Security

WebSphere Single Sign-on

As distributed applications continue to grow several options are available that allow for security information to flow between distributed tiers within the infrastructure. Lightweight Third Party Authentication (LTPA) is a protocol that is designed for distributed as well as clustered application server environments. LTPA allows servers to securely communicate by sharing a secure token that can be encrypted and signed to identify an authenticated user. Figure 9.15 illustrates the flow for LTPA tokens in a single sign-on scenario.

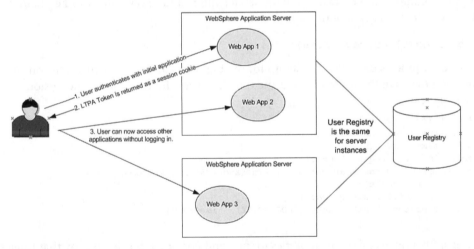

Figure 9.15   LTPA single sign-on

This feature allows a user to authenticate only once within the environment and be provided access to other applications within the domain. LTPA is highly secure; however, it is not an open standard, which means that LTAP tokens cannot be shared between other applications. WAS single sign-on is a little limiting in that LTPA tokens can only be shared with other WAS servers and Domino servers. For enterprise single sign-on, look to the Tivoli brand and Tivoli Access Manager series of products.

WebSphere Authorization

In a multi-layered application passing user credentials between layers is often necessary to ensure that the user, who authenticated at the front end of the application, has the necessary authorization to perform the requested function in the back end. Web applications and EJBs authenticate a client request in different ways, but the credentials are shared across the two. This means that when a user authenticates via the web app, those credentials are made available to EJB calls within the same application server. Figure 9.16 shows the authentication options available within WAS.

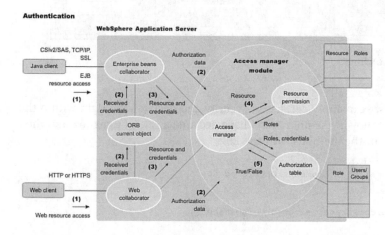

Figure 9.16   WebSphere authentication

Identifying the user role within the application can be performed using several available methods:

- EJB can use the `getCallerPrincipal()` and `isCallerinRole()` method to determine the user role.
- Servlets can use the `getRemoteUser()`, `isUserInRole()`, and `getUserPrincipal()` to identify the same information.

You may have noticed in Figure 9.11 that two special roles or subjects were available for role/user mapping: **AllAuthenticatedUsers** and **Everyone**. These represent special sets of users that would probably not be identified within the user registry.

Revisiting the OrderWebServlet

Chapter 3 outlines an EJB3 application and a separate web app as the client, as shown in Figure 9.17. We can revisit this application with some security applied. The same approach is used for applying security on the web application as the previous example. However, a different approach is used for applying security to the EJB layer.

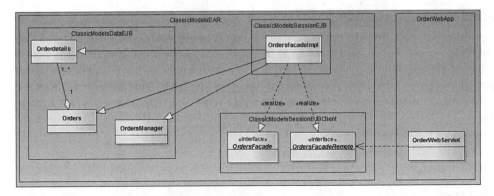

Figure 9.17   Distributed example

Using EJB3 annotations we can apply declarative security and declare roles right within the application code. In the following sample code I have declared a role of manager and then applied that role to both of the methods with the EJB.

@DeclareRoles("manager")
```
public class OrdersFacadeImpl implements OrdersFacade,
OrdersFacadeRemote {

        OrdersManager orderManager = new OrdersManager();

        @RolesAllowed ("manager")
        public List<Orders> getOrders() {
            …
        }

        @RolesAllowed ("manager")
        public Orders findOrdersByOrdernumber(short ordernumber) {
            …
        }
```

Once security is applied to the EJB application the methods will require the proper access rights to access the application. Running the application again the application will fail because no groups are mapped to the manager role.

```
4/8/08 20:38:24:906 EDT] 00000022 SecurityColla A    SECJ0053E:
Authorization failed for defaultWIMFileBasedRealm/User1 while invoking
(Bean)<null> findOrdersByOrdernumber(short):1 securityName:
defaultWIMFileBasedRealm/User1;accessID:
user:defaultWIMFileBasedRealm/uid=User1,o=defaultWIMFileBasedRealm is
not granted any of the required roles: manager

[4/8/08 20:38:24:953 EDT] 00000022 ServletWrappe E    SRVE0068E: Uncaught
exception thrown in one of the service methods of the servlet:
OrderWebServlet. Exception thrown : javax.ejb.EJBAccessException:

SECJ0053E: Authorization failed for defaultWIMFileBasedRealm/User1 while
invoking (Bean)null findOrdersByOrdernumber(short):1 securityName:
defaultWIMFileBasedRealm/User1;accessID:
```

```
user:defaultWIMFileBasedRealm/uid=User1,o=defaultWIMFileBasedRealm is
not granted any of the required roles: manager
```

The final step in this process would be to map one or more user groups to the `manager` role. As of this writing the available tooling is not quite ready to illustrate that portion of the exercise.

Conclusion

Most architects will understand that as with most of the chapters in this book we have only just scratched the surface of what security options are available, and what your responsibilities are in this area. For example Java 2 security has not been mentioned; however, it may be a key component of your strategy if you need that granular of a security model. Java 2 security can be a big step for an organization, especially within a shared environment. You can learn more about Java 2 security and how it is implemented in the WebSphere Application Server InfoCenter at http://publib.boulder.ibm.com/infocenter/wasinfo/v6r1/topic/com.ibm.websphere.nd.multiplatform.doc/info/ae/ae/csec_rsecmgr2.html?resultof=%22%4a%61%76%61%22%20%22%6a%61%76%61%22%20%22%32%22%20%22%53%65%63%75%72%69%74%79%22%20%22%73%65%63%75%72%22%20.

I should note that much of the form login example was adapted from the technology samples that come with WAS. I simplified the stock example a bit and added some role mappings to show how everything can work together. The technology samples are a good place to start looking when you are not sure how to do something, or do not know what features even exist within the server.

 ## Links to developerWorks Articles

A9.1 Application Architecture Security, Thomas Myer, http://www.ibm.com/developerworks/library/ar-apparch7/

A9.2 Seven lesser known system attacks and how to defeat them, Sean-Phillip Oriyano, http://www.ibm.com/developerworks/library/ar-sevatt/

A9.3 WebSphere Application Server V6 advanced security hardening, Keys Botzum, http://www.ibm.com/developerworks/library/ar-sevatt/

Chapter 10

Managing Your Applications

W
e have just spent the last nine chapters talking about how to build applications. It makes sense then that we spend a little bit of time talking about how to manage your applications and environment as new applications come online. This chapter delves into that topic and outlines some of the options that are available to you as you put together this management, or dare I say, governance, strategy. Instead of getting too deep into the theory this chapter tries to outline some practical suggestions that you can easily implement within your organization or project.

Managing Applications

Governance has become a hot topic over the last few years. Although it's nothing new to many organizations, as technology changes and adapts so do governance strategies and approaches. **Governance** is the concept of managing your application and how changes are made to the existing environment. This can include items like updates to a particular application, applying maintenance fixes to the infrastructure, or deploying and using new services within the enterprise.

A10.1

But governance is about so much more. Most importantly it helps to manage what changes are being made to the environment, when the changes should be made, and why. IT governance has been around for a long time and takes many different forms. This chapter explores some aspects of governance as well as how to make common sense decisions to help maintain your environment. At the end of the day governance is all about controlling resources and minimizing risk on current investments to ensure value delivery as a return.

Much of the resurgence around governance has been due to the widespread acceptance of service-oriented architectures (SOA) and approaches. This is because SOA has raised many questions around how to manage these reusable assets within the enterprise, questions like:

"What services exist?" and "Who is using a particular service?" In this context, services can be considered discrete applications that are made available to other applications within the organization. An example of a service could be a unique user profile service that provides information about a user, or it can be an actual LDAP infrastructure that is made available to other applications.

Enforcing Architecture Adherence

We talked about enforcing architecture adherence a little bit in Chapter 2, "Setting a Standard." How do you enforce the architecture, processes, and standards that you have put into place? Later this chapter offers a look at some tooling that may help with this task, but when it comes down to it, someone has to actually look at the code. You might refer to this as "Putting eyeballs on the code!" I mentioned in Chapter 1, "Application Architecture," the idea of "sleeves-up architecture"; looking at what is being built and guiding the direction of the application is one place where adhering to the architecture matters.

The fact is that you actually may need some tooling to help with some of these review aspects. Understanding how different layers within the architecture are being used can be difficult by simply looking at code, so you can use some simple tools that tell you a lot at a glance through package and dependency analysis. Figure 10.1 shows an example package analysis from one of these tools.

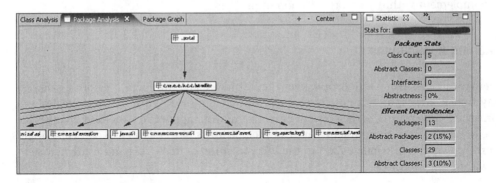

Figure 10.1   Package analysis

Several commercial and open source products can help provide this type of analysis within Eclipse or Rational Application Developer, such as Structure Analysis for Java or the Code Analysis Plugin. Rational Software Developer also has some built-in tools for performing some code analysis. This type of analysis combined with spot checks and formal code reviews can go a long way toward ensuring that architectural decisions and standards are being followed or applied correctly.

Standing by Your Decisions

Flexibility is the key when building applications, but constant change can be a death knell when it puts timelines and delivery schedules at risk. Change for change's sake is not always a good option. In fact, it is probably a common anti-practice. Change that improves the delivery of your application in some way, even if it means slipping the schedule a bit, should be carefully considered. For example, what if you had decided on a particular library that developers should use for some aspect of the application, then several weeks into development a developer comes to you and explains that the team just found a different library that did the same thing in a better way?

Consider the following:

- What is the amount of effort needed to change to this new library? How much testing is required to ensure there are no conflicts with existing code or the application server?
- How much effort will really be saved by moving to this new library? Are there performance enhancements, better security, or less code for the development team? Weigh these benefits against the effort to change out the old library.
- How will this change affect the rest of the development team? Are there other changes that have been denied or accepted that may cause a cascade effect? Will other team members propose additional changes to parts of the application?

Many other options should be considered such as licensing costs, if necessary, and supportability of the new library.

All things considered, in many cases the recommended changes can be a good idea, but the consequences may go way beyond what is initially realized. The last question to ask yourself is, "Does this change add business value to what we are doing?" Consider the reason the developer proposed the new library: Was it because it was one that he or she happened to be familiar with, but not the organization standard, or because there is real difficulty in using the current standard for this particular task?

Documenting Libraries

Open source, third-party, and custom libraries should be well managed within your environment. This really means documenting what you will allow and how it should be used. Poor library management is one of those problems that you never want to encounter. Imagine two different developers who have decided to use different and incompatible versions of the same open source library package. You might imagine that finding this fact out at deployment time can be quite a nightmare (if you haven't lived through this scenario yourself already).

A simple table, like Table 10.1, is one approach to documenting the allowed libraries. Additions or changes to this table are something that should be considered within your governance strategy using some of the criteria I mentioned earlier in this chapter. Remember that documenting your standards beforehand is the only way to ensure that they will be followed.

Table 10.1   Library Management Example

Name	Extension	Version	Usage
Log4J		1.2.8	Logging framework
Axis		2.1.0	SOAP implementation
Axiom	.api	1.0	XML processing
Axiom	.dom	1.0	XML processing

Most library discrepancies can be found at compile time, if you put together a global or project build process. Certainly you don't want to find this problem out at the end of a project, as mentioned earlier, but a build process should be put in place way before this event can occur. Problems occasionally are found at runtime so you should take care to ensure that consistency within your libraries is maintained.

Managing Organizational Process

IT service management is not a new concern of organizational and vendor IT shops. Understanding and managing the processes, work products, and deliverables of any IT organization is an ongoing concern. There are several industry attempts to normalize and improve quality standards both within and across industries. Six Sigma is one such approach to improving quality of service within an organization as is the popular Capability Maturity Model (CMMI) or the Information Technology Infrastructure Library (ITIL).

CMMI

Capability Maturity Model Integration, or CMMI, is a defined approach for process improvement within an organization. This robust set of guidelines allows an organization to measure current processes or implement new processes using a well-defined set of goals. CMMI is offered by the Software Engineering Institute (SEI) at Carnegie Mellon University, which works to continually improve the guidelines set forth in CMMI. Currently, the SEI provides a set of guidelines called CMMI for Development; it is designed as a reference model for development and maintenance activities (SEI, 2006). Process areas of the model include

- Causal Analysis and Resolution
- Configuration Management
- Decision Analysis and Resolution
- Integrated Project Management
- Measurement and Analysis
- Organizational Innovation and Deployment
- Organizational Process Definition
- Organizational Process Focus
- Organizational Process Performance
- Organizational Training

- Product Integration
- Project Monitoring and Control
- Project Planning
- Process and Product Quality Assurance
- Quantitative Project Management
- Requirements Development
- Requirements Management
- Risk Management
- Supplier Agreement Management
- Technical Solution
- Validation
- Verification

It is apparent by this list alone that CMMI for Development is pretty comprehensive. Within each of these process areas are detailed sets of goals and processes that you can implement to achieve new capability levels. Each level has a set of goals that must be accomplished to achieve the next level. The available capability levels are as follows:

- **0: Incomplete**—Usually everyone starts at incomplete. This means that the process is not performed or not completely performed. Project success at this level is hit and miss at best. Usually it depends upon the team or team leader being successful in bringing things together and not on repeatable processes within the organization.
- **1: Performed**—This level satisfies the goals of the process as defined. It is performed on a one-time basis. Additional work must be done to maintain these improvements through subsequent levels.
- **2: Managed**—A managed process builds on the capability of level 1 by instating the right training and infrastructure to repeat and maintain the process.
- **3: Defined**—Once a process is in the managed state, further refinement can be done to tailor the process to the organization. This definition allows the process to conform to the organization's way of doing things.
- **4: Quantitatively Managed**—Defined processes within the enterprise can now be quantitatively managed using statistical analysis or other quantitative approaches. This allows the organization to track and manage the processes across the organization.
- **5: Optimizing**—The goal in any organization should be for continuous improvement of all work. Once a process is quantitatively managed it can be optimized through incremental changes and improvements.

Moving through the process levels is done by applying the practices and goals that are defined within the model. As additional levels are achieved the organization will realize greater benefits to improved process and well-defined practices.

ITIL

Information Technology Infrastructure Library or ITIL is a set of documented best practices for IT management that is maintained by the Office of Government Commerce in the United Kingdom. According to the ITIL Open Guide (Guide, 2007), "The Information

Technology Infrastructure Library (ITIL) defines the organization structure and skill requirements of an information technology organization and a set of standard operational management procedures and practices to allow the organization to manage an IT operation and
associated infrastructure. The operation procedures and practices are supplier independent
and apply to all aspects within the IT Infrastructure."

One of the major benefits of adopting ITIL is to gain the benefit of 20+ years of experience
within the IT industry. Many of the contributors of ITIL have worked within the industry
and understand what works and what doesn't. In addition there are many quickstart
processes and measurements that are available for immediate use within your organization.
Sustained high levels of business performance are not possible without high-quality IT
Services (Murray & Mohamed, 2007).

It is interesting to note that ITIL was originally heavily influenced by work performed by
IBM. According to IBM (IBM, 2004), "In the early 1980s, IBM documented the original
System Management concepts in a four volume series called A Management System for
Information Systems. These widely accepted "yellow books," were key inputs to the original
set of ITIL Books."

In addition Version 3 is an attempt to update ITIL to understand new standards and
approaches in IT. A focus on services and service management has been incorporated into
the five new books to assist organizations with defining and managing services within the
enterprise. A quick look through the five texts can provide an immediate view into the comprehensive nature of ITIL. ITIL Version 3, which was released in May 2007, provides the following core texts (Kelly & Fred, 2007):

- **Service Strategy:** Provides information on defining organizational capability in the
  form of services. This lays the foundation for organizations that are looking to
  define the services that IT should provide to the business.
- **Service Design:** Provides information on the design and development of services.
  This book provides for the development of a service catalog and service-level agreements (SLAs) for service components.
- **Service Transition:** Provides for the transition of new services to operations allowing for change management of new and existing services within the organization.
- **Service Operation:** Provides for services that are running and allows for the continued delivery and support of existing services by operations. Key in this phase is
  incident and problem management.
- **Continual Service Improvement:** The final book in the series, it allows for the
  constant improvement of services, SLAs, support, and change management.

Adoption of ITIL is not a simple process, although there is benefit to be gained by simply
understanding what is available and how it may be put in place within your organization.
According to Stuart (Stuart, Jim, Ronald, and Sue, 2007), services account for more than 75%
of the world's economy and this paradigm maps nicely to IT shops looking to support the

business in the best way possible. Adopting a service approach willing to provide the organization with the right services at the right time is quickly becoming the focus of IT worldwide. A service approach and IT governance go hand in hand within the organization and ITIL assists in defining and managing both. Governance reflects the leadership and organizational structures and process that ensure IT sustains and extends the organization's strategies and objects (Raghupathi, 2007).

Avoiding Common Process Malpractices

In 2006, IBM (IBM 2006) published a set of common malpractices that can result in customer problems. The practices range across the entire spectrum of the project lifecycle but with many of them you will probably find common ground with your own organization. Figure 10.2 outlines those common malpractices.

A10.2

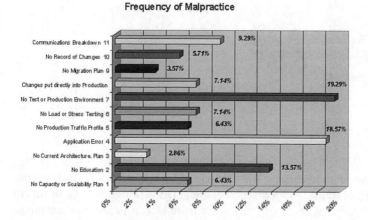

Figure 10.2   Common malpractices

No organization can do everything perfectly, but avoiding the trouble areas can be difficult without some process in place. We can break these malpractices down by project lifecycle, as shown in Figure 10.3, to determine where in the project they are most likely to occur. Many of us have encountered one or more of these malpractices, but the goal should be to strive to put some processes in place, with which to provide better guidance for solving issues that might occur.

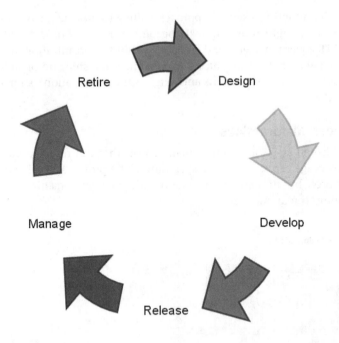

Retire   Design

Manage   Develop

Release

Figure 10.3   Malpractices by project phase

Organizations have to get better at managing the lifecycle of their applications and components that make up new applications. As mentioned earlier, SOA is bringing some of this to light, but non-web service type of services still can suffer from lack of proper management. When a reusable service is defined and eventually brought to life, there has to be a mechanism to record, track, find, and reuse these components. Another way to look at a component lifecycle is shown in Figure 10.4. This outlines the major phases that a component or possibly a library may go through in its lifetime and defines the malpractices that may occur during any particular phase.

One of the most common complaints from many organizations is around reuse of current application code. The feeling is that a lot of rework is being done because an accurate way to provide for and enforce reuse within the enterprise does not exist.

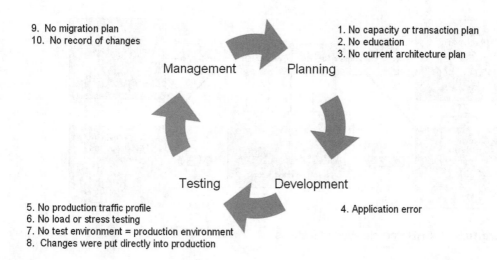

9. No migration plan
10. No record of changes

1. No capacity or transaction plan
2. No education
3. No current architecture plan

Management

Planning

Testing

Development

5. No production traffic profile
6. No load or stress testing
7. No test environment = production environment
8. Changes were put directly into production

4. Application error

Figure 10.4 Component lifecycle

Enforcing Adherence and Reuse with Technology Solutions

Many teams are looking for technology solutions to help with managing their process and environment. This desire can be a double-edged sword, as you either need to customize the tool to work within your process, or you have to change your processes to work with the tool. For new areas where no processes are in place, a tool can help you learn from industry best practices and formulate a strategy. But for those processes where you often hear, "This is the way we have always done it," putting any type of tooling in place can be a challenge.

Definitely consider these challenges when shopping for tooling to help take some of the pain out of managing your infrastructure. If your organization is strong on its own internal processes then a build versus buy decision should weigh heavily toward build, so that custom processes can be taken into account. Too often off-the-shelf tooling is not flexible enough, when it requires heavy customization.

Using a Registry and Repository

WebSphere Service Registry and Repository (WSRR) is a relatively new product from IBM that derived out of some major SOA project work. The product is designed to be the metadata repository for services within the enterprise. It allows an organization to provide a central location for storing and perhaps more importantly finding available services. Figure 10.5 shows the major functionality of WSRR. The definition of services that you can manage with WSRR is fairly broad and includes most of the traditional types of services that we usually think of, and includes newer types of services such as Web Services for Remote Portlets (WSRP).

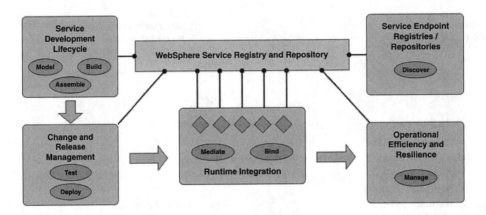

Figure 10.5   WSRR lifecycle support features

The value of this approach with all things that need to be managed is undeniable. The concept of a Registry and Repository has to be extended across the enterprise. We often think of a source code management system as such a repository; however, usually this type of product does not include the lookup and management features of a true registry.

A component registry can be as simple as a wiki designed for that purpose. Many organizations do have a file-based repository where static documents are held, but these often get out of sync, or overloaded with version, subdirectories, and access permission issues. Figure 10.6 shows a wiki example that provides for data type management within an organization. A wiki is an open community-based approach that allows everyone to contribute to the development of standards, publishing of components and services, and management of artifacts within the infrastructure.

When teams are distributed in different locations or across the globe, communication often becomes a problem; however, a registry allows for 24-hour access to what services, components, or libraries are available. Potential benefits include promoting reuse of components and preventing the reinvention of the same services or libraries, which helps with adoption of available components across the organization.

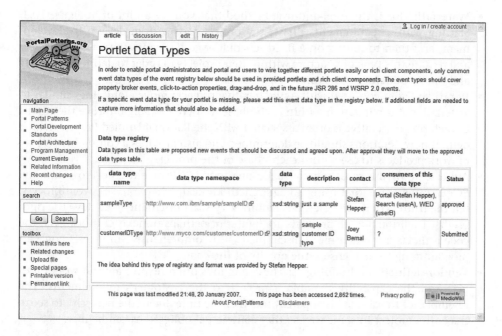

Figure 10.6 Wiki as a Component Registry or Standards document

The number of other products that are available to help you manage your IT environment could fill a set of books. However, categories of tools that you would look at for helping to manage the process within your environment include

- Requirements management systems
- Version control systems
- Defect management or trouble ticket systems
- Build and configuration management systems

When combined with some type of registry and when all the pieces are working together, these management tools can play a critical role in helping to control your environment and code artifacts.

Project Methodology

Methodology is one of those areas where science and art seems to come together. A methodology is a set of practices and processes that are combined with a set of rules. These items combined help to guide a team or group of people to find a conclusion within their set parameters. IBM's Global Services Method, recently retooled as the Global Services Unified Method, and the Rational Unified Process are two well-known methods. Some of the most common methodologies include

A10.3

- **Waterfall:** This is the tried-and-true method that you see a hint of in Figure 10.4. Starting with a requirements phase, the project moves from design, to development, and then to testing on a fixed schedule. Many organizations work this way and require this type of structure within their projects in order to define the budget and time requirements of a project.
- **Iterative:** Often confused with Agile, iterative projects move along lines similar to waterfall, but use iteration within each phase to incrementally improve the results of each phase. Iterative is often associated with the Rational Unified Process, which defines how iterations should be determined and also provides a comprehensive set of work products to use within each phase of the project.
- **Agile:** One of the most popular agile methods is XP or eXtreme Programming. People often think that using an agile method means that you can avoid process, but the truth is that agile methods require very strict discipline to achieve the right results. Traditional work products are lighter or perhaps nonexistent; however, the code artifacts are much more disciplined with comprehensive unit tests and pair programming to help ensure the quality of the code.
- **Vendor-defined methodologies:** These methods often revolve around work products and the capability to mold a project to the customer's requirements. The resemblance to waterfall is apparent much of the time due to the necessity to scope the entire project in some way so that contractual obligations can be met.

The key is to have some type of methodology. When teams don't have a defined set of processes then no one is sure of the next step or when things should be done within the project lifecycle.

Common Methodology Problems

It is easy to fall into the trap of thinking that your method is working without understanding how it may be hindering your process within the development cycle. The following options are meant to put those occurrences in a humorous light and allow you to recognize where you might need to shake things up a bit.

- **Ad hoc:** This is the team that has no process and doesn't think it needs a process. No process means no way to measure your progress, and no accountability for poor deliveries or nondelivery of key functionality. There are a lot of things that can go wrong, but you won't know because you didn't do a risk analysis.
- **Stone idol:** Many organizations have adopted well-defined industry standards such as Six Sigma or ISO 9001, but have left the troops or the group lacking the skills and experience to really follow through. The common mantra through the organization is to chant the required phrases; however, the team is only paying lip service or adhering by filling out the required forms. The real value of repeatable and quality deliverables is lost.
- **Latest craze:** This team jumps on the latest buzz such as SOA or agile for a variety of reasons. Sometimes there is an honest attempt to improve processes, but other times it is simply because something is new and exciting and the team members are looking to pad their resume.

Hopefully you haven't seen your own organization in this list and you can continue to improve your already well-defined process.

Change Control Board

So what is missing? Well, the act of governing the environment for one thing. This means that controls need to be put into place, along with some checks and balances to be used when changes are requested to the system. Often this control takes the guise of a Change Control Board (CCB) that approves change requests on a regular basis. Those changes are then scheduled and implemented at the next open maintenance window.

Won't a CCB Get in the Way?

A change control process along with a governing board will absolutely get in the way. That is actually the point. To slow down the rate of change to something that is manageable. A team cannot stabilize and maintain a system that is undergoing constant changes. Scheduling as illustrated in Figure 10.7 needs to occur and be followed so that casual change requests do not become an everyday occurrence.

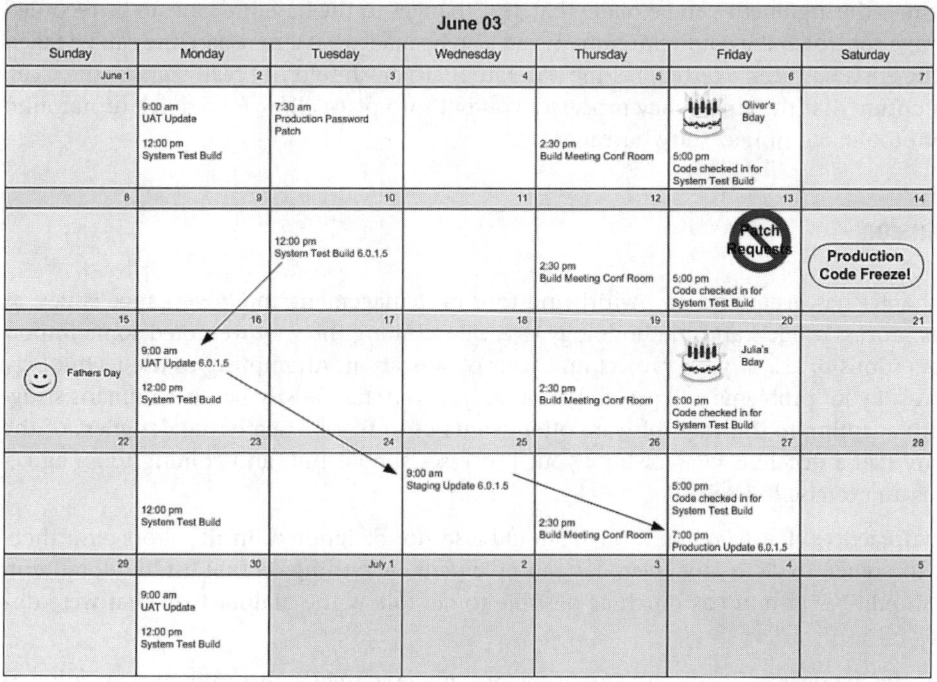

Figure 10.7   Change control schedule

The CCB also acts as a communication medium across organization boundaries and to act as the enforcer when necessary within the enterprise. This can help ensure that changes to one application or part of the environment do not adversely affect another application.

This idea of constant change request most often occurs when an application is first rolled out. Sometimes not all the requested functionality has made it into the first release, or perhaps the schedule slipped, or there was not enough time for thorough testing. The first reaction from the business is to make daily requests to fix this function, or update some piece of content. Unfortunately, this is also the worst time to make these changes because operations will be working to get the new application stabilized.

When to Ignore the CCB

There *are* times when you should ignore change control; for example, during critical situations when the system is not operating. Well, not actually ignored, but emergency process can be put into place in crisis situations. Sometimes things go wrong. Anyone who has been in the IT business can relate to that, and a quick reaction to stabilize the environment is necessary.

Sometimes the argument can be made that any changes to the baseline have to be recorded in change control, but a counterargument can also be made that a new baseline can be taken after the crisis has been averted. Let me reiterate that you should not really ignore the CCB; rather ensure that the emergency processes you put into place allow for a quick turnaround without too much unnecessary bureaucracy.

Conclusion

This chapter has been kind of a whirlwind tour of management and governance issues, as well as process models and methodology overviews. Along the way we noted some important questions to ask of your project and your organization. Attempting to use technology to solve all your problems will probably not get you very far, mostly because humans struggle with adapting to the way software often wants us to work. Usually the designers of the software had a different view of how your processes should run, and coming to an agreement is an exercise in itself.

The malpractices that were mentioned should also not be ignored. In the short term there is just too much to do in any given day to implement everything on that list, but long-term goals should be set to do as much as possible to *not* follow the malpractices that were discussed.

One of the major benefits of implementing as many governance processes and avoiding as many antipractices as possible is that there is a lot of spillover to any new projects. These items provide mostly organization-wide benefits so implementing them as fully and correctly as possible offers few downsides.

References

IBM. (2004). *IBM and the IT Infrastructure Library*. Retrieved November 17, 2007, from http://www-935.ibm.com/services/us/igs/pdf/wp-g510-3008-03f-supports-provides-itil-capabilities-solutions.pdf.

IBM. (2006). *Common Process Malpractices*. Retrieved April 9, 2008, from http://www-1.ibm.com/support/docview.wss?rs=180&uid=swg27007543#Introduction.

Kelly, M., and Fred, D. (2007). *American ITIL*. Paper presented at the Proceedings of the 35th annual ACM SIGUCCS conference on User services. Retrieved October 2, 2007, from http://doi.acm.org/10.1145/1294046.1294106.

Murray, A., and Mohamed, M. S. (2007). The role of ITIL in building the enterprise of the future. *KM World, 16*(1), 22-23.

Raghupathi, W. R. (2007). Corporate governance of IT: a framework for development. *Commun. ACM, 50*(8), 94-99.

SEI. (2006). CMMI for Development version 1.2. Retrieved March 22, 2008, from http://www.sei.cmu.edu/pub/documents/06.reports/pdf/06tr008.pdf.

Steinberg, R., and Goodwin, M. (2006). ITIL Crash Course. (Cover story). *InfoWorld, 28*(43), 22-30.

Stuart, G., Jim, J. Q., Ronald, D., and Sue, C. (2007). *Information technology service management: an emerging area for academic research and pedagogical development*. Paper presented at the Proceedings of the 2007 ACM SIGMIS CPR conference on 2007 computer personnel doctoral consortium and research conference: The global information technology workforce. Retrieved October 2, 2007, from http://doi.acm.org/10.1145/1235000.1235010.

Links to developerWorks Articles

A10.1 Operational IT Governance, Murray Cantor, John D. Sanders, http://www.ibm.com/developerworks/rational/library/may07/cantor_sanders/

A10.2 Common WebSphere Malpractices, http://www-1.ibm.com/support/docview.wss?rs=180&uid=swg27007543

A10.3 Getting started with application development methodologies, Christopher P. Caserio, http://www.ibm.com/developerworks/library/ar-apparch3/index.html?S_TACT=105AGX20&S_CMP=EDU

Setting Up the Data Sample

This appendix is all about getting the database set up and working correctly. It is assumed that you have WebSphere Application Server up and running and have even built some simple projects with Rational Application Developer or the latest version of Eclipse. This book doesn't cover these applications, but you need some basic knowledge of them to follow and build the examples.

Many of the examples focus on a specific set of data provided by eclipse.org. Because it has been adapted for the purposes of this book it is necessary to explain how to set up the database and create a usable datasource. This exercise will lay the groundwork for building your own sample applications.

Getting Started

This exercise makes use of an existing database provided by Eclipse.org. The BIRT (Business Intelligence and Reporting Tools) sample database provides a simple set of tables and example data that form the basis for BIRT sample reports. The examples are based around a company called Classic Models (see Figure A.1), which is a retailer of scale-model classic cars and other vehicles.

Figure A.1   Classic Models logo

The database is typical of what you might find in a small business, with data such as customers, orders, order detail items, products, and so on. It was designed to illustrate many of the features of the BIRT report designer, but it also happens to be perfect for building many of the examples presented within this book.

The sample database is open source; you are free to use it for your own experiments with other tools or projects, to create samples for other tools, and so on. It is provided under the terms of Eclipse.org, located with the sample downloads provided with this book or available at www.eclipse.org/legal/epl/notice.php.

IBM has done substantial research in the area of common scenarios that customers need to solve. One common use case is for setting up a new account for customers. Additional use cases include order entry, order status, and payment history. This book cannot present all these use cases. It instead focuses on different approaches to integrating a breadth of tools, rather than building out a single application that illustrates one business scenario. This book shows you some of them, and the general guidelines for building these types of applications.

Database and Schema

The Classic Models database consists of seven tables completely populated with sample data. Figure A.2 illustrates the data model associated with those tables. The tables are

- Offices: Sales offices and locations
- Employees: All employees, including sales reps who work with customers
- Customers: Customers of Classic Models
- Orders: Orders placed by customers
- Order Details: Line items that are contained within a single order
- Payments: Payments made by customers against their account
- Products: The list of scale model cars
- Product Line: Types of products offered by Classic Models

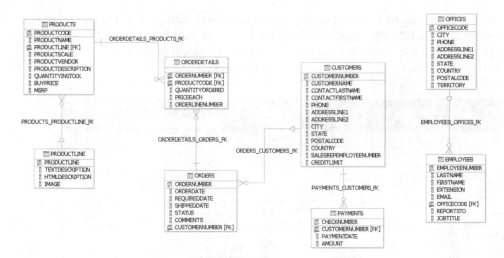

Figure A.2   Classic Models database schema

Using this schema with the prepopulated data makes available a large set of sample data and use cases to build upon: Everything from simple lookup tables to complete business transactions can be explored within this environment.

Setting Up Your Data Environment

The classic models database is available from eclipse.org at www.eclipse.org/birt/ phoenix/db/. It is provided in a variety of formats except for the main one that we need, which is DB2. Because this appendix works with WebSphere and focuses on IBM software you want to have this database available in DB2. In some cases you might consider Oracle, or even Derby for development purposes.

Fortunately, after much trial and error a script has been developed that will simplify the steps to create and load the Classic Models database in DB2. The download site that hosts the code samples for this book provides the data sources DB2 setup script along with any changes to the latest instructions for creating the database.

The setup process consists of three main steps:

1. Creating a CMODELS database

2. Running the CMODELS data script

3. Creating a WAS data source

If you don't have access to a DB2 workgroup or enterprise edition then I recommend you download and use IBM DB2 Express-C for these examples. All the examples are tested with this platform. You can download and install this version, shown in Figure A.3, from the IBM website at www-306.ibm.com/software/data/db2/express/.

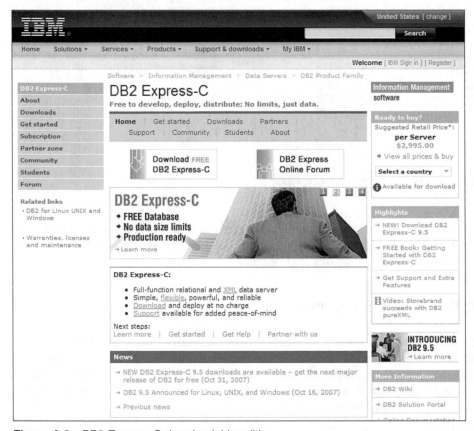

Figure A.3   DB2 Express-C downloadable edition

AA.1

IBM DB2 Express-C is a no-charge community edition of the DB2 database server. It is designed for small businesses, developers, and business partners who serve small business clients. DB2 Express-C can be set up quickly, is easy to use, and includes self-managing capabilities.

Creating the DB2 Database

After you have DB2 installed and running, the next step is to create the Classic Models database. After you have created the database you can then run the CreateCMDB2.sql script, which creates the required tables and populates them with sample data.

When setting up the database keep in mind the following points:

- The DB2 admin used in these examples is **db2admin**. This is also the schema name for the tables that is hard coded in the load script. If your admin name is different you will have to modify the load script.
- In this example the database is loaded on the same machine as WAS. If you are creating a remote database you will need to load the local drivers on your WebSphere instance and change any reference to **localhost** in this example to the correct host name.
- Versions used in this set of examples are DB2 Express-C version 9.5 and WebSphere Application Server version 6.1. Some of these steps or screenshots may differ slightly from what is shown.

After you install DB2, the First Steps screen appears (see Figure A.4).

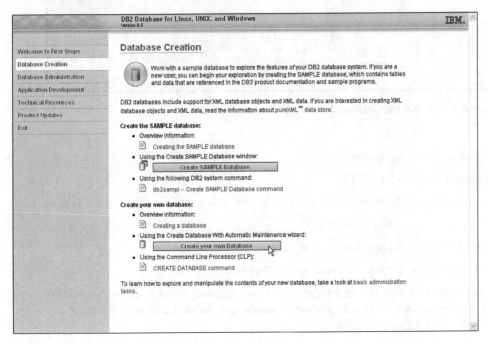

Figure A.4 Start the database creation wizard

Follow these steps to create the database:

1. Choose the **Create your own Database** option to launch the database creation wizard. This wizard allows you to quickly create the Classic Models database (see Figure A.5).

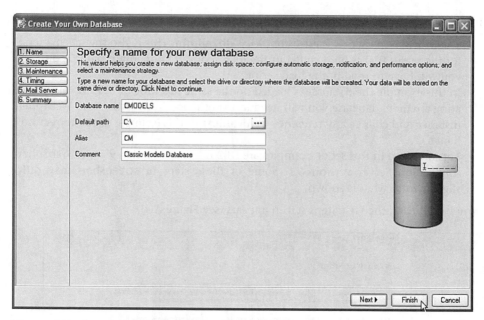

Figure A.5   Create the Classic Models DB

Choose the following options:

Database name	CMODELS
Default path	Your preferred path; make sure this path exists on the file system.
Alias	CM or CMODELS
Comment	Classic Models Database

After you have the setting configured click **Finish**.

A window appears that shows the database being created. Allow it to finish and then close the First Steps window. At this point the database is created and you can now create the tables and load the sample data.

Load the Classic Models Data

I have provided a load script that you can use to create the tables and load the sample data. Figure A.6 shows the command line steps that should be followed. Just follow these steps:

1. To load the data, use the DB2 command-line processor to connect to the database.

```
C:\>db2 connect to CMODELS

   Database Connection Information

   Database server        = DB2/NT 9.5.0
   SQL authorization ID   = ADMIN
   Local database alias   = CMODELS
```

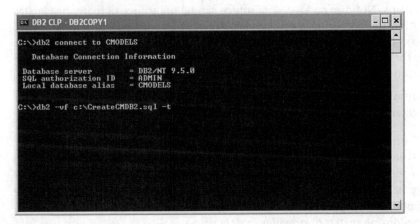

Figure A.6   Load sample data

2. Enter the following command to run the script:

   ```
   C:\>db2 —vf <your path>CreateCMDB2.sql —t
   ```

   The "v" is the verbose flag, which is not required, but it does provide detailed output so it is recommended. Check the output in the command window to ensure that there were no errors during the load process.

3. Copy the script to your local machine then open the command window and enter the following commands.

...

```
GRANT SELECT, INSERT, UPDATE, DELETE, INDEX, ALTER, REFERENCES ON TABLE
   DB2ADMIN.PRODUCTLINE TO USER DB2ADMIN WITH GRANT OPTION
DB200001 The SQL command completed successfully.

GRANT CONTROL ON TABLE DB2ADMIN.PRODUCTS TO USER DB2ADMIN
DB200001 The SQL command completed successfully.

GRANT SELECT, INSERT, UPDATE, DELETE, INDEX, ALTER, REFERENCES ON TABLE
   DB2ADMIN.PRODUCTS TO USER DB2ADMIN WITH GRANT OPTION
DB200001 The SQL command completed successfully.

C:\>
```

Now the database is fully populated with sample data that you can start to use. The next step is to create a WebSphere data source so that your applications can properly connect to the data source.

Creating a WebSphere Data Source

WebSphere data sources provide an approach for managing connections to databases and other back-end systems. Not using a WAS data source can be the source of many headaches within an application design. Using a proven data connection manager to handle things such as database connection pools, monitoring capability, and transaction management just makes good sense for any application or environment. You can set up data source providers and data sources through the WebSphere administration console.

Access the WAS console using the username and password you used when you installed your server. After you enter your username and password, click **Log in**.

Create the JDBC Provider

A JDBC provider is really the driver that you will be using to connect to your data source. You may, in fact, have one provider for each type of data source that you will be using. For example, you may have one provider for DB2 databases and one for Oracle databases. The granularity or number of JDBC providers can vary depending upon a number of factors. In this case it is a one-for-one match of provider to data source.

1. From the opening screen in the admin console, click on **JDBC Providers** to access the JDBC Providers screen (see Figure A.7). From it you can set up the scope of your provider. WebSphere provides several different levels at which to scope your resources, which allows increased security and better management of them.

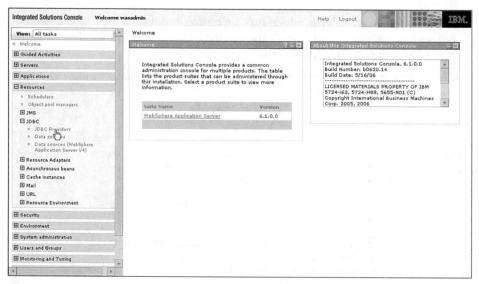

Figure A.7   Navigate to JDBC providers

2. The scope of a datasource is used to determine which servers, clusters, or cells can access that datasource. Figure A.9 shows the page where the scope can be changed. Click on the drop-down menu and select 'Cell' scope (see Figure A.8) for the scope options that should be available.

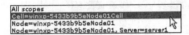

Figure A.8   Change to Cell level scope

3. Click the **New** button as shown in Figure A.9, to continue.

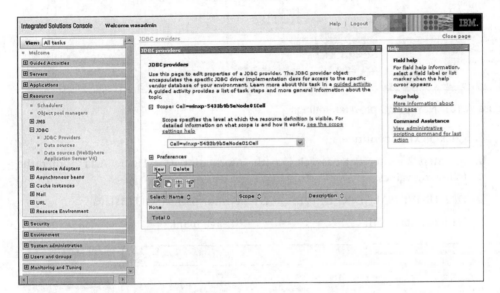

Figure A.9   Create a new JDBC provider

4. For Step 1: Create new JDBC provider (see Figure A.10), enter the following settings:

Database type	DB2	
Provider type	DB2	Universal JDBC Driver Provider
Implementation type		XA data source
Name	Classic	Models DB2 JDBC Driver Provider (XA)
Description	Classic	Models XA DB2 Universal JDBC Driver compliant Provider

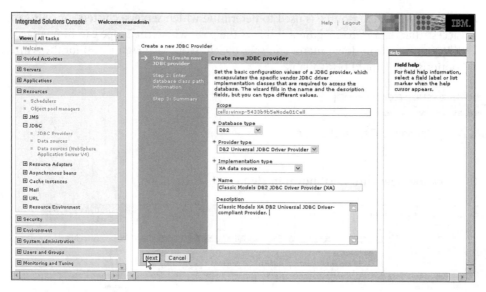

Figure A.10   New JDBC provider settings

5. Click **Next** to continue.

6. For Step 2: Enter database class path information (see Figure A.11), enter the following values:

DB2_UNIVERSAL_JDBC_DRIVER_PATH   <your path>\SQLLIB\java

Native library path   Leave blank

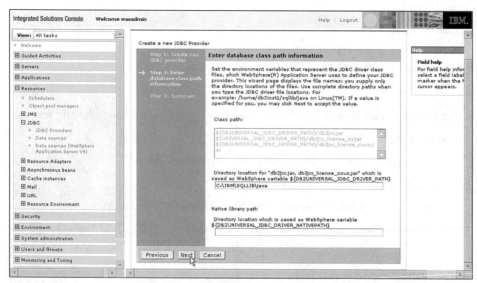

Figure A.11   Driver class path information

7. Click **Next** to continue. On the summary screen, validate the settings and then click **Finish**.

8. After your provider is created be sure to click **Save** in the messages area at the top of the screen (see Figure A.12). Doing so ensures that your changes are saved to the WebSphere master configuration. Additional steps such as creating and testing data sources will not be possible until you save the JDBC provider configuration.

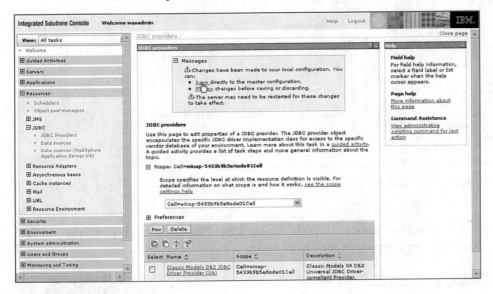

Figure A.12 Save changes

Create an Authentication Alias

Before you can create an actual data source you need to set up an authentication alias for your database. Doing so allows you to connect to the database without providing a username and password within your actual application code. Generally this alias allows the DBA to manage the username/password for the database separately from any code that is developed. Using this feature may not always be the best practice, depending upon your security requirements.

1. To start, click on the **Classic Models JDBC Provider** (see Figure A.13) that you just created.

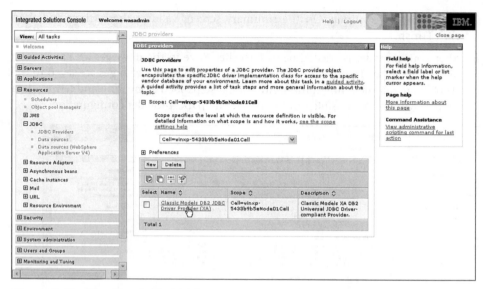

Figure A.13   The Classic Models data source

2. Click the **Data sources** link (see Figure A.14). Currently you can see that no data sources are defined within this provider.

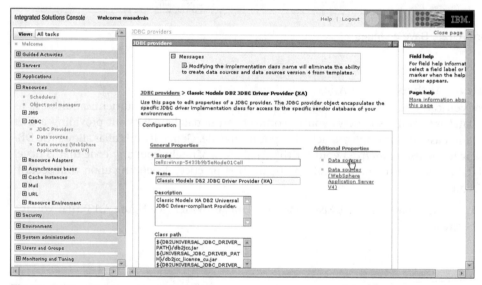

Figure A.14   Create a new data source

3. On the Data Sources page click the **New** button. At this point you could start to create a data source; however, without an authentication alias you would not be able to finish this process. If you are using a different version of WebSphere you may not have this option at this step. In this case it may be better to back up and create an authentication alias separately before creating the data source.

4. Click on the **create a new J2C authentication alias** link (see Figure A.15). In the JASS – J2C authentication data screen that appears, click the **New** button. A form appears that allows you to create the authentication alias.

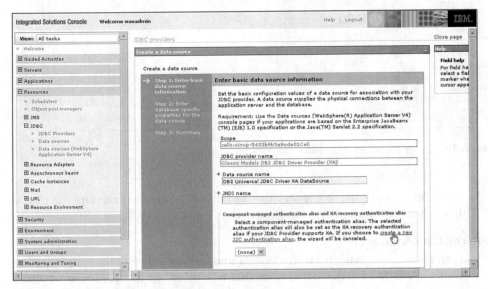

Figure A.15   Accessing the Authentication Alias screen

On the JASS-J2C authentication data screen (see Figure A.16), enter the following values:

Alias	classicModelsAlias
User ID	db2admin or your user id
Password	Your DB2 password
Description	Classic Models Authentication Alias

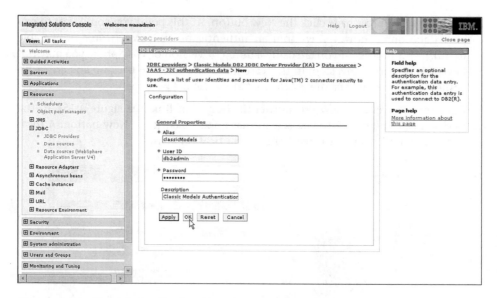

Figure A.16   Enter Authentication Alias data

5. Click **OK** to continue; in the Messages section click **Save** to make sure the alias is properly stored to the WAS configuration.

Create the Data Source

Now you can go back and actually create the data source. After you save the authentication alias it is time to create an actual data source that references our classic models database. Follow these steps:

1. Click on the **Data sources** link in the breadcrumb navigation trail at the top of the screen. This will return you to the data source setup screen. Figure A.17 demonstrates how to use this breadcrumb trail.

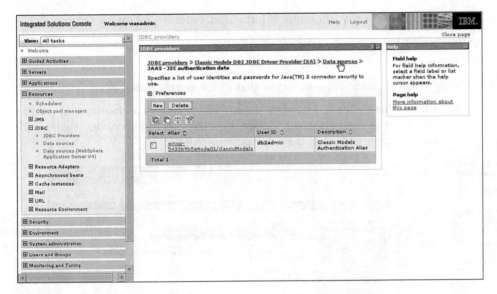

Figure A.17   Return to create data source

2. Click the **New** button. You are now back to the original data source screen; how-ever, this time you have an authentication alias to use in the setup. Figure A.18 shows how to setup the basic datasource information.

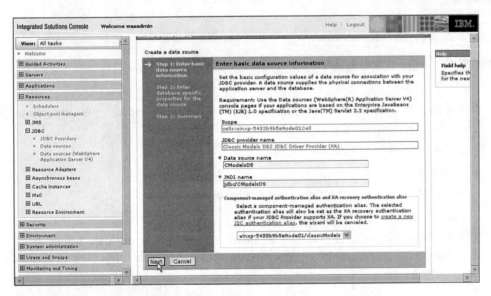

Figure A.18   Enter data source information

3. For Step 1: Enter basic data source information, enter the following values:

Data source name   classicModelsDS

JNDI name   jdbc/classicModelsDS

Component-managed authentication alias <your newly created alias>

Note that in this example, I have picked my newly created authentication alias in the drop-down at the bottom of the screen. Click **Next** to continue. Figure A.19 shows how you should setup the database properties.

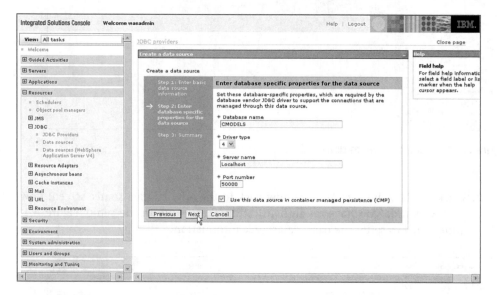

Figure A.19   Database setup parameters

4. For Step 2: Enter database specific properties for the data source, enter the following values:

Database Name   CMODELS

Driver type   4

Server Name   Localhost or <your server name>

Port number   50000 is the default

5. Click **Next** to continue. On the summary screen, review the data source setup parameters and click **Finish**. Again, save the data source once it has been created by clicking **Save**.

Test the Connection

After you have saved your newly created data source navigate back to it to test that it was set up correctly as shown in Figure A.20.

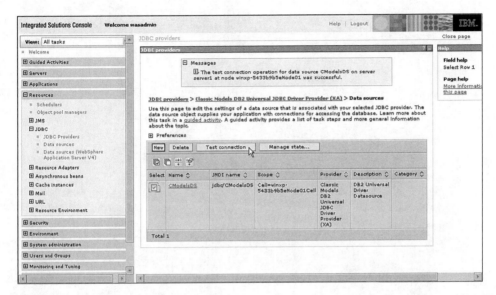

Figure A.20 Testing the data source

You can test the configuration in several ways; however, the simplest is to check the Select box next to your data source and click the **Test connection** button. The system will return a message at the top of the screen indicating success or telling you about any errors in the setup.

Conclusion

If you were able to set up your environment as outlined in this chapter then you should be ready to go for most of the examples in the book.

 Links to developerWorks Articles

AA.1 developerWorks Information Management Zone: http://www.ibm.com/developer-works/db2/

Appendix B

Running the Examples

We have covered many examples in this book and because many of them illustrate relatively new technologies, this appendix is designed to provide you with some information about running these examples. All the samples are available at the download site for this book, located at http://www.ibmpressbooks.com/title/0137129262.

Chapter Code Samples

All the samples were built using Rational Application Developer (RAD) 7.0.0.3 or using RAD 7.5 beta. The WebSphere Application Server 6.1 runtime was used for most of the samples, with some feature packs used in a few chapters (as specified in the following relevant sections). Example files are available in two flavors:

- **Deployable packages:** Any file that ends in a .war, .ear, or .jar extension is a deployable unit that you can install directly in WebSphere. There is no source code in these example files.
- **RAD source code projects:** Any project with a .zip extension is a Rational Application Developer Interchange Project and is designed to be imported into RAD directly as an independent set of projects. Once they are imported, you can examine, compile, and test these projects from within the RAD framework.

Some chapters have code that builds upon earlier examples. For this reason it is best to create a new workspace for each chapter to avoid conflict and to avoid overwriting an earlier example.

Chapter 2

Chapter 2 contains one file called `JavaLoggingProject.zip`. You can import this file into Rational Application Developer as a RAD Interchange Project. This example illustrates the logging approach described in this chapter.

Chapter 3

Chapter 3 contains several sets of example files. It contains the `ClassicModelsDataEAR.ear` file, which holds all the deployable samples for a multilayered EJB3 application. This includes the EJB session beans and a sample web application for viewing the data.

The file `OrderWebApp.war` is a deployable .war file that illustrates how to access a remote EJB3 project. This file requires the `ClassicModelsDataEAR.ear` file mentioned earlier.

The file `ClassicModelsRemoteSourceProjects.zip` contains all the RAD Interchange projects for examining the EJB3 examples and using them with a local and remote interface. This includes the source for the OrderWebApp project, which is deployed as a separate .war file.

The files `CMIbatisDAOTestWebProject.war` and `CMIbatisDAOTestWebProject.zip` illustrate how to use Spring and Ibatis to access a WAS data source from within a single web application.

The file `CMIbatisDAOService.zip` contains the source code examples for building an Ibatis-based persistence layer that can be used as a shared library.

The `ejb-jpa-example.zip` contains the source code projects for an EJB3-based example that uses the Java Persistence API.

The file `BaseLibraries.zip` can be imported RAD to provide some additional libraries for the project `CMIbatisDAOService`.

The samples in this chapter depend upon the EJB3 Feature Pack for WebSphere Application Server 6.1.

Chapter 4

Chapter 4 contains several files that will be useful in understanding the examples. The file `bizlayerdeploy.zip` contains the example shared library and associated files. This file should be unzipped in the Websphere/lib directory so that it can be configured and accessed by other files as a shared library.

The file `bizlayerprojectinterchange.zip` is the RAD Interchange file for all the projects in the chapter. You can import this file into RAD to view the source code of the examples.

Finally, the two sample web applications `BusinessWebApp1.war` and `BusinessWebApp2.war` are available for deploying into a WebSphere web container to illustrate how the shared libraries can be used by the presentation layer.

Chapter 5

Chapter 5 provides an example JavaServer Faces .war file along with the associated project. The files available are ExampleJSFProject.zip and ExampleJSFProject.war.

Chapter 6

Chapter 6 provides a set of sample portlets that are available within a single deployable unit. The available files are SamplePortlet.zip and SamplePortlets.war, which can be deployed into WebSphere Portal V6.x.

Chapter 7

Chapter 7 required the WebSphere Application Server 6.1 Feature Pack for Web Services. The standards supported within the feature pack are discussed within Chapter 7. As of this writing both RAD 7.0.0.3 and RAD 7.5 beta supported the installation of this feature pack along with a WAS 6.1 test environment profile. You can modify the RAD installation to include this feature pack as shown in Figure B.1 using the Rational Installation Manager. Once you are in the installation manager choose to modify your installation package of RAD to find new features (see figure B.1).

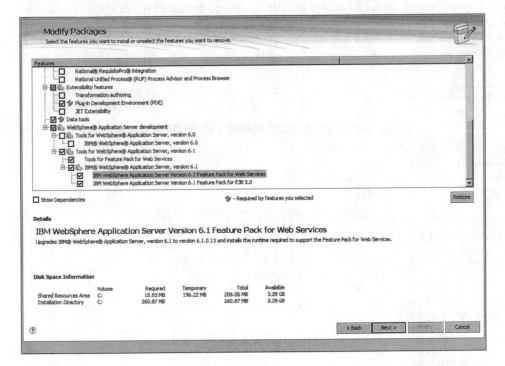

Figure B.1   Feature Pack for Web Services

The files `CreditLimit.zip` and `CreditLimitEAR.ear` are an example web service that features usage of the Web Services Feature Pack for WAS 6.1. This package contains both the service and a generated client application.

The examples `CustomerView.war` and `CustomerView.zip` illustrate how to build your own client for the CreditLimit web service.

The files `CreditLimitREST.war` and `CreditLimitREST.zip` are samples for building a simple REST-based service using a servlet, and for building an Ajax client to access the service.

Chapter 8

Chapter 8 provides an example that is adapted from Chapter 3. These samples implement a caching solution into the application. The example files available are `ClassicModelsData EAR.zip` and `ClassicModelsDataEAR.ear`.

Chapter 9

The samples in Chapter 9 were tested on a standalone WAS 6.1 server. While it is possible to enable security within the RAD test environment, by default security is enabled on standalone servers. Several users and groups have to be created to enable the examples to run correctly. Because roles are defined within the application examples it is not as important what groups are created. Figure B.2 shows an example of creating users and groups in the WebSphere Integrated Administration Console.

Figure B.2 Creating users and groups in WebSphere

For simplicity I created the following user and group mapping using the administrative console interface.

Group1   →   User1

Group2   →   User2

The code example files for Chapter 9 are `SQLInjectionWebApp.war` and `SQLInjection WebApp.zip`. These examples illustrate how SQL injection could be used against an application where input data is not validated correctly.

`FormLoginWebApp.zip` and `FormLoginWebApp.war` illustrate how to configure a login form for your application using `j_security_check` and WebSphere Application Server.

The `ClassicModelsDataEAR.ear` and `ClassicModelsDataEAR.zip` files and the `OrderWebApp.war` and `OrderWebApp.zip` files illustrate security within an enterprise application and how the security context can be passed across tiers.

Conclusion

The Web site mentioned at the beginning of this chapter is where you can download all the sample code mentioned in this book. Also any updates of fixes to the code samples will be posted on the Web site as they become available.

Index

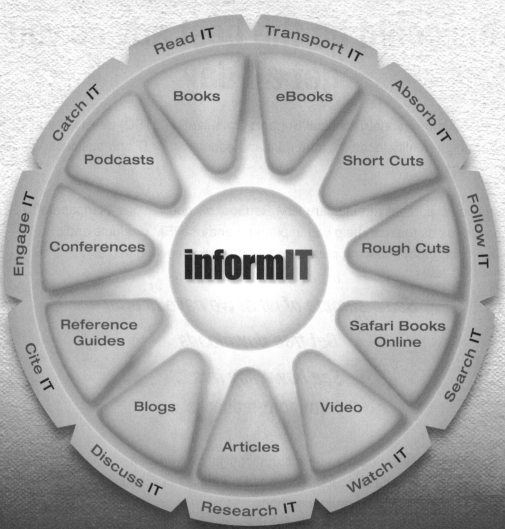

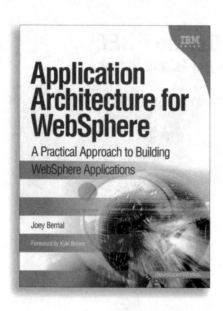

Your purchase of **Application Architecture for WebSphere®: A Practical Approach to Building Websphere Applications** includes access to a free online edition for 45 days through the Safari Books Online subscription service. Nearly every IBM Press book is available online through Safari Books Online, along with more than 5,000 other technical books and videos from publishers such as Addison-Wesley Professional, Cisco Press, Exam Cram, O'Reilly, Prentice Hall, Que, and Sams.

SAFARI BOOKS ONLINE allows you to search for a specific answer, cut and paste code, download chapters, and stay current with emerging technologies.

Activate your FREE Online Edition at
www.informit.com/safarifree

> **STEP 1:** Enter the coupon code: VLPLRFA.

> **STEP 2:** New Safari users, complete the brief registration form.
> Safari subscribers, just login.

If you have difficulty registering on Safari or accessing the online edition, please e-mail customer-service@safaribooksonline.com